RUSH
on the
RADIO

RUSH
on the
RADIO

A TRIBUTE FROM HIS
SIDEKICK FOR 30 YEARS

JAMES GOLDEN
aka Bo Snerdley

All Seasons Press

All Seasons Press
6800 Gulfport Blvd. Suite 201-355
St. Petersburg, FL 33707

Interior design by Timothy Shaner

FIRST EDITION: NOVEMBER 2021

Library of Congress Cataloging-in-Publication Data has been applied for.

ISBNs: 978-1-7374785-4-6 (hardcover), 978-1-7374785-5-3 (ebook)

Printed in Canada

10   9   8   7   6   5   4   3   2   1

To the Golden and Kerley families,
without whom I would not be.

Mom and Dad, I love you.

CONTENTS

RUSH
on the
RADIO

Over the years a lot of people have been very nice, telling me how much this program has meant to them, but whatever that is, it pales in comparison to what you all have meant to me.

—RUSH LIMBAUGH

1

ON LOAN FROM GOD

I was driving my Beemer, with music blaring, to the EIB Southern Command complex in Palm Beach, Florida, when my cell phone lit up. There would be a staff meeting with Rush before today's show.

Instantly, there were butterflies in my stomach—more like bricks, actually.

On most commutes, I entertain myself with a playlist of tunes from my ever-growing music library. But when something's weighing on my mind, as it was on that day, February 3, 2020, I turn off the music festival and drive with silence as my companion.

We never have meetings. Maybe two over the last thirty years. What's going on?

I don't remember the rest of the drive, but as soon as I arrived, I headed straight for the media room. Everyone was there, and we all knew something was very wrong.

Every eye was on Rush as he walked into the room. His demeanor seemed normal. "I asked you all to come today," he began in a very controlled manner, without giving way to emotion, as he told us about his recent medical diagnosis. Rush had advanced lung cancer. A second opinion had already verified the first opinion that it was indeed advanced. Rush, being Rush, looked around the room and said, "I'm sorry I let you down."

I let out an involuntary shout. "No! You can't apologize to *us*!" I was mortified that he apologized on what had to be one of the worst days of his life.

Rush was stoic throughout the short meeting—not a hint of self-pity, fear, or anxiety on his face. He assured us he was seeking the best treatment available. He thanked everyone for coming together, then calmly turned away and walked down the hallway back into his broadcast studio. As usual, his presentation was executed flawlessly with zero mistakes.

After I exchanged stunned, worried glances with the rest of the EIB family, I took a deep breath and proceeded down the hall, opened the huge soundproof door, and went into his studio. I gave Rush a hug, told him I loved him, and reassured him that everything was going to be okay—I felt confident about it.

What I've not revealed publicly until recently is that I had just finished the most grueling phase of treatment for my own bout with prostate cancer. Rush—along with Kraig Kitchin, one of the founders of Premiere Networks; Julie Talbott, the current president of Premiere; Brian Johnson; and our other engineers on the West Coast—moved mountains to allow me to work from Maryland, where I relocated for almost six months for medical treatment. I needed to keep working as if everything was normal, and it was. Kind of. I had treatments in the mornings then went off to work each day.

If I can beat cancer, Rush is going to beat this, I assured myself as I walked back to my desk. *He can beat anything.* I believed Rush was invincible. But at the same time, that word—*advanced*—and the way he emphasized it in the meeting, really stuck in my head.

Letting Everybody Down

It was showtime. Along came the theme music. Rush opened the show in the usual way, leading off with stories of the day. During the next two hours and forty-five minutes, the show cruised along as normal. Rush cracked jokes, went through a detailed analysis of the news, and bantered with callers.

It was surreal.

Three of us were in the control room that day—Dawn Bachinski, Brian Johnson, and me, along with Mike Maimone, our engineer who worked in our New York studios—doing our jobs and doing our best to keep our composure. I screened calls as usual. We kept looking at each other and trying not to cry. *Rush is on the air. We have to be engaged in the show. He can't see us crying. When he says something funny, we need to smile.*

We did our best, but the air was thick with dread. We knew what was coming. After the "43 break"—a little inside radio term—Rush took a deep breath. And that's when he told you, his listeners, and the rest of the world. Hearing the announcement a second time was just as horrific and shocking as it had been that morning.

"Ladies and gentlemen, this has been one of the most difficult days in memory for me because I've known this moment was coming in the program today. I'm sure that you all know by now that I really don't like talking about myself and I don't like making things about me, other than the usual, satirical parodic joking way. [. . .] So I have to tell you something today that I wish I didn't have to tell you. And it's a struggle [for] me because I had to inform my staff earlier today. I can't help but feel that I'm letting everybody down with this.

"The upshot is that I have been diagnosed with advanced lung cancer." —RL

You could almost hear the collective gasp of twenty-seven million people. In the control room, we finally let the tears roll.

"I wish I didn't have to tell you this. And I thought about not telling anybody. I thought about trying to do this without anybody knowing because I don't like making things about me. But there are going to be days that I'm not going to be able to be here because I'm undergoing treatment, or I'm reacting to treatment." —RL

Never the Same

"I told the staff today that I have a deeply personal relationship with God that I do not proselytize about. But I do, and I have been working that relationship tremendously, which I do regularly anyway. But I've been

4

focused on it intensely for the past couple of weeks. I know there are many of you in this audience who have experienced this, who are going through it yourselves at the same time. At the moment, I am experiencing zero symptoms other than, look, I don't want to get too detailed in this.

"What led to the shortness of breath that I thought might have been asthma or you know, I'm 69, it could have been my heart. My heart's in great shape, squeezing and pumping away. It was not that. It was a pulmonary problem involving malignancy so I'm going to be gone the next couple of days as we figure out the treatment course of action and have further testing done. But as I said, I'm going to be here as often as I can and as is the case with everybody who finds themselves in this circumstance, you just want to push ahead and try to keep everything as normal as you can, which is something that I'm going to try to do."—RL

Within the first five or six minutes of the announcement, the first breaking news story showed up on television. We knew life was never going to be the same. And it wasn't. At least now, the EIB family and I didn't have to pretend to feel anything other than extreme anxiety and sadness, mixed with prayerful hope. We had to give Rush our best support because, as always, it was all about our audience.

"Over the years a lot of people have been very nice, telling me how much this program has meant to them,

but whatever that is, it pales in comparison to what you all have meant to me. And I can't describe this, but I know you're there every day. I can see you. It's strange, but I know you're there. I know you're there in great numbers and I know that you understand everything I say. The rest of the world may not when they hear it expressed a different way but I know that you do.

"You've been one of the greatest sources of confidence that I've had in my life, so I hope I will be talking about this as little as necessary in the coming days but we've got a great bunch of doctors, a great team assembled. We're at full speed ahead on this and it's just now a matter of implementing what we are gonna be told later this week, so I'll be back here, hopefully, Thursday. If not, it'll be as soon as I can and know that every day I'm not here, I'll be thinking about you and missing you. Thank you very much."—RL

After the big announcement, Rush and his wife, Kathryn went to the airport, where I assume EIB One was waiting, and off they went to begin his treatment. In his absence, my thoughts were consumed with the unbelievable reality. *Rush has advanced cancer.* There were plenty of tears among the staff. This was the radio host who'd gone completely deaf, which would have been a career ender for almost anyone else. And yet he came back and delivered—and never stopped delivering—excellent work. *This is Rush,* I insisted. *He can do anything.*

The show went on, because it had to. Wonderful guest hosts graced us and our listeners with genuine love and their best efforts to do the impossible, which in this case meant providing assurances to the audience that things would turn out well. How do you do that? As great as our guest hosts were, it simply couldn't be done.

Born to Host

When Rush was young, his dad didn't necessarily support his passion for radio wholeheartedly. But at the age of nine, Rush broadcast from his bedroom using a toy given to him by his parents. The tiny gadget could only transmit throughout his home.

> *"There was a device called a Remco Caravelle, and it was the most amazing thing. My parents got it for Christmas for me one year, and my mother actually, dutifully, put a radio on her lap and I would go upstairs where the bedroom was, and my phonograph. You had to move the microphone to your mouth when you were doing DJ stuff and then you'd hold the microphone near the speaker for the phonograph to play the record. My mother would dutifully sit down there and listen to this. And the quality was just horrible. But you know, it allowed me to get started on living out my dreams.*
>
> *"Even though the family didn't understand it, the fact that I hadn't quit it was enough for them to encourage me to stay in it. And I did. And all that happened, happened. And it's been so rewarding and*

*it has been so meaningful to me and there have been so
many people who have made it possible, among them,
all of you."—RL*

Pandemic and Pain

When we next saw Rush, a few weeks after the announcement,
everything was different. How could it not be? We were in a
pandemic. Rush had advanced lung cancer and the treatment
compromised his immune system. Any germ that touched him
could be fatal. Not only were we masked in the building, there
was no more physical contact. His studio was off-limits. We had
to remain behind the glass in the control room. When Rush
left his studio during breaks to go to the kitchen, nobody else
could be there. We couldn't even be in the same room. There
were two exceptions. One was our gifted engineer, Brian, who
sanitized his hands, gloved up, masked up, and would enter
Rush's studio for a few moments to bring him my stack of show
prep and to hook up Rush's cochlear implant clip to the back of
his shirt. The other was Rush's private chef, who would enter,
masked and gloved, to bring his pre-show meal.

For us, the lack of physical closeness was a very real hardship. I know that might sound selfish. But we were family, and
had been for decades. It was my habit to go into the studio
every single day before the show and talk with Rush. No more.
I think we've all learned, since COVID, that phones and video
screens will never really replace face-to-face interaction.

After his treatments started, for the first few weeks it
seemed like everything was going well. Then the side effects

came. From day one, Rush said he didn't want to be "a cancer patient." He didn't want cancer to define him—on the air or off.

Many of us, if we received a diagnosis like his, would say, "OK. Thank you. I had a great run at this career. I'm gonna do my bucket list and enjoy myself. I'm going to spend time with the people I want to be with." And guess what? That's what Rush did.

He spent time with the people he wanted to be with—his audience. Rush's bucket list was to give everything that he could to his listeners, out of a sense of gratitude and appreciation for the wonderful life that they had provided for him.

"I understand now, what Lou Gehrig meant. Because I certainly feel like that. I feel extremely fortunate and lucky because I have outlived the diagnosis, I have been able to receive and hear and process some of the most wonderful nice things about me that I might not have ever heard."—RL

There were only a few times on the air when Rush talked about his treatment. One was particularly grave when he indicated they would have to try "a new approach." That was a red flag for me.

During what would be the final Thanksgiving show in 2020, Rush made it a point to speak very poignantly about how much the audience meant to him. I still think about this a lot. He said, "There will come a time when I will no longer be able to do this, but until then, I'm going to do this as many days as I can." I tried to ignore the first part of his statement, but that was the reality.

We all experience changes in life. But I can't imagine living on a stage before tens of millions of people. Our audience, by the way, never stopped growing, even into our thirty-third year. Rush's passion to "do this as long as I can do this" showed where his heart was. He loved his wife, he loved his friends, and he loved helping others through philanthropy. But Rush made no secret about his calling.

> *"I was born to host. And you were born to listen." —RL*

This was always said with a trademark smile, but it was no joke. And until the very end, that was Rush Limbaugh. Born to host with talent on loan from God, and we were there to enjoy the broadcast.

The Gift of Christmas
"I've been very lucky, folks, and I can't tell you in how many ways. You, I, when this kind of thing befalls you, it's hard not to become self-focused. It's hard to not just think of yourself. It's hard to think that everybody's going to drop what they're doing and deal with me. You have to guard against that because this is, to the family, this is as disrupting, it's as upsetting as it is to me. And in some cases, even more so. So, you can't, I can't, be self-absorbed about it when that is the tendency when

you are told that you've got a due date. You have an expiration date. A lot of people never get told that so they don't face life this way."—RL

The Christmas broadcast in December 2020—his final Christmas broadcast—was incredibly special. To me, it was the advent of the worst Christmas of my life. I was so devastated emotionally after that broadcast that I didn't go out during the holidays. I didn't want to be around anybody. I just wanted to stay home, mope, cry, and feel miserable. I could tell in that broadcast that this man—who'd spent the entire year giving everything he had to give—might not be with us the following Christmas.

"My point in all this is gratitude. My point in everything today that I share about this, is to say thanks and to tell everybody involved how much I love you from the bottom of a sizable and growing and still-beating heart."—RL

There was something in the way he delivered the message. Only later did I realize he was preparing his audience—and us—for the end. After the show, he privately confided, "You know, I didn't expect to be here this long after that diagnosis."

In the weeks leading up to the Christmas broadcast, I had noticed a new word in his lexicon. *Terminal.* Instead of referring to *advanced* lung cancer, he called it *terminal* lung cancer. Rush knew the prognosis and wanted others to know it.

I refused to accept the reality. I still believed some new approach would turn back the clock. But at the same time, I saw my friend's intense suffering.

Rush gave it his all, and some days at the end of the show, we could see what giving it all meant. Rush could barely move. I saw just how much those three hours had taken out of him. Those broadcasts were flawless, some of his best. But when that show was over, he was exhausted. "I can barely stand up," he told me one day.

We could see steady weight loss. He grew a beard, which reminded me of Ernest Hemingway at first, but after a few months, even his thick, gray whiskers couldn't hide his narrowing face and gaunt complexion. Most listeners probably did not notice a difference because his energy and excellence never faded. Even after the disappointment of election day 2020, he still maintained a positive attitude through that painful holiday season.

One day that stands out in particular was a celebration of Christmas the four of us had together—Rush, Dawn, Brian, and me. He asked us to come into the studio with him, which was the first time in a year we were allowed in the same room with him. The gathering was such a special gift that I won't divulge the details, but I will tell you this. Rush Limbaugh was the greatest broadcaster of all time, in my eyes, and I've known many great broadcasters. Beyond that, he was one of the most courageous human beings I've ever had the pleasure of knowing.

His life changed my life. And the way Rush handled his final challenge—giving his all every day—changed me.

The Voice

Rush Limbaugh did something that very few broadcasters are able to do. He earned the heartfelt trust of tens of millions of listeners.

In the months since Rush passed, people are still grieving. I certainly am. Maybe you are, too. In one of the final broadcasts, a man called in and tried to explain why the show mattered so much to him. He fumbled around with a few explanations, but finally broke down crying, and told Rush, "I just want to hear your voice."

Even Rush said people wouldn't remember what he talked about, but they would remember how he made them feel. His voice became a familiar part of people's lives for more than three decades.

Rush also had an emotional connection with people because he was not afraid to admit that he had failed many times at something he really loved. He'd been fired many times from a profession that he passionately pursued. After seven firings, he temporarily left the field and figured he wasn't going to make it. But he came back to give radio one last try, and that one last try was unimaginably successful. His voice was a living reminder to not give up, even after experiencing failure.

We had many calls over the years from listeners who related to Rush's story. They talked about the failures and disappointments in their own lives, and how Rush's positivity gave them confidence to try again. Now, that's a rare commodity in broadcasting—a voice speaking into *your* life, inspiring you to do something with *your* life. Thousands of people over the years called and expressed those sentiments to me. They found inspiration through his optimism.

"I Became a Doctor Thanks to You"

RUSH: "Hey, Larry, great to have you. I'm glad you waited, sir. Hi."

CALLER: "Thank you, and dittos. I wanted to say thank you, and I'm glad I got the chance to do this. I became a doctor thanks to you. I've been a doctor a long time now, but it's thanks to you. And my second point is, I remember—"

RUSH: "Wait. What kind of doctor are you?"

CALLER: "I'm a spine specialist."

RUSH: "A spine specialist. And how did this program make you want to become a doctor?"

CALLER: "I was a schoolteacher, and you talked about following your passion and how you've never worked a day in your life because you love what you did. And I was convincing myself that, *you know what, I should do that, too.*"

RUSH: "I love hearing stories like that. I really do. Because, see, it was in you all the time."

CALLER: "Yes."

RUSH: "This passion was in you all the time. You just needed a little kick that told you, *you could do it.*"

CALLER: "Absolutely. And the money and everything just appeared. It was a miracle, if you want to use that term. But it just occurred. And I've been practicing a lot now, and still passionate about it.

I'm getting a little older in my years and long in
the tooth, but I have as much passion today as the
day I walked into the school and walked into the
anatomy lab. So, it's there."

RUSH: "Well, thank you very much. I love hearing
stories like that, when anybody is able to get out
of a rut, find out what they really love doing, and
go do it. That's fabulous. Thank you very much!"

I remember when Larry called in and told me about his
decision to pursue his new career in medicine. I knew Rush
would want to hear his story and talk with him. And I had
the honor of speaking with tens of thousands of callers, just
like Larry, whose lives were literally changed for the better
because of Rush's voice—and his example. Fifteen hours a
week for thirty-three years, he gave us all a little kick that
reminded us, *we can do it.*

Rush did more than just *talk* about political and social
issues. As professor of the Limbaugh Institute for Advanced
Conservative Studies, he educated us about the way the various systems in this country *really* operated. His voice inspired
young skulls full of mush and older skulls full of doubts. A
weapon of mass instruction indeed.

As part of the fourth branch of government, he brought
issues to light—issues the establishment of both parties
preferred to keep in the dark. He debunked propaganda with
facts and reason. He championed capitalism and celebrated
success. Rush discussed the same headlines we all read and
heard about, but his take on those stories was unique. He

would often say that he was well aware of what the "conventional wisdom" was on an issue—but he rarely agreed with it.

Those of us who care about the fate of this country, what our children and their children will inherit, must keep important issues front and center, and we must put what we've learned from Rush into practice.

Most conservatives don't know who our de facto leader is today. Many feel betrayed by the establishment Republican Party, whose members seem to forget the values that energized their constituents to send them to Washington, DC. Rush was a liaison between us and those officeholders, always reminding them what people wanted and what they were failing to deliver.

Rush held true to conservative values and articulated them—loud and clear. Will anyone else step up to the microphone in the same way? I don't know. But history shows us that where there's a void, someone—or millions of someones—will fill that void.

I've been content and grateful to avoid the spotlight. I worked under a not-so-secret alias for goodness sake! But I must tell this story. Rush mattered. The show mattered. The ideas embraced by millions of his fans—including me— matter. Instead of Bo Snerdley, it's James Golden, but my voice has never changed. I'm the same man you heard agree *and disagree* with Rush for thirty-three years. The lessons and stories must not be lost. Most of all, Rush's legacy must be framed truthfully and properly.

SHOW NOTES

The broadcast was always about this great nation. And more specifically, about appreciating the people who make this nation what it is. Rush was a force of optimism; he believed in America and her people. I also believe and will do my part, however small, to keep that optimism alive and express my profound gratitude to our listeners who share the values Rush Limbaugh articulated—all the while, "having more fun than a human being should be allowed to have."

A Recent Message from a Listener

Dear Mr. Golden,
I am deeply sorry for your loss of Rush and
your Mother. I am a Rush Baby who is raising
three Rush Babies. When Rush passed away,
I mourned him like I mourned my father. I lost
both of my parents to cancer, my mother to lung
cancer. I know exactly what y'all went through. I
was amazed at Rush's stamina while undergoing
treatments. He truly was a gift from God.

A Word from One of Our Amazing Guest Hosts, SEAN HANNITY

"We lost our best player, we lost our team captain, we lost our franchise, everything. And it does now fall on all of us to up our game and carry the torch—every one of us—and strive to live with the courage, the compassion, the conviction, patriotism that Rush did every single day."

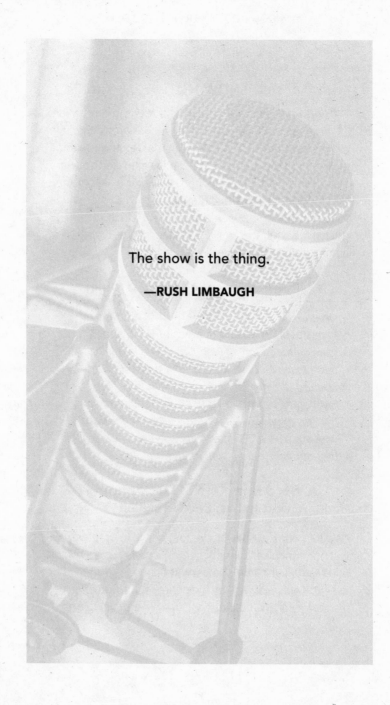

The show is the thing.

—RUSH LIMBAUGH

2

MEETING OF THE MINDS

It takes me about five seconds to figure out if someone is being honest or not.

It's not that I haven't been played before, or don't get fooled from time to time. But I do have a pretty good batting average when it comes to sizing up people—which went to another level during my time working with Rush Limbaugh and speaking with hundreds of thousands of callers. According to my math, I screened calls from almost a million people during my radio career.

I read people. I read voices. And I discriminate. We all do, by the way, and I had the honor of getting paid to make many tough choices in my radio career, whether it was about songs or people. As a call screener, I would often know within ten words if the caller would make it on the air or not. That was my job as chief discriminator. A good call can make a show, and a bad call can derail it. This principle is as true in music radio as it is in talk radio.

Rush Hour

Rush and I first met in the summer of 1988, on the day he came to New York City to work with my longtime mentor, Ed McLaughlin, whom I got to know very well through my work at WABC. Ed left his leadership role at ABC, where he ran the entire radio empire, to form a new company, EFM Media, which had acquired satellite access time to launch new radio programming. This included a "new talk radio guy" out of Sacramento, California, who was slated to host a midday show—Rush Limbaugh.

As a radio professional, I really hadn't given much thought about the potential for a sizable audience in this midday time slot, simply because most listeners tuned in during morning and late-afternoon drive times. This program's success was a long shot, according to "industry experts," but change was in the air. The idea of nationally syndicating talk radio seemed to be gaining ground, even though it went against the conventional wisdom that listeners wanted local hosts and topics.

As I walked down the stairs from the ABC building, I spotted Ed walking up from the sidewalk with another gentleman. Somehow, I knew it was Rush. After Ed introduced us, I found myself saying, "Oh, you're gonna be the new Paul Harvey—the next big thing in radio!"

We all had a friendly chuckle about that prediction and chatted for a few minutes. Even in the midst of the chaotic city street, what struck me immediately about Rush was his quiet, confident charisma.

In order to have WABC carry his national show, Rush had to first co-host a two-hour local show, which aired on WABC with news director Kathleen Maloney. Station management dangled that as a requirement, but it did benefit the newly syndicated *Rush Limbaugh Show* because it allowed them to go to national advertisers with a New York radio giant as their flagship affiliate. Any ad that sponsors across the nation bought would air in the biggest market in the country: New York City.

About a week after our initial meeting, I was walking to a meeting at ABC and heard Rush's new program through the speakers in the hallway. There was something different about the show, even down to his choice of music. Then I heard Rush Limbaugh behind the microphone for the first time. The man had a unique gift.

"I was brought to New York by Ed McLaughlin, to whom I probably owe everything as far as this national career of mine has gone. And we wanted to try something that everybody in the business said wouldn't work. We were going to syndicate a national program in the daytime without local issues without local phone numbers and so forth, and nobody in the business thought it would work. [. . .] I say what I say to the American people and any chance I have a chance to speak to them, I do. And I am so grateful and so honored for the overwhelming change in my life that they have brought. Regardless of what I mean to them,

I am certain that I will never mean as much to them as they mean to me." —RL

Bo Is Born

I instantly became a loyal listener to Rush on the radio. Everything about the show was so fresh—the attitude, the humor, and the smart takes on taboo issues. It didn't take long for the local show to explode, and it was apparent that Rush was destined for a big national audience. Because we worked in the same building, I'd sometimes bring him unusual news stories that I thought he'd appreciate, and that's how we first got to know each other.

WABC provided a call screener and an engineer for the program. One of the first screeners was a woman who didn't want her friends to know she was working with a conservative show, so Rush called her Marva Snerdley. And there were other Snerdleys in the radio family. Even then, being known as a conservative was not always socially acceptable. Nicknames would become a tradition as the show grew—not to provide aliases, but just for fun.

About two months after the program's launch, "Marva" moved on to a different show and I gladly stepped into the role. I'll never forget the day I walked into Rush's studio as an official part of the team. There was just five minutes before the show began. "Well, James, you know everybody on the show's gotta be a Snerdley. Which Snerdley are you?"

I looked down on his desk, scanning headlines from countless scattered newspapers. The *Daily News* had a story about Bo Jackson the baseball player. "Uh. Bo!" Little did I know that over three decades later, people would still refer to me as Bo Snerdley.

Hello? Am I on the Air?

Whenever I was screening, especially for a news or a topical show, I'd try to think like the host. I worked to position callers in the best order, and at the right time within each hour. Much of this approach had become second nature to me, which was one of the reasons why Rush and I clicked. One of our staff said that I had "mind meld" with Rush. He was able to tell me what he wanted—and didn't want—from calls, and I'd go through hell or high water to make sure we had those callers lined up.

Call screening can be a tough gig, if done correctly. At the end of three hours, you feel like you've been through the wringer—because putting other people through the wringer is hard work! In a typical day, I may have spoken with a hundred people, and only five of them might make it on air.

I knew Rush wanted excellence, and my radio career was all about delivering excellence, from years of pioneering music research, on the air as a disc jockey, to producing music and talk programs. What I didn't know—and there was plenty— he would teach me, especially during the first few months of working together.

The Show Is the Thing

One of the biggest lessons I learned from working with Rush came during my first week on the job. In my normal routine, once we reached the final segment or two, I'd make sure we had a few callers ready, then I'd work on various postproduction tasks. One particular afternoon, I had three or four callers primed and ready. Rush had a computer screen to see who the callers were, where they were from, and what they wanted to talk about. I figured everything was good to go, since there was only one short segment of the show left, so I switched my focus to other tasks while continuing to listen to the show.

By the time he welcomed the first of those callers, there was no one on the line. Crickets.

Rush being Rush, he winged it with humor and professionalism, and switched to the second caller. Dial tone. I froze. There was no time to screen more callers. Then he tried the next in line. Every caller had either hung up or been disconnected. We had dead air, and I was dead meat.

As soon as the show was over, he called me in and asked what happened. "I'm sorry," I said. "I was doing postproduction work and had several callers stacked up."

He stopped me dead in my excuses. With a forgiving but firm voice he said, "Listen. The show is the thing."

That was a phrase I heard throughout the decades. *The show is the thing.* Everything else waits. Don't start on anything else until *after* the show. Pay attention to every single moment we are on the air, up to and including the last second.

His professionalism and love for our audience was on a different level from anything I'd experienced in all my previous years of radio production. *Excellence in broadcasting* was more than a slogan or brand name.

A few days later, I made some stupid political joke about Ronald Reagan, who, I'd soon learn, was one of Rush's heroes.

Rush looked up at me and sighed with a weary expression of, *I really hope this guy isn't one of those flaming-ass liberals who's gonna badmouth Reagan.* I didn't mean anything disrespectful by the attempted humor, but I realized this was not a guy who sat around and cracked jokes. Rush took politics seriously. He loved America—and loved Americans. He loved his listeners. And that's why he was so successful.

Thankfully, Rush also cared about his team and understood we were all growing as we went along. Good thing, because the broadcast was about to grow beyond all of our imaginations.

> *"In 1988 when I started, all of the wizards of broadcasting, God love them, they were not being mean, they just said it will never work. 'You can't take a national program in the middle of the day, syndicate it, and have anybody listen to it. Radio is local, you have to have local topics, local phone numbers, local hosts.' But it worked. There are a whole lot of lessons there. The wizards of broadcasting were wrong; they were presiding over the eventual demise of their own genre." —RL*

Making Air Waves

We started in August 1988, with fifty-six radio stations across the nation, in a two-hour time slot from noon to two. The ratings grew so quickly that we added a third hour, and that's how we became a three-hour broadcast. After only three months, we were airing on one hundred stations. Then two hundred. It was a whirlwind ride that didn't stop. Less than two years later, Rush was on more than six hundred stations. Amazingly, the show continued to grow nationwide without the help of a major syndicator. The program changed talk radio and rescued the AM radio industry. Before Rush's national program, there were less than two hundred stations in the United States with a "news talk" format. Twenty years later, there were over two thousand.

When listeners inquired about Rush's network affiliation, he began referring to his team as the Excellence in Broadcasting network, later dubbed the EIB network.

> *"Now, 1988, you have to remember, there's no conservatism nationally other than, what, National Review magazine. And that wasn't really national. It was the three networks, and CNN, and the Washington Post, and the New York Times. That was the media. USA Today had just popped up. CNN was the only thing outside the three networks. It had started in 1980, so it was eight years old, and it was on cable. And it was a much different CNN then from the CNN that you know today.*
>
> *"So the conservative movement of that era didn't know what to make of me. The conservative movement has been burned many times over the decades by people who they thought were conservative, invested in them, and it turned out that they were weak, not like-minded, and eventually faded and ended up either ignoring, betraying, or walking away from*

conservatism. And so there were people at arm's length. Nobody mistreated me, nothing of the sort. It's just it was a natural instinct. 'Who is this guy? OK, so he's a conservative, but is this gonna help us or hurt us? This guy on the radio, he's doing weird things. He's cracking jokes about liberals and I don't know if we want to be associated with this.'

"They were very cautious because, again, they had no idea who I was and standoffish a little bit. They were, on one hand, thrilled and excited that somebody had come along that was articulating what they had been writing and speaking of and slaving over in basements and crowded rooms trying to get published here and there. And here comes some guy who they've never heard of espousing things they believe in. So it was a mixed bag. They wanted it all to be legit, but because of betrayal and an image, frankly, that some people had of anything not on television, they were standoffish." —RL

Within about two years, Rush went from being a no-name to a household name across America. Television and newspaper interviewers started showing up, including Peter Boyer of *Vanity Fair* and Steve Roberts, husband of Cokie Roberts, from *U.S. News & World Report*. This media attention was our first taste of what was to come. For me, the Steve Roberts interview was the first time I realized the huge difference between what Rush was saying and how it was perceived by the political left.

In the early years, Rush did cover politics, but the show also contained a lot of off-the-cuff commentary and pull-no-punches parody on a wide variety of topics. Maybe you remember the stories about the Arkansas Toe Sucker. Nick—a caller from the high mountains of New Mexico—told us about grilling dogs. Stray dogs. Rush told the nation about his plans to make a delicious omelette, made from bald eagle eggs. That bit generated a few calls. He truly had an irreverent sense of humor, and the bald eagle prank was one of thousands to follow over the years. It was a gentle stab at the endangered species list, which, for all the good it did, also had absurdities that adversely impacted farmers. The spotted owl was also on that list. Protecting its habitat would lead to thousands of job losses in the timber industry, and, as Rush would point out, the birds had been spotted (no pun intended) living in broken K-Mart signs and other places where environmentalists proclaimed it would be impossible for them to survive.

"When I moved to New York, I didn't plan on becoming a political spokesman. In fact, politics was the last thing I factored in, in determining whether or not I would be a success. I was coming to be on radio, a media guy and I love radio. I do television, too, but that microphone is right here and that camera is twenty feet away. And there's intimacy on the radio and there's naturalness on the radio that can never be replicated on TV. TV is the medium of our time, there's

no question, but I am proud to be part of the marvelous resurgence of radio as a political force in this country. Four years ago, when people went to vote, people said, 'My gosh, there aren't enough people voting. There's apathy. The people don't care.' Today, the Congress of the United States is attempting to shut talk radio up because people care too much. And I am proud to be a part of that." —RL

Rush used to define the show as "the relentless pursuit of the truth," combining the news of the day with irreverent humor. And his humor was fearless. It was also shocking, not because he was trying to be a shock jock, but because people had never heard anything like it on the radio. There were no sacred cows—or sacred politicians.

I remember taking a call from an elderly woman who was nearly sobbing because she was so concerned about Rush. She was worried because he was making fun of Senator Ted Kennedy. In America, nobody made fun of the Kennedys, and no one dared to even whisper *Chappaquiddick.* This caller was afraid that Rush would be arrested and thrown off the air. In case we've forgotten, that's just one example of how ground-breaking the show was.

Listener response was stunning—and affirming. We were beginning to see that half the country felt the way Rush did. Maybe more than half. And Rush was their champion. He said what people never heard from the media. There was no Fox News. There was no internet as we know it today.

National Review magazine espoused conservative ideals, but it was a highbrow publication. There wasn't anything relevant or relatable—or funny—for average Americans to tune in to. It simply didn't exist before Rush.

His sense of humor wasn't mean, it was pointed. He also illustrated absurdity by being absurd. He was polite with people who disagreed with him. In fact, a rule he gave me was to place callers with opposing views at the front of the line—he didn't want those who disagreed with him to wait. He wanted to have the debate head on.

Wrong about Bill

The era of Bill Clinton changed everything for us. That's when the show became mostly political. In fact, it was in the lead-up to Clinton's first presidential campaign that Rush offered up one of his classic bits.

More and more people referred to Bill Clinton as "Slick Willie" because he could weasel his way out of any question and deflect from blatant contradictions in his past. His adversary, Bob Dole, asked, "Why doesn't character matter?" Senator Dole wanted to be a bridge to the past.

Yeah, I thought, *just what I want from a president, a bridge to the past.*

And of course, Clinton hopped all over Dole's comment and changed the subject: "No, no, no. We need a bridge to the future!"

One day late in the campaign season, Rush opened the show and continued for the entire first hour of his monologue explaining that he'd been all wrong about Bill Clinton. After careful review, Rush confessed that Clinton was probably the best candidate to become president, and as such, he endorsed Bill Clinton.

We had already reached the point where what Rush said made national and international news. Within minutes, we started getting calls from the major news organizations preparing to write the story that Rush Limbaugh had endorsed Bill Clinton. We even got calls from the Bush White House team. "What the hell is this endorsement?!"

The second hour opened and listeners were outraged. Some were even crying, "How dare you? How could you do this to us?"

Rush was completely nonplussed. He responded to callers' questions with puzzlement. "Why are you asking me about this?"

"You endorsed Bill Clinton!" an exasperated caller blurted.

"No, I didn't. I didn't endorse Bill Clinton."

"Well, I heard you say it."

"Well, no, you didn't. I never said that."

One of the mantras Bill Clinton had repeated in defense of past statements was, "Oh, that was a long time ago. Let's move past that." So, when callers pointed out they'd heard the endorsement of Clinton in the past hour, Rush didn't miss a beat. He acted just like Slick Willie.

"Oh, that was a long time ago," Rush replied. "Please forget that. No one can take that seriously. You can't hold me to that. I said that a long time ago. I do not endorse Bill Clinton. I've never endorsed Bill Clinton."

For the rest of the show, we hosted furious callers who swore they heard him endorse Clinton. Rush steadfastly denied that he had *ever* or *would ever* endorse Bill Clinton. It was the perfect example of illustrating absurdity by being absurd—and also calling out the media coverage, which had ignored almost everything Bill Clinton had done and said during the campaign, especially his blatant contradictions.

It was hysterical. It wasn't planned, and at the time, I didn't even know what was happening.

I'm One of Them

When I first heard Rush "endorse" Bill Clinton, I was in *Oh crap* mode. *What the hell is he doing?* The first of countless such moments. Yes, over the years I became wise to his satire, but even up to our final months of working side by side, he'd still manage to fool me.

I was never obsessed with politics, but I realized something significant was going on in our republic, and the show was forging new impact and new importance in political dialogue. I followed politics, I knew what I liked, didn't like, and believed, but I never identified myself as a conservative.

Years earlier, I had worked as producer and call screener with Bob Grant, a pioneer of the conservative talk radio format. During the late Reagan years with all the Sandinista craziness going on in Nicaragua, someone called in . . . from Nicaragua. Jackpot! I put him on the air, telling Bob that we had a perfect man-on-the-street perspective. *This is gonna be a great caller,* I thought, *confirming Bob's take on the threat of communist-backed Sandinistas!* Just one problem—the guy on the phone was a communist and spewed all sorts of propaganda to our listeners. I never thought to ask deeper questions about what his views were and why he was calling. Once Grant understood the man's agenda, he cut the caller down to size and eviscerated him. That's when I realized I needed a clearer ideological and political perspective, so I could filter callers and present them to the host accurately. I had let Bob down. And I had let the caller down, because I never want anyone to feel ambushed.

As a creator and consumer of news media, I agreed with most conservative ideas while producing a variety of political shows. I wouldn't necessarily have expressed my ideas in the same way other hosts did, until I worked with Rush. He gave a name to the beliefs I held my entire life. Rush called it conservatism. That's when I had another *Oh crap* moment and realized, *He's articulating exactly what I believe. OK,* I thought. *I'm a conservative. I'm one of them!*

Of course, Rush knew what he was doing since day one on WABC, and he spelled it out in his 2009 speech at the Conservative Political Action Conference (CPAC).

"I thought it would be helpful to define conservatism for people, because nobody else was. Everybody just assumed it was this or that—small government less taxes and all this stuff. But it's really about people; it's about our understanding of people; it's about our faith, trust in people. It's about the knowledge that it is people that make a great nation. It's ordinary people pursuing and accomplishing extraordinary things with

*the freedom, the ambition to do so. And I just thought
it needed to be pointed out—the love and compassion
that you in this audience have shown consistently for
thirty-one years."—RL*

This clarity is what Rush was all about for millions of
Americans, and I do mean millions. Not two million, not
ten million. For almost thirty million people, Rush clearly
stated what they believed, and that was one of the reasons his
show always grew and was always successful. He was able to
communicate what so many people were *already* thinking.
And he called it conservatism.

Rush defined and clarified what was already ingrained in
my political belief system. And he helped me form and articulate my conservative beliefs, in ways that helped me communicate with people of various political ideologies.

Our nation is at a crossroads. We have amazing technology, breakthroughs in medicine, and unprecedented opportunity for every American. But we're still wrestling with
problems that could have been solved fifty years ago. Health
care is one. Prison reform another, although President Trump
did his best to deliver on these issues instead of just talk, as so
many politicians have done.

I believe this country would be much better off if, instead
of reacting to phrases and sound bites, we had *real* tolerance,
not just fake civility. We should be able to ask each other
honest questions without fear of being canceled. Then we
open ourselves up to hearing answers that might take us out
of our comfort zones.

Political Odd Couples

If any two people can enlighten us on listening and loving each other, it's my dear friends Mary Matalin and James Carville. You probably know them as outstanding political strategists—Mary on the Republican side, and James on the Democrat side. James was the lead strategist with former president Bill Clinton's campaign, and Mary worked with President Ronald Reagan and was campaign director for President George H. W. Bush. They've been married since 1993. Here's what they shared with me about Rush in an interview from July 2021.

> MARY MATALIN: "Rush and James [Carville], ironically, hit it off. And I knew Rush before he was Rush. I think my dad turned me on to him in the late '80s and we've been constant companions since then, as James will tell you, since I never turned him off."

> JAMES CARVILLE: "When you become famous, and I've noticed this in my own life, people only know you for what you're famous for. So if you're a baseball player and you're famous, you have a life outside of baseball. People are just not that interested in it or are marginally interested in it. Well obviously, probably the two people that Mary was closest to was Rush and Vice President Cheney, and as a result of that, I had to spend a fair amount of time. What both of them were,

they were multidimensional people, so I wasn't going to talk politics because I sure as hell didn't agree with anything they said, and they would say the same thing about me, but we could talk about other things very easily. It wasn't a stilted or forced conversation, they both were multidimensional people, so you didn't have like uncomfortable small talk.

"He saved AM radio. The way that you know a person's legacy is how many knockoffs did he create, you know. Let Mary go through the list of names of people. Well, in a nation that is really divided, and to people I think that divisiveness is a problem, you kind of want to say 'what a divisive guy,' but having said that, what I'd like to focus on is you know, he created a lot of knockoffs and none of them ever became him. And that's when you know you've done something, when you've got successful people imitating you. [. . .] I'm sorry, but I couldn't do three hours of programming five days a week for anything in the world. He was not an overly modest man, but to be honest, in terms of his professional career, he didn't have a lot to be modest about."

MARY MATALIN: "There's things that people didn't know about Rush, I mean of course he was talented, he was a talent on loan from God and you, too, James [Golden], but picking up on that point that James [Carville] made, in real life,

Rush was overly modest, humble, he knew what the data was, but I think to the very end he was moved, struck, shocked, awed by his own reach. He also was a gentleman, he was courteous, he was gentle, he was patient. He taught me how to use an iPhone in the flip phone days. [...]

"One of the problems I had with Rush early on was, I was kind of a hippy dippy, you know, environmentalist in my old days. And he, when it started to turn into a racket and he connected it to environmental whackos, which I kind of understood, but I couldn't understand the motivation. That was the other thing that he could suss out and explain. And he never attributed ill motives. He attributed the reality. He *was* the mayor of Realville so he knew what they were going to do, and he would say these things, and people would go, 'Oh, Rush.' And he was always, literally, sometimes decades, always years ahead of where the culture and the zeitgeist was.

"You [James Golden] would challenge him, particularly as he was thinking—that was another thing he did that I've never seen anybody do with the aplomb that he did it, he would think out loud and he would think in full paragraphs and complete narratives—but you would push him and prod him and pick at him and understand what he understood, what was in his head that he thought everybody knew. You guys were a great team."

JAMES GOLDEN: "I wanted to know how he arrived at these conclusions. And you know, he gave me the freedom to disagree with him publicly, which was just amazing and astounding. And he could sometimes tell by a look because I would look at him a certain way. 'Why are you looking at me like that? Do you not agree?' If I didn't, OK, I don't and why. And then he would explain it. He was wonderful that way."

MARY MATALIN: "That is the hallmark of a genius, is somebody who is always challenging their own perspectives, their own ideas, and is trying to understand how other people think and how they're perceiving what he is, that the person, he or she is saying. He always had that, and he liked to be disagreed with. Didn't you all just tee up the liberals first?"

JAMES GOLDEN: "That's right. He would demand that if someone disagreed, put them up at the top. 'I want to talk to them first!' Mary, explain 1994."

MARY MATALIN: Republicans were wandering around in the desert and they had been in the minority for over half a century and he [Rush] became an honorary member of the 94th Congress [. . .] I credit, and many do, too—and anybody who knows anything about politics and how a message is delivered and penetrates—would attribute the victory and the finest victory in the last century for Republicans to Rush Limbaugh's 1994, and

I can't call it anything else but a *campaign*. His other completely transformational act was Operation Chaos. He had so much influence on politics, way more than anybody who's in politics. Well, I shouldn't say that, that's a little hyperbole. But he had as much influence as every day operatives have on politics, but in the big picture, the historical picture, he had more influence than anybody else, and that is fair to say.

"I don't think he could have done it without you, James Golden, without the whole team of course, but you were like his constant touchstone. Everything he said, he would take a look at you. How many times has he said, 'You don't think that? You disagree with me?' You never talked, which is so cool, but we knew where you were and he would describe you sitting behind the [glass], and that was a beautiful relationship and I think a legacy, too, because it's something when somebody can have, for the length of time that he had, the same team. You have to be a good person with loyalty, which goes both ways, to have the kind of team that he had, which you were the spearhead of, so we thank you Bo Snerdley, James Golden."

More Talk or More Action?

I cannot even begin to fill the void left by Rush's departure, but I have to do *something*. I had many discussions with Rush on the subject of "activism." He was not an activist, and his show was not about activism. Rush was a matchless educator. He believed that people had the innate wisdom to decide for themselves how and where to act, if they chose to.

I respect that position, but I don't hold the exact same view. The time has long since passed where conservatives can walk around with their tails tucked between their legs and settle for being on the defensive. How has that worked out for us and our beliefs? There is a time and place for action—and I have a particular vision for what this means in our world.

It's going to take millions of voices—including mine and yours—to fill the void.

We need to aggressively articulate our views and our values. However, in doing so, we don't have to demean other people. We can act from a position of love—love for the country and love for others with whom we disagree. We don't have to hate those who disagree. We don't even have to dislike them. All we have to do is defeat them politically.

Here's what Rush told me in a 2008 interview.

"Well, James, one thing hasn't changed from what I wrote in my first book. Elected officials come and go; my success does not depend on who wins elections. Theirs is a different business than mine. They have to go get votes. They have a different attitude on things. I am on constant offense, defeat-the-opposition mode. Politicians have this notion, we've got to work together. I don't want to work together with these people that I find pose a great threat. I have never moistened a

finger and stuck it in the air to see what people want to hear and said it. Just the opposite." —RL

Even though some people despise us, disparage us, and try to cancel us, we must not sink to their level.

SHOW NOTES

I love to talk politics. I've made a career out of talking and listening. Longtime listeners to the Rush Limbaugh program have the equivalent of a college degree in political science. We have the education. May I suggest that it's time to put what we know into action? I'm not talking about marches and counter-protests. I'm talking about letting people on the political left know we are not going to be quiet.

We will play the incrementalism game, celebrate limited victories, and keep coming back until we win. That's how the left plays it, and it works very well. Why don't we play politics like they do—but in an honorable manner? We have to face the fact that our political adversaries fight like pit bulls, and we have to be equally determined about our beliefs and our ideals.

We need more talk *and* more action.

A Recent Message from a Listener

"Mr. Golden, how blessed you are to have known and worked with Rush. I admire the obvious love and devotion you had for him. I visited his grave site today and paid my respects. Yes, I cried. Anyway, thank you for what you have shared and God bless you."

A Word from One of Our Amazing Guest Hosts, MARK STEYN

"I know precisely when I first heard Rush. It was not long after he started the show and not long after I bought my pad in New Hampshire. I was driving some visitors from London through the North Maine Woods toward New Brunswick in that dead zone where the only thing that comes in is the soft-and-easy station on 94.9 FM from the top of Mount Washington. And then that died, and there was nothing, and I forgot to switch it off so it was automatically scanning up and around the dial as we chitchatted in the car. And then suddenly it found some guy, and there he was talking about 'the arts-and-croissants crowd' moving into your town, and reading out press releases from NOW [the National Organization for Women], whom he called the NAGS [National Association of Gals], and playing Andy Williams's version of *Born Free* punctuated by gunfire to accompany any environmental story.

"And, in my car, conversation ceased. My friends were what you might call slightly skeptical lefties, so they disagreed with what Rush said on the issues but they were rapt by the way he said it. Because they had never heard anybody say it like that before. It was a unique combination—absolute piercing philosophical clarity, and a grand rollicking presentational style honed through all the lean years of minor-market disc-jockeying.

"First, he perfected the style, and then he applied it to the content. When Clinton was elected, Rush opened his shows, for years, with 'America Held Hostage, Day Thirty-Nine . . . Day Seventy-Three . . . Day Hundred and Twenty-Four . . .,' and when Newt's Republicans won the 1994 mid-terms he started with James Brown singing *I Feel Good*.

"One man doing what he wanted to do saved an entire medium—AM radio—and turned all its old rules upside down. Traditionally, morning drive is your big audience, and everything tapers off from there. Rush figured that everyone needs a local guy at that time, with traffic and weather updates, and that the opportunity to build a national show lay in the hitherto somnolent slot of noon-to-three Eastern/nine-to-twelve Pacific. And within a couple of years, hundreds of stations were building the entire schedule around the midday guy."

I wanted to issue a special thanks to the
. . . I call them *highly overrated staff*,
they may be, but they're incredibly
valuable. They're incredibly loyal. They
are incredibly committed. And they are
exceptionally, exceptionally devoted, and
none of this could happen without them.

—RUSH LIMBAUGH

3

THE HIGHLY OVERRATED STAFF: SOUTHERN COMMAND

The first time Rush mentioned the "highly overrated staff," those of us in the control room at EIB's Southern Command Headquarters laughed our heads off. He said it so nonchalantly, looking at us and smiling. But we knew what he was saying. We knew he was proud of us, all of us in New York, Florida, and other locations.

> *"I'm sorry, folks, it's just a little inside baseball here, because you know, the staff and me, we love each other. Actually, in their minds, I'm one of the staff. So when I talk about the 'highly overrated staff,' they always think I'm talking about myself, too. It's what allows me to get away with it." —RL*

The Excellence in Broadcasting staff was a family. What I still find amazing is that Rush brought together such a talented and wonderful group of people, all of whom had strong personalities. At our peak, there were about twenty-four on the immediate staff, doing the newsletter and website, the three of us in Florida, and others who worked with the show in New York and Los Angeles. I maintain that everyone who worked with Rush could have done something different and been hugely successful. Yet they chose to invest their talents in the program.

Everyone at EIB was self-motivated and always brought their A game. It was a testament to Rush that he kept so many gifted people, with very strong personalities, in his orbit. Almost every staff member reported directly to Rush, but "reporting" was simply doing your job. He would lay out what he expected from you and left you to do your job. We were employed by the broadcast company and got paid the industry rate, but Rush would reward us all generously with bonuses at the end of the year. He didn't have to do that, but he did.

I looked forward to putting this chapter together because no perspective on Rush Limbaugh would be complete without an understanding of the amazing crew of people he surrounded himself with, and how close we became over the years. But the part I dreaded about this writing was the daunting task of whom to write about, since there have been dozens of wonderful people on the EIB team through the years.

So I decided to focus on the two people I sat beside during most of the broadcasts at the EIB Southern Command Headquarters for twenty years, Dawn and Brian—and one other very special person. I could write an entire book about all the amazing staff I had the honor of working with through thirty-three years, and I hope those I could not mention here will understand.

I must begin by honoring the late H. R. "Kit" Carson.

Hail to the Chief

Before I started working with Rush, there was a tall, skinny, redheaded guy I saw once in a while at ABC corporate headquarters, 1330 Avenue of the Americas, in New York, which was in the heart of broadcast central. ABC, CBS, NBC, the Associated Press, and other media headquarters were all in the media district of Manhattan. In the '80s, we were all dressed up to go to work. One day I noticed this young man—wearing shorts, polo shirt, and Keds sneakers—walk into Rush's office. *Who the hell is this guy?* I wondered.

That guy was Kit Carson, Rush's first hire. Rush had his own nickname for Kit: "H. R. Kit Carson," which was a reference to H. R. Haldeman, the keeper of secrets and White House chief of staff to President Nixon. He was initially brought in because Rush needed someone to handle all the mail that was coming in. When I started working with the show, it didn't take long before Kit and I became really close. As the show and the staff grew, Kit took on more responsibilities and ultimately became the chief of staff for *The Rush Limbaugh Show.*

He handled the correspondence, the requests for interviews and appearances, and postproduction work, which included helping Rush cut commercials or customize promos for the affiliate stations. Kit's job also included saying *no* to the hundreds of requests that came in every day for Rush. This took a lot of pressure off Rush. Every year, Kit organized a radio-thon fundraiser for the Leukemia & Lymphoma Society. He handled the media, he was the public liaison, and he had the freedom to suggest issues he thought Rush should talk about on the show.

As a teenager, Kit wanted to be an actor. He was funny, about six-foot-two, and very knowledgeable about so many subjects. He was so pale, I used to call him Casper, and he used to call me Shaka Zulu. We sometimes enjoyed arguing about political issues, but we were never contentious. People sometimes compared us to the *Pulp Fiction* characters played by John Travolta and Samuel L. Jackson.

Kit had two bouts with cancer. The first time, he went into remission and we were all so happy he beat it. But it came back. Kit never complained or made any kind of a big deal about it. Sometimes, we'd be talking about something, and Kit would just stop and look at me and say, "You know, James, you're a great guy." I still hear that voice. It was a special relationship. His death in 2015 came five years to the day before Rush announced his own cancer diagnosis in 2020. I always thought there was something a little cosmic about that.

Because Kit was one of a kind, there was no attempt to replace his role at EIB when he passed. Other people absorbed some of his duties, but there was never going to be a replacement for Kit. Rush echoed those sentiments in a radio tribute.

"I speak for everybody here at the EIB network when I say we feel an overwhelming absence. We feel an overwhelming hole in the normal ebb and flow of energy and presence in our network because of the passing yesterday morning of chief of staff Christopher Kit Carson. And it's going to take a while. [. . .] Been with me longer than anybody at twenty-seven years. I can't possibly personally respond to everyone who is sending me email condolences but they're beautiful, and the people who are writing me who knew Kit are telling me stories that I didn't know. Things that have happened when they interacted with Kit. Funny stories. They were descriptions of his magnanimous and gracious and hilarious personality. Don't misunderstand, it's not that I didn't know of the aspects of his personality, I didn't know the specific details of these particular stories. [. . .]

"Kit Carson, he took all kinds of pressure off of me just so I could focus on this, and he was able to do this, getting to know me and studying the program, he could do it in his sleep after a while. That's why this is going to be such a big void. And he knew that when the program is over, this is tough to explain, when the program is over, it's over. I don't want anything related to the program for at least three hours. I am wrung out. But I'm not allowed. I've often said other things. 'I've gotten to the point where I don't have to do what I don't want to do.' That's not true where Kit was involved. Program would end every day [at] three o'clock and I *would record the morning update, both the audio and video version of it.*

"Kit would routinely say, 'That's it! That's it. I got nothing here.' And I'd say, 'Fine, that's cool.'

"'Except . . .' And then he'd launch into ten things or five or whatever it was. But he always prefaced it by saying, 'Look, I got nothing. There's nothing here. I'm free and clear. Oh! Wait.' It always softened my reaction. He had it down to a science. We just miss him. There's a void and emptiness here. It's going to [take a] long time to get used to, but we hope God blesses Kit and his family." —RL

The first time Rush referred to us as the "highly overrated staff," Kit had T-shirts made for us all.

I still have mine.

"I'm just teasing the highly overrated staff. The staff went out, and they've even had some of their own shirts printed: 'Highly Overrated Staff: Excellence in Broadcasting Network.' They're having fun with it." —RL

Clark Kent, aka Brian Johnson

Brian Johnson says he was born in a radio station, and I believe it. His parents worked in radio, that's how they met, and his father built a successful radio engineering business in which Brian worked. He can fix or build anything.

When Rush lost his hearing, Brian invented a system of lights in the studio we used to let Rush know where we were at in the show. When Rush received the cochlear implant, Brian came up with a way to actually wire it into various audio sources—TV, staff intercom, and phone calls. It was really complex, but Brian could always figure it out and make it work flawlessly. The implant used a lot of batteries, but Brian built a power source Rush could plug the device into. He basically customized that studio to meet Rush's needs.

If Brian creates something, it has to be perfect functionally and aesthetically. But nothing rattles Brian. When something goes wrong, there is no "What am I going to do?!" kind of panic. You can see his Superman brain working, figuring out how he's going to fix it. Unlike me, he was always Mr. Calm—I used to call him Clark Kent. And he did it all with a smile.

Brian also occasionally answered the phone at EIB Southern Command. Here's Rush describing one particular call from someone who would sing at Rush and Kathryn's 2010 wedding.

> "Back in, I guess it was March, I'm sitting here in the morning doing show prep, getting ready for that day's busy broadcast, and all of a sudden Brian comes storming in here and says, 'There's somebody on the phone, some practical joker says he's Elton John.' And I said, 'Brian, you did not get this call. You do not remember.' [. . .] Well, I found out later Elton John's on the phone with Brian and Brian doesn't believe it. He's accusing him of being a practical joker and wasting his time.

"So Elton John actually started singing on the phone to Brian to try to prove to him that it was Elton John, and Brian still didn't believe it. But finally something compelled him to come in here and tell me that it was Elton John, so I picked up the phone and he said, 'Hi, I'm in New York, your guy didn't believe it was me.' [laughing]

"So I asked, 'What did he sing to you, Brian? You don't remember it, right? You have no idea what the tune was.' And I'm thinking, Here's Elton John on the phone singing to my broadcast engineer to try to prove to him that it is indeed Elton John. *It is very tight security. I mean I can't complain about the security aspect of it, but I mean that's just hilarious."* —RL

Rush's Boss

Dawn Bachinski is a brilliant, hardworking person. In addition to what she did for us all those years, transcribing and interpreting callers' words for Rush after his hearing loss, she launched and ran her own successful court reporting company. I maintain that she's a better lawyer than most lawyers because she notices things in legal documents that they miss.

To be an excellent transcriptionist, you have to create your own dictionary and input certain words into your word processing software. Dawn worked for countless hours over the years to curate an extensive dictionary for Rush, with all the political and cultural references. For example, have you ever tried to spell "Mahmoud Ahmadinejad" while Rush

Limbaugh and twenty million listeners were waiting? She knew that if she heard that word twice, it needed to be in her dictionary for quick access. Until the show's very last day, she kept her dictionary fresh and updated so that she could deliver what Rush needed, almost instantly.

Beyond that, she was the glue in the office, the person who made sure everybody's birthdays and anniversaries were remembered. She was also a great encourager, delivering strong and motherly wisdom to the entire staff—including Rush. I know he respected and trusted her completely.

"Dawn, are you irritated by this? You don't like this? I thought I detected a facial expression. Dawn transcribes calls to this program. She's sitting in there and her face getting contorted and so forth. And I knew it. I knew it." —RL

Dawn is also a person of faith. There were times after Rush's cancer diagnosis when the three of us—Dawn, Brian, and me—would instinctively hold hands and pray for a minute. Or if something happened in our personal lives, Dawn would gather us together and lead us in prayer. This was never pushy or forced. It's just how we were.

Every year she bought a birthday card for Rush and collected everyone's signatures. One year the card had a monkey on it, and I saw an opportunity to mess with her head. I looked at the card for a few moments, then brought my angry gaze to her eyes. "I ain't signing no card with a big monkey on it." Dawn, bless her strawberry blonde head, was horrified. "What? What are you talking about?" I said, "Can you truly be this oblivious that you don't know what I'm talking about? Me, a Black man in America, I am not signing my name under a picture of a monkey."

"I call my daughter Monkey," she gasped. And I kept the circus rolling.

"Well, your daughter is not an African American. You call her Monkey all you want to. I wouldn't call my daughter a monkey!" When I saw how upset she was, I finally relented, and we had a big laugh.

There was the Rush Limbaugh show, and there was the EIB show, behind the glass. Both were endlessly entertaining.

"You can't have a better prize than this. Four very lucky grand prize winners, four of 'em, are gonna win a full-ride trip for two to the EIB Southern Command in South Florida. As a grand prize winner, you and the person of your choice will spend the day at the highly fortified Southern Command. You'll meet me and spend the day with the overrated staff on the other side of the glass. You'll watch the show be engineered. There's not really a producer. I don't have a producer, but you'll watch Snerdley screen the calls. If it's a good day for Snerdley, that is a show unto itself." —RL

We Are Family

Special guests often dropped by the Southern Command. On one occasion, Supreme Court justice Clarence Thomas visited Rush, but we knew he was *really* there to see the highly overrated staff. As we all gathered in the production room, we stood for a photo with Justice Thomas—and handed Rush our cameras and smartphones so he could take our pictures. This was normal practice, and I know Rush got a kick out of these moments.

Rush had an incredibly diverse staff—straight, gay, every racial background, and even some liberals—because there wasn't a litmus test about your conservatism or any other ism in order to work for the show. The only test was the quality of your work. He wanted the best people around him and enjoyed unleashing them to achieve the best results.

Of course, there were occasional disagreements. Wait, that sounds too tame. We would sometimes get pissed off at each other and express opinions, loudly. But what we didn't have were power struggles and turf wars. We were clear about Rush's leadership and sincerely wanted to make Rush—and each other—proud of the work we produced.

We also knew that whatever pressures and controversies surrounded the show, Rush was the guy in the spotlight, not us. He took great care to shield us from the spotlight because he didn't want us or our families targeted. Now, for me, that wasn't an issue. I did radio and made appearances under my own name, so he treated me a little differently in that way. In fact, I wanted to go out and do battle on his behalf. That hasn't changed to this day. If anything, he had to hold me back.

"It's a lot of years and everybody on the staff contributes in their own way. But I just have decided

that based on the things I've learned on my little success track here, they don't need to go home and have their families scream at them about, 'Why are they saying that about you? Why doesn't Rush protect you?' It's just better and safer for them if they remain out of the line of fire, pure and simple. That's why you haven't heard a whole bunch of names mentioned all the time." —RL

When I was going through cancer treatment in Maryland, Rush and the crew heard I had a few days off from appointments. They immediately bought a plane ticket for me to come home so that I could be in the studio with them for one day and stay at my home for the weekend. They knew I missed them so much, and I guess the feeling was mutual. Those were the kinds of things Rush would do all the time. A new iPad would come out, and the next day I had a delivery with a new iPad. Those gestures might not have seemed like a big deal to him, but they were very meaningful to me.

And despite his decrees to not do anything for his birthday, we happily ignored him—every year. Here's his reaction on what would be his final on-air celebration.

[Highly overrated staff interrupts and starts singing Happy Birthday*] "Oh, yes, that's right. Here we come. Happy delayed birthday. Thank you. Thank you. Thank you. Thank you. What kind of flavor is that? Looks like orange something or other? All right. Cool. I picked it out. So, yeah, I was seventy years old*

on—what was it? Tuesday? I don't even remember. I have to back count to the twelfth. Anyway, they have a delayed seventieth birthday.

"*The staff constantly ignores my expressed wishes to not make a big deal out of it. This one, however, is. Look, I don't want to make—but I, frankly, about eleven months ago didn't think I would see my seventieth birthday, so for the first time in my life it's a big deal." —RL*

People often ask me if the relationship with Rush was professional or personal, or something more complex. I never compartmentalized or analyzed it. Rush was part of my family. He let us know that he loved us personally, and appreciated what we brought professionally. We were both family and friends, but knew we were there to deliver excellence.

I was truly honored to be a guest at Rush and Kathryn's wedding, which was the most beautiful and remarkable event I had ever experienced. Yes, the concert by Sir Elton John was amazing, but observing the bride and groom was the most impactful aspect of the day. Kathryn captured the spotlight—a glorious bride and partner—with her unique grace. Rush beamed like the happiest man on the planet, and I'd never seen him so exuberant.

Here's a favorite memory of mine, for many reasons, as Rush told his listeners about wedding photos he posted to his Facebook page.

"The picture of me and Snerdley on the Facebook page is getting more comments than any other picture except for the opening page. You're a popular guy. And, you know, some of these comments: 'Rush, you better be nice to that guy.' [laughing]

"I said, 'Whoa.' [laughing] 'Rush, you better be nice to Snerdley.' You know, even after twenty-two years, this is the first day for millions of people to learn that you are African American. Stunningly so, but that's the conclusion that is inescapable. So you're a popular figure on the El Rushbo and Kathryn Facebook page."

SHOW NOTES

Again, I'll just say it plainly. I love the guy, as deeply as I love any of my family members. And I was as loyal to him as he was loyal to me as a human being. The bond will never change. It's that simple. I still grieve the loss of my boss and my friend. Like any family, the EIB family is still grieving the too-soon departure of our leader and lovable little fuzzball.

A Recent Message from One of Our Listeners

"It was around twenty-nine years ago and my now late, beloved husband was getting ready for work and putting on his Green Beret. He wore that beautiful Green Beret for twenty-three years. I was channel surfing and hit on Rush. I quickly flipped the channel and mumbled the BS I'd been fed, that he was a bigot

and racist. My husband, having adjusted that beautiful Beret, saw who I was referring to and asked if I'd ever listened to Rush. I replied, 'No!' Then he said, 'Well, you obviously don't know him.'

"My husband bet me that I would change my mind if I listened to Rush for two weeks. Easy win, I thought! I'd sit and write all the bad things Rush said on the air. Well, you already know how that turned out. I've been a Rush girl since then, and we raised a 'Rush baby' who is now twenty-three years old. I've been crying for several days now, both for the loss of Rush as well as for my beloved husband, who I lost five years ago. God bless you, Bo. It was SO obvious over the airwaves how much you both loved one another."

A Word from One of Our Amazing Guest Hosts, TODD HERMAN

"If you were an animator and you got to fill in for Walt Disney, or your favorite illustrator, what would that be like? Or the people that invented your medium, not even your favorite, but who *invented* your medium. That is what this is like.

"That's the level we're talking about here. In terms of Rush's legacy, anytime you turn on a radio show and you hear an opinion-based show, you will be hearing the legacy of Rush Limbaugh. Opinion radio would not have survived without Rush. It simply wouldn't have."

Mark Steyn had a great comment. He said, "People join EIB and they never leave," and that's one of the reasons why this show works so well. It's because we've been a team here.

—RUSH LIMBAUGH

4

THE HIGHLY OVERRATED STAFF: NEW YORK TO LOS ANGELES

You knew I couldn't have only one chapter about the EIB family, didn't you?

Here are a few memories of some more dear friends with whom I had the honor of working for many years, along with some of their words from recent conversations. Whether at Southern Command, New York City, Los Angeles, or points in between, the highly overrated staff delivered excellence every day. It truly was a marvel of technology and teamwork.

A Premiere Talent: Kraig Kitchin

In my view, one man is responsible for more radio talent successes than anyone else. Kraig Kitchin was one of six cofounders of Premiere Radio Networks. They bought into Rush's original company, EFM (a partnership between Rush, Ed McLaughlin, John Axten, and Stu Crane) and expanded the reach of *The Rush Limbaugh Show*. But if you look at everyone they've touched, you realize the phenomenal impact they've had, working with hosts such as Sean Hannity, Mark Levin, Glenn Beck, Steve Harvey—and Delilah on the music side.

Kraig Kitchin has an amazing track record, he's one of the nicest guys you'll ever meet, and he can be tough when he needs to be. Don't recognize his name? His EIB moniker is Ray Donovan. I don't know how he finds the time to do everything he does. He runs the Radio Hall of Fame, does charity work, yet he still finds the time to respond if we need him. That's because he genuinely cares. I have no problem saying I love Kraig. The same with Julie Talbott, the president of Premiere. They've been there for us professionally and personally. They let us know they value us as people, not just employees. Here are a few insights from Kraig, from a recent conversation.

"In 1997 when I met Rush for the first time, I had no idea how focused he was between 8:30 a.m. and noon, when he first went on the air. But for some reason, the meeting time that he had set up was at 10:30 in the morning. I went to our meeting thinking we're gonna spend the next hour, hour and a half talking, until noon. Rush made it look, and listen, so easy. The microphones open, the music plays, and he just starts talking to you as your best friend. I had no idea that he spent the better part of fifteen hours leading up to that moment preparing for that show.

"I find the equivalent suit and tie for that meeting and went to WABC to meet the man that I'm about to sign a new four-year agreement with, and start working with, and I'm thinking we've got the better part of ninety minutes just to get to know each other. I found out very quickly we had about eight minutes. And those eight minutes better count. And so we had a great eight minutes together. But he could not have been warmer and more gregarious in that short time. Rush had an ability to be singularly focused on you and make you feel like you are the most important person in his mind."

What most don't know, and will never know about Kraig, is that he has a heart to help people, and he puts his money where his heart is. He reluctantly shared a few details with me.

"One of the other radio personalities that I work with is Delilah. In 2004, she received a letter from a woman in Africa asking if she would adopt Black children from Africa, from Ghana in particular. Delilah thought the letter might have been bogus, but when she confirmed it was real, Delilah traveled outside the United States for the first time. There, she met a population of 80,000 Liberians living in a refugee camp in Ghana who had fled a civil war in Liberia. She came back a changed person and saw these people in Ghana had an urgent need for fresh water. So I, from afar, helped Delilah find a way to raise the money to build water wells. Unfortunately, the first ones we drilled turned out to be salt water wells. So in 2008, I went to Ghana four times to negotiate with the country of

Ghana, and the municipalities there, to bring fresh water to that population of Liberians. Still, to this day, they drink fresh water for the equivalent of about twenty-five cents per family per week because of the generosity of Delilah, and in small part because of the intestinal fortitude I somehow found in making a deal that the country of Ghana could not refuse."

Kraig Kitchin gets it done. During one particular show in 2019, I had three bad callers in a row, which never happened. Rush looked at me through the glass and blurted, "Listen. If that's the best that you can do, you might as well go home!" I freaked out.

First, burning tears involuntarily ran down my face. I immediately shot back, "Well, I'm not going home, so you can forget that!" I wiped every caller off the board and started over. But I was furious. And I was hurt. But at the same time, I was appreciative.

Mommy Dawn said, "Stop it, James. It's OK. We're all family in here and you know that he doesn't mean to hurt you." Brian was stoic and kind. "C'mon, everybody has a moment."

After the show, I was still emotional and wondered if I was up to the job. When I talked with Dawn, she looked at me and delivered a much-needed dose of reality. "Don't go there, James. You know he doesn't mean that to hurt you." She was right of course.

After the show, I went back to my office and called Kraig. "You won't believe what just happened. He just told me to go home!" And Kraig—aka Ray Donovan—did what he always did. He patiently listened. Then he said, "I understand how you would feel that way." I appreciated his understanding and tone. I don't remember his exact next words, but they were something to the effect of, "Now get your ass back to work, James."

Was I having an emotional day? Undoubtedly. Rush and I had always communicated openly, and we trusted each other. The next day, and to this day, I look back at that exchange and smile. Why? This was Rush being Rush. Even after thirty-one years, the show was the thing. This is one of the reasons I loved Rush.

The Ever Flawless Mike Maimone

I've known Mike Maimone since the music days when I first walked into WABC. He was the longest-serving broadcast engineer with the Rush Limbaugh program, and he has the distinction of being the only engineer in America responsible for a billion-dollar business—which he had no part of. That enterprise is Snapple. Here's Mike's take about this remarkable story.

"I used to take the Long Island Railroad into the studio because, at that time, the network studio was at 2 Penn Plaza. Penn Plaza was a pit but, at that time, the delis there sold the most amazing assortment of beverages. I found Snapple one day. Oh, Raspberry iced tea, this looks good. And it was. After a couple of weeks, Rush asked, 'What is that? That looks really good.' I said 'It's Snapple. It's iced tea. I'll bring you one tomorrow.'

"The next day I brought him one and he loved it. Rush even talked about it on the air. So, every day I'd bring one for him. After one of his long spiels about how wonderful it was, and sipping it during the broadcast, 'Slurp, mmm, this is such wonderful stuff,' I gave a recording of this to one of the advertising salespeople for the show. I asked, 'Could you do something with this?' and he did. They became an advertiser, and the rest is history.

Here's what Rush had to say about the experience.

"I knew that I was gonna have to demonstrate to advertisers immediately that their advertising on this program worked. And I knew that it would work if we could find the advertisers, because I had done it in Sacramento. So I guess the best illustration that I can give of this is Snapple. I'd never heard of Snapple until I got to New York, and the last thing I thought it was was an iced tea, when I heard the brand name. The broadcast engineer one day, who was the same broadcast engineer then as today, was in his studio, in his broadcast engineer studio complex, and he was pouring a bottle of this stuff over a cup with cracked ice in it.

"I tasted it. I said, 'Whoa.' It was delicious. [. . .] At the time they were a three-state business. And the short version of this story is, after a couple of years, they were in fifty states, and there were people all over the country wanting to be Snapple distributors, and

they became a sponsor and eventually the three guys
that owned Snapple sold it for two billion dollars to
Quaker Oats, who then proceeded to ruin it. But the
Snapple story was the thing that illustrated that adver-
tising on this program got results." —RL

Beyond this tale of tea, Mike Maimone was, and is, an
incredible broadcast engineer. Basically, every element you
heard on the radio was cued up and mixed by him. It took
a high degree of coordination to pull off a show like this and
everybody had to pay attention, working together to make it
go flawlessly. Mike was also a brilliant innovator and created
many of the tools and protocols that allowed us to broadcast
from Florida.

Diana Allocco, the Editrix

From day one, the show grew and ditto heads across the
fruited plain multiplied. Rush always wanted to find ways to
connect with his audience, and he dreamt up the idea of a
snail-mail newsletter listeners could subscribe to.

Diana Allocco came to us from her work at *Reader's*
Digest. She's a highly gifted editor and writer, and was one
of the editors at that publication, back when it was a big deal.

She's the person I turned to in the early days, when I
was still getting my bearings. She would immediately have
a resource that I could use to learn what I needed to know.
Like Rush, she has her own political mind that does not follow
conventional wisdom. She's a creative thinker, and much of
the credit goes to her for making the *Limbaugh Letter* the

most successful political newsletter in the country. As the editor, Diana was able to anticipate where hot topics would be three weeks out. The process that she and Rush worked out was amazing. She also edited the morning updates that I wrote. Yeah, she's a pretty big deal.

Here is Diana's take on how she came to join the EIB family.

"I was one of the four issue editors at *Reader's Digest*, and in 1991, I read a profile of Rush Limbaugh. That was the first time I had ever heard his name. It was a wonderful, positive article, and I thought, *He will be just perfect for this issue. It'll round it out, it's different, this guy has such personality and it's radio*, which we didn't have a lot of material on. After condensing my article, one of the copy editors said, 'You should listen to this guy. Nothing compares with hearing him yourself.' By the way, I later hired her for the *Limbaugh Letter*.

"On my lunch break, I went to my car, turned on the radio, and was immediately hooked. From that day, I spent every lunch hour in the editorial library at *Reader's Digest* listening to Rush's show as much as I could.

"A month or two later, I heard through the grapevine that Rush was starting a publication, and I thought, *I'm made for that!* So I looked in the employment ads in the *New York Times* and saw this little, two-line ad, 'Wanted. Editor for new publication. Combines humor and conservative politics.' And I knew there was only one person on the planet who combines humor and conservative politics.

"I made it through the first interview, and the second interview was with Rush himself. What I didn't know at the time was the fact that something I *didn't* do in the interviews helped me get the job. I didn't ask about benefits. I didn't ask anybody about anything other than what they wanted in the job itself. And I learned later that that was just a bugaboo that Rush had, that he couldn't stand people who just wanted to know what the benefits were."

The *Limbaugh Letter* began as a very basic two-color, eight-page piece. Diana's job was, in her words, "to absorb Rush as much as possible and try and contain lightning in a bottle." Of course, that's just what she did, every month for three decades. Every few years, the page count increased, and the publication was soon printed in full-color. And every year, Rush's respect for Diana increased—to the point that she was given her official EIB title. I'll let Diana tell the story.

"In 1994, he wanted to do a reprint not only of the 35 Undeniable Truths of Life, but also update them. He was standing in my office discussing it, and I corrected him on number 24 on his list: 'Feminism was established so as to allow unattractive women access to the mainstream of society.' I said, 'Hey Rush, you've got too many words in there. It should be 'feminism was established to allow'—you don't need the 'so as to,' it's just superfluous.

"After giving me that one-eyed look, he said, 'Lemme tell you, when you have 325 radio stations you can write it however you want.'

"'Point taken,' I said as we laughed and moved on to other matters. From that day, he started calling me editrix. I suppose it's a mix of editor and dominatrix, because I had argued with him and I wanted to correct his writing."

Here's one of Rush's many shout-outs to Diana.

"*Diana Schneider [Allocco], the editrix at the* Limbaugh Letter, *has been toiling away, trying to figure out, what is it that Hillary Clinton has done for women? Her husband out there, on* Good Morning America, *said that he's done more for women than anybody he can think of. And Diana said, 'Well, you know, she did do something that's worthwhile for women. She taught women to wear pink to distract from their guilt in certain matters. Wear pink when you're lying and sit under a portrait of Abraham Lincoln when one is handy.' You know, the Pretty in Pink press conference. [Laughing] So there's something that we can say that she has done.*" —RL

The February 2021 issue of the *Limbaugh Letter*, which reached subscribers just a few weeks before Rush's passing, had a title that I believe was inspired. "God Is with Me," the cover read. Diana noted those words when Rush said them on air and put the phrase on a list of suggestions for Rush to choose from in January. After Rush read the list of possible titles, he chose that one. He also chose the cover art that depicted him with praying hands.

> *"We don't get a lot of calls about the* Limbaugh Letter, *but when we do, everybody on that staff just loves it. The* Limbaugh Letter *is sixteen, people don't know how difficult that is because, look, fifteen hours a week here on the radio, that is then reproduced on the website and then here's this sixteen-page monthly publication that's not on digital. What do you do to put things in it that haven't been said? It's a monthly challenge and the people that put that together are excellent at it.*
>
> *"They follow my example, that's why it's great. But really, in all candor, it is fifteen hours a week, what is there not said? It turns out a lot, and the newsletter is the repository for us." —RL*

Creativity on Loan from God—Denise Mei

When you have a newsletter, you need a graphic designer. When it's the *Limbaugh Letter*, you need excellence and unbridled creativity. Denise Mei was the talent behind the visual impact of the newsletter for almost thirty years. Here's a story I love, told by Denise.

"When we were in New York, we used to go out all the time to like fancy restaurants like Ruth's Chris and 21 Club, and we'd always have a private room in the back. One time, I remember, I had just started and I think Rush was curious about what I was like, or who I was, you know, so I was sitting next to him at dinner and we had a great time. But at the end of the dinner, he turned to me and said, 'You know, Denise, we're going to smoke cigars, do you mind moving?' And he kind of like gave me this sheepish grin.

"I didn't want to move, I was having way too much fun, so I said, 'Well, Rush, you're not going to offer me a cigar? I like smoking cigars.' And he started to laugh. 'Sure you can have a cigar. I didn't know you smoked cigars.' It was a different time, it was a long time ago. And he opened up the humidor and, of course, now is the challenge. He asked, 'Well, which one do you want?'

"I know nothing about cigars. I was totally bluffing. 'Well, which one's the most expensive one?' And he's starting to laugh, because that was the only thing that I knew, that there were probably inexpensive cigars in there and there were probably really expensive cigars, and if I was going to do this, like, I gotta have the best, right? So he said, 'Well this one is the most expensive one.'

"'Well then, I'll have that one,' I replied.

"I love that story because that was him, he liked to test you a little bit. It was fun. I didn't smoke the whole thing, I *couldn't* smoke the whole thing. But I kept it because it was just such a great memory of us all hanging out and having such a good time."

Two Particular *Limbaugh Letters*

After Rush's passing, Diana and Denise, and the entire EIB family, faced a daunting task. How would they deliver the next issue of the *Limbaugh Letter*? Not only were there editorial challenges, the emotional weight was almost too much for any of us to bear. Yet they knew Rush would want them to finish and deliver the publication.

Every cover featured Rush's likeness, but the March 2021 issue featured only the golden EIB microphone. Rush also chose this cover design, just weeks before he passed.

Denise recently told me, "We had a couple of different ideas for that cover, and honestly, we were surprised he chose that one. And you know what, Rush is never wrong. Sometimes Diana and I showed him concepts and he went with something else, and it was always perfect."

The Fifteenth Anniversary *Limbaugh Letter*

"Snerdley interviewed me. We have pictures of the interview taking place, by the way, at the EIB broadcast complex. I figured it was the fifteenth anniversary issue of the Limbaugh Letter, *we'd make it about me since it's my newsletter, and we did, and there's an extensive interview with me in there that Mr. Snerdley*

conducted. I don't know how, but he got stuff out of me I've never said before anywhere about growing up and some other things. And when we finished with it, I said, 'Oh, jeez, send me this when you've edited it down.'

"'We're not editing it, we'll add pages if we have to,' he said. So before I had seen the finished product—I really didn't need to see it because I knew what I had said since I'm the interview subject, and I remembered what I said, but Diana Schneider, the editrix of the newsletter, they were all going nuts. 'Wow, I can't believe you said all this.'

"Well, blame Snerdley or praise Snerdley. Snerdley put me to sleep in this interview, relaxed me so much. We did this interview over two days and his first question was ten minutes long. Second question was five minutes long. We had to do two days because his questions were statements of adulation, idolatry, praise, and so forth. I'm kidding about the last." —RL

Queen and King of Screens—Cookie and Koko

Rush's TV show launched in 1992 and was groundbreaking on many levels. It was a rare, live-to-tape format where not everything was scripted. Even standup comedians rehearse their jokes and deliveries while being spontaneous on stage. Rush delivered the news of the day *and* did a spontaneous performance, as far as the medium would allow. The nature of television requires a lot of preparation, given the fact there are different cameras that have to capture different shots. But planning was kept to a minimum. Rush explained what he wanted, and the production crew had to figure out how to deliver.

These were long, grueling days because every weekday morning Rush would do his radio show prep, then meet with the TV crew about that evening's taping. From noon to three, he did the radio show and then we'd head over to the television studio. When the show was about to begin, Kit would explain to the audience how things worked if they wanted to meet Rush or have him sign their books. After Kit finished, I'd go out and warm up the crowd until we got the signal that Rush was ready. The place would go wild and the show began.

Rush pioneered both political and comedy television genres, and many of the team's innovations are still emulated today. His man-on-the-street interviews quickly became common on late night talk shows, as well as video montages. But liberal television executives put the show in the worst possible time slots—around one or two a.m. People used to tape it (on VHS, which was not easy) or would stay up to watch it. Even so, the show still had good ratings. Had the Rush Limbaugh TV show been put on a mainstream network in a respectable time slot, it would have been an undisputed hit.

After four years, Rush realized he didn't really like TV because it wasn't spontaneous enough. One day he decided not to do it anymore, and that was it.

Whether it be television screens or computer screens, we can thank Cookie and Koko for excellence in those mediums. As executive producer and vice president of digital, respectively, Kathleen and George Prayias—known as "Cookie" and

"Koko" to millions of listeners and viewers—worked with Rush for almost the entirety of his broadcasting career.

Kathleen was the first producer hired for the TV show. Later on, Rush brought her to the radio side. As her responsibilities grew, she took over what we called the "War Room," where the quotes (called "actualities" in media jargon) were pulled from all the media from various places. Anytime Rush was mentioned in the media, she had that video or audio clip. She had all the top news stories of the day, anticipating which ones he might want to discuss, or which clips he might want to hear.

Before the advent of digital recording, her office had a twenty-foot-long row of shelves stacked with VHS videotape recorders, all programed to record different shows. Astoundingly, and on a daily basis, Kathleen perused all the relevant recordings and created a "cue sheet" with ten to thirty actualities that Rush could choose from. She had a small staff, but it was a hell of a lot of work. She was an amazing TV producer, but she turned out to be an amazing radio producer as well.

> *"If you haven't done so yet, you've gotta go to RushLimbaugh.com. You've not seen anything like this. It is indescribable. I would not do it justice trying to describe this. But the web team has been working on this for months, and it is stunning. The video is actually taken from the control room. What you see is the back of the broadcast engineer's head, Brian Johnson, which is as close to fame as Brian says he wants to get." —RL*

After the television show ended, George decided he wanted to move into the IT realm and ended up running Rush's website. He had his own staff of four or five people— all of whom were the best at their job.

"The EIB Network now has an official Obama criticizer, he is Bo Snerdley. I got Cookie working on the sound bite even now. You might be confusing Cookie with Koko. Koko is married to Cookie. Koko runs the website. Koko is the gorilla at the TV show that now runs the website. He's the webmaster." —RL

Here are some insights from Kathleen and George that might bring up some happy memories from the television show.

KATHLEEN: "When I was working on the Rush TV show, there was a story in the *Washington Post* about ABC news reporter Cokie Roberts, that she had to go to a gala immediately after her report that evening, so she had her evening gown under her raincoat. They put her in front of a green screen with the Capitol behind her. She pretended to do a standup live from the Capitol, in front of the green screen. Well, the story got out and we did a skit where I was the EIB reporter, Cookie Gleason with EIB News. The green screen behind me kept changing location. From that day on, I was always Cookie. My real name is Kathleen Gleason Prayias."

GEORGE: "I came to the Rush TV show in 1995 and I was a production assistant, and they were going to do a skit about Koko, the sign-language-speaking gorilla. Rush thought this was hilarious that people thought a gorilla could speak sign language. So the bit was Rush would deliver a segment, and someone would wear a gorilla suit and appear in the corner of the screen—translating into sign language for other gorillas who were watching.

"They were looking for somebody to put on the gorilla suit, and the rest is history. That'll be a chapter in my life story, 'Never be afraid to put on the gorilla suit.'

"We started the skit and Rush got one look at me in that gorilla suit and he cracked up. He could not stop laughing. It was one of the few times that Rush kind of lost it because he always was the king of cool when he was performing. From that point on, I was Koko. He didn't know my name before that, but after that, every day I'd see him, 'Koko, how are you?' We were friends from that point on."

It wasn't all fun and games and gorilla suits on television or radio, but being a part of the EIB family was never boring. We did whatever it took and enjoyed the challenge. Hearing Rush's appreciation, on and off the air, was always an honor.

"You know, I was telling people here during the break that I was kind of stressing over this program

today. Thirty years is a big deal to a lot of people. It's another day to me, but it is a big deal. But the people that have worked with me for all the years, it's a huge deal to be part of something that has been number one, that has been dominant, that is winning.

"I mean, the number of people on the highly over-rated staff who have left this program in thirty years, you can count 'em on one hand. I think only one of them's been fired, two of 'em have been close. They're still here. There are some people barely cutting it here, but we hang onto 'em because we're good people. They don't know who they are.

"No, seriously. It's a big deal to them, because everybody wants to be on a successful, winning team. It's a source of great pride, especially when you are an important contributor to it. And so I realize this. And it's something that I want to acknowledge for all of the people who have enabled me and helped me and assisted me to do this. And one of the main ways they do it is by not distracting me. They take care of things without having to ask me about it. That's a luxury, folks, to have people who you just trust to do what needs to be done, whatever it is, whatever area they're working on." —RL

Guest Hosts Behind the Golden EIB Microphone

As the years progressed, another branch of the EIB family grew—the crucial guest hosts. Because of my background in radio, I sometimes suggested possible hosts—like Mark Steyn and Walter Williams to name two—when Rush could not be behind the mic. And it was an honor to help them have the best show possible. Here's a quick recap.

"B-1" Bob Dornan was one of the early guest hosts and, in a funny way, helped me solidify my role as a producer on shows when Rush was away. On one of his earliest guest spots, Bob told me he was going to read General MacArthur's farewell address on the air. *What a snoozer*, I thought. I could almost hear the sound of radio stations being changed by the millions. I spoke with John Axten, president of EFM, and said, "As much as I love Bob Dornan, you can't have guys reading lengthy speeches from World War II generals on the air!" And that's when I started becoming involved in producing the show.

One of the first people I suggested they hire to guest host was Michael Medved. What I didn't know at the time was that he was the author of one of my favorite political books, *The Shadow Presidents*. Michael always did a great show and brought in a contemporary cultural aspect. Many years later, he recommended me for a position with a new, internet-based broadcasting company. We'll talk about that spot later.

I suggested Mary Matalin as a host, and as we know, she was brilliant and insightful. Mary was just a dream to work with. She was a dear friend of Rush's right to the end, and she was a dear friend to me and the program. I just love Mary so much, it's hard to even put it into words.

I get teary eyed when I think about the late Tony Snow. Tony went on to become co-host of *Fox News Sunday* and then the White House press secretary before his tragic death. He was exceptionally gifted as a writer, and as a political mind, he knew the inside players. Even people on the other side of the aisle respected him and liked him personally. He was one of those guys who kept his humanity despite being on the front lines of the political arena. It broke my heart when he passed.

Tim Russert sat in for us one time, which was really funny. Tim liked Rush. He used to annoy the hell out of me on *Meet the Press* with those endless charts about Social Security, which he would only use when Republicans were on his show. But he was a great journalist and a great guy. Tim Russert asked tough questions of everybody and for a Democrat—which I assume he was—he was pretty evenhanded. When Tim was with NBC News, *Meet the Press* was a "must see." Now it's a barely seen. Who wants to watch an hour with Chuck Todd?

Sean Hannity guest hosted *The Rush Limbaugh Show* right before WABC decided to syndicate him, and of course, once his syndication began, Premiere Radio signed him. Sean is a good friend, and before his career took off, I told him at dinner, "Sean, get ready, you're about to ride the rocket." He said, "What do you mean?" I replied, "Within a year or two you're going to be on TV, you're going to have a syndicated show yourself." He looked at me and laughed. Sean is one of the good guys. During the time Rush was sick, Sean would often call me and members of our staff to see how we were doing. He was one of the few people Rush would agree to do interviews with, and when he came down, it was like a big family reunion because his staff and our staff all knew each other so well.

Jason Lewis is smart as a whip and steady as he can be. Knowledgeable, and a policy wonk, but Jason is also able to express himself clearly and is a wonderful guy to work with. He was one of the few talk radio hosts who actually put his career where his mouth was. He ran for, and won, the Congressional seat for Minneapolis-St. Paul in 2016.

Buck Sexton was young, ambitious, and very smart actually. He still is—except maybe the "young" part. It was always clear he had a very bright future ahead of him. He was the first guy in our guest host lineup who came from the intelligence community. Buck now hosts in the coveted noon to 3:00 p.m. time slot with Clay Travis.

Mark Belling would come to New York to do the show. He didn't like hosting remotely because he wanted the interaction with us, and we always enjoyed having Mark in the studio. He was with us for almost twenty years and was Mr. Reliable. He was actually sick as a dog the very first time he filled in, but he did the show anyway. Mark thought it was a terrible performance, but he did great.

I could write a book about Mark Steyn. (*Don't mess with me, Mark, or I will!*) He is one of the most brilliant men on the face of the earth. He also has a unique wit. I suggested Mark based on reading his columns. He has the most comprehensive grasp of history of any talk show host I know. He can talk to you about things going on in countries that you've never heard of because he's either been there or has extensive knowledge about the place. He has a command of the English language that only the Brits (and Canadians educated in Britain) have, which also makes him fun to listen to. When he goes on a rant, I can barely contain myself because of his use of language and his passion. Mark Steyn is one of the most brilliant people in the media world. I never had to have a conversation with him about what the show looked like. We sent him links to a couple dozen stories worth paying attention to, which I did for all the hosts because I knew what our audience expected.

The Doctor, Walter Williams. *Oh my God!* Walter was not a professional radio host and that bugged program directors because Walter would sometimes stumble his way into the spot breaks. He was an economist, not a radio professional. Walter took it upon himself to mentor me. He invited me to his house many times. Walter never missed a chance to teach and help people. He was a prolific writer and an educator at George Mason University.

He gave me a lesson that really started me reading economics differently, and his lesson was in the form of one simple question to me: "James, how many people does it take to create a pencil?" That opened up a world of economics to me that I had never understood before. He was brilliant and I miss him. Our audience loved him. Walter would have Dr. Thomas Sowell on with him—both economists with brilliant minds and enough books on policy that they wrote together to fill a library.

Douglas Urbanski is a Hollywood and Broadway icon. Doug was the youngest producer in his time of a successful Broadway show. He conquered theater in both the United Kingdom and the United States, and he has his hand in so many hit movies. If you do a search of his life history, it will amaze you. Occasionally, I did the show from California with him, and he's also a very devout religious man, so Doug and I would sometimes go to mass together. He's an original. It was a joy to work with Doug.

Erick Erickson is a dear friend. He has a really clear moral underpinning and it comes through on the air, as it does in person. Erick is a very competent talk show host and a very kind man.

Chris Plante did one show for us. *Hil-ar-i-ous!* Chris is a consummate professional and wicked smart. His show on WMAL was a go-to show for the inside political class of Washington, DC. Chris did one show for us and quickly became a syndicated host based on his performance. He's an amazing talent.

Roger Hedgecock, in the early days, was one of our standby guys. He was in the rotation with Walter Williams. I used to go to San Diego to work with Roger. He was mayor of San Diego at one point. I'll never forget the show I did with Roger right after Princess Diana died. We were on the show talking about that, and then we heard that Mother Teresa passed. Roger was also one of the strongest voices on the immigration issue long before it became popular.

Ken Matthews is a sweetheart of a guy. He has a unique sense of humor and can cover many news stories and many different takes within an hour. He has a quick mind and is a great host.

Nick Searcy did the show for us once. Rush became aware of him when he was on the TV show *Justified.* Rush talked about it, and soon enough, Nick called in. Nick is a remarkable human being and a great filmmaker. When Nick sat in for us, he gave a performance that will never be equaled or duplicated. It was a fun hour of him spoofing Hollywood and spoofing himself.

Derek Hunter is a good friend. He came to us and sat in on one of the last shows. Sadly, he only guest hosted for us once, and he did a great job. Derek has an amazing future in front of him.

Todd Herman has to be one of the best prepared broadcasters in history. This guy lays out a show like I've never seen anyone lay out a show. Every aspect, every minute is planned. Now, he doesn't always stay with the plan, but he begins with a great map. At six a.m., I'd sit down to send the latest show prep, open my laptop, and he would have already emailed his ideas with stories, links, everything. My job at that point would be to suggest lineup changes, maybe moving his lead down to the second hour, or suggestions like that.

The first few times Todd did the show, he placed a note on his computer monitor that read, "Pacing. Relax." I'd noticed that Todd's cadence was off a little bit. He was going too fast. That's the adrenaline that comes from sitting in the prestigious Attila the Hun Chair. One day I had a conversation and told him he could relax a little more and have fun. He wrote it down on a piece of paper and was back in his top form from that moment. This guy is an amazing force unto himself. He's a compassionate human being, a man of deep faith and conviction, who understands people in a way very few conservatives do.

Having Chris Matthews—yes, *that* Chris Matthews—as a guest host was Kit's pick. God bless Kit. If Kit was still alive, I'd still razz him about it.

Brett Winterble took my place as the call screener during my absence, then came back as one of our guest hosts during the last days of the show. Brett is the only host who was on the "inside" with us on staff. The audience would know him as Mr. Winterble, Rush called him that all the time. Brett has extensive knowledge of world history and politics. All of us just eat this stuff up, and Brett is no exception.

With other talent, I was glad to be a little more involved, along with the always-on-it Mike Maimone. For those unfamiliar with radio, we'd help get in and out of breaks because we had "hard stops." For instance, you have to be out at 58:50, not 58:51. Two people always worked with a guest host, never one. There are two sets of ears on a guest host, the engineer and the producer, so you can't have an ego about being the only one who can talk to the host. If the engineer hears something he thinks is off, he needs to have the freedom to speak directly to the host. If I'm busy screening the calls, I've got to trust that Mike is listening to the show. If he hears something that needs interaction with the host, at that moment, he's the producer. He's been doing this a long time, and his ears are as finely tuned as mine. I could always count on Mike to have my back in there. If I was caught up with callers, Mike's ears were on the talent, his eyes were on the clock, and he was always ready to make sure we did what needed to be done.

Producing and call screening also involves knowing where the pieces of the jigsaw puzzle go. It sounds weird, but I always had a vision of how the callers would fit in the time-clock puzzle. If we're coming up on ten minutes before the hour, is this person so long-winded that the host will have to cut them off? Or do I have a person who can make a point and end the segment with a bang with just two minutes available? Unlike music, you don't know how much time each call will take.

All that said, because Rush was the best in the business, our guest hosts were the best. That's one reason why I've included quotes from as many of these EIB family members as possible at the end of each chapter.

> *"Yes, over thirty years, a lot has happened, a lot has changed. But some things remain the same. America is the greatest nation on earth. The American people, those who make the country work, are the most generous, the most compassionate, the hardest-working people on earth. And when unleashed from Big Government, our freedom lights up the world.*
>
> *"And you, my audience, you are the greatest of the great. For thirty years! Everything I have achieved, I couldn't have achieved without you. And I thank you from the bottom of my heart.*
>
> *"As well as the highly overrated staff. You all mean everything to me." —RL*

Excellence—in broadcasting or any endeavor—is the key to success. It's one thing to pursue something you love, it's another thing to apply consistent excellence to your daily pursuits. For Rush, and the entire EIB family, the show was the thing. I don't believe we ever had a mediocre broadcast. We always brought our best, and Rush always inspired us to be our best.

SHOW NOTES

As I was planning this book, Kathleen Gleason Pray-ias (aka Cookie) told me that she and the other staff members always felt kind of proud when I was on TV talking about Rush. This meant the world to me. I had always felt *guilty* about any media attention because I know there are so many people who worked just as hard as I did.

I still feel guilty when all the spotlight is on me and because every single person on our staff feels the same way about Rush. We all worked hard, and we all respected each other's work. We all had the same pride about working with Rush and of the show's success. We also felt equally bad when he was under attack.

I cried when Kathleen told me, "Well look, we all felt really proud seeing you on TV because you represent us. You're the one who represents all of us." That made me feel a *little* bit better about it.

Now, we're trying to comprehend what it all meant, we're trying to organize our lives going forward, and we're also trying to come to terms with this incredible void. Rush Limbaugh was larger than life. Not just as a media personality. This organization that he created was a unique place that will never, ever be replicated.

A Recent Message from a Listener

"Hello, Mr. Snerdley. I've been with you on the phone and you're a big tough guy there, but when I hear you on the radio I know you're just a big, softie, teddy bear. I had only spoken to Rush very briefly one time and written a couple of letters to him on the website.

"On a particularly dark day in my life, I took a walk, and when I got home there was a huge box on my front porch. I opened it up, and inside there was this big white box that said Rush Limbaugh on it, with his signature. I was blown away. There was a beautifully framed, autographed photo of Rush receiving the medal from President Trump, and another photo with a letter from Rush. And there was a mug, which has been the only liquid receptacle I've used ever since that day. But the real treasure, the most incredible gift, was the folded up American flag.

"Bo, thank you again for continuing to share the legacy of this great man. I think I love you as much as I loved Rush. Thanks again."

A Word from One of Our Amazing Guest Hosts, KEN MATTHEWS

"I started out as a listener like millions of other people, then I ended up as a guest host and Rush made me a better guest host, but he also made me a smarter person and a better thinker. And a lot of that came from being a Rush listener because Rush was an intellectual giant, but he wasn't a snob about it, and he had fun and he liked to laugh and he was a smart aleck. And I think a lot of those characteristics appealed to the American people. It was a wonderful environment to work in and the listeners are outstanding. And why wouldn't they be? Rush loved the listeners."

I knew what I wanted to do when I was eight years old. I hated school. It was prison. I'm locked in this place having to learn about whatever you learn about in first grade, you know, how to paste things and stuff. So every morning getting ready to go to this prison, this school, my mother had the radio on and she's listening to the guy, a local jock, and this guy sounds like he's having fun. [. . .] I said, "That's how I want my day to be."

—RUSH LIMBAUGH

5

BACKGROUND CHECK

We know Rush was born to host, but I always wondered if I was born to be in radio.

As a kid, our family life centered around school, church, books, and music—not necessarily in that order from my mom's point of view. I was part of the church choir from about age six and into my teens.

Perhaps the earliest memory of my childhood is me sitting on my dad's knee in the kitchen of our small house—which seemed like a mansion back then. My dad was reading a book to me. I believe I was three or four years old at the time, but it is a moment that's deeply ingrained in my mind, one I still find comforting. I used to think it was strange not to have an early remembrance of my mom. But then I realized she carried me from conception and was always there for me in ways I still can't comprehend, as mothers are for their children.

The modest house in Queens, New York, featured a big library in the dining room. I remember my dad and one of his work buddies, "Uncle Milton," building those expansive shelves. Up until the day we packed up the house after my mother's passing, that room was still full of books. The three of us kids also had our own personal libraries in our bedrooms. Even when I finally got to rent my own places, no matter how small, there was always room for books. It amazes me to walk into so many homes today and not see a book anywhere in sight.

School was a very big deal to my parents. My mother, who was born and raised in Alabama, was a school teacher for some of her career. My father was a social worker, but he was always interested in furthering his education. While we kids were still attending school, he went back to college and earned his master's degree, and later he returned to school to work on a PhD.

I enjoyed certain aspects of school. I liked Sunday school more than "regular" school. But music was my first love.

Can't Help Myself

I was about eight years old when my older brother, my younger sister, and I went to a store on Long Island to buy our very first record: "I Can't Help Myself (Sugar Pie Honey Bunch)" by the Four Tops. I was already in love with music, and after that first purchase, it just continued to grow with intensity. Our home was always filled with music. My mother's record collection included everything from bebop to doo-wop, from John Coltrane and Frank Sinatra to the early Motown music, and even spoken word.

Piano lessons began at age nine, and despite my lack of progress, I had my first recital. The piece was "Elephant Walk," but the joke afterward was that the elephant didn't walk very well. I didn't think it was funny.

When you're a kid and you screw up in public, it's traumatic. A few years later in a school play, I had the part of the captain of the HMS *Pinafore*, in Gilbert and Sullivan's opera. My singing role required a dramatic octave jump, but my voice box jumped ship as I went for the high note. I don't know how to describe the sound I produced, but the audience instantly exploded in laughter—not a crescendo from polite chuckles. Full-on howling.

I finished the show but was traumatized. *Never again*, I promised myself. So, the stage life would have to take another form. The next consequential step in my musical career was to join a band with my brother and another set of brothers who were our close neighbors.

Around that time, in 1967, sixteen-year-old Rusty Sharpe (aka Rush Limbaugh) landed his first job in radio at KGMO in Cape Girardeau, Missouri.

Cripple Crab

By age fourteen, sometime in 1969, I'd transitioned to brass instruments and developed relatively decent chops on the trumpet. My older brother and I started a band with our neighbors across the street, Darrell and Victor Rogers, with whom we were very close. Darrell and I were the same age, as were Victor and my brother, Kim. We practiced a lot with another friend whom I'd known since the first grade, Antonio Norris—a gifted guitarist and the most advanced musician among us. I stayed away from the microphone. We started performing R&B cover songs, but as we grew musically, we incorporated contemporary jazz and rock into our repertoire.

We started off as the Famous Flames. (Yeah, we stole the name from James Brown's band.) A few years later, we

re-branded as New York City Part Two. During the last iter-
ation of the band, our handle was Cripple Crab, taken from
a local DJ's sign-off, which said he was "funkier than a crip-
pled crab without the crutch." By then, the band had grown to
twelve members, including singers.

We were never a great band, but we were pretty damn
good. Within a couple of years, we were pulling down $600
to $1,000 per show and traveling as far away as Albany, New
York, and occasionally Connecticut and Pennsylvania. We
had gigs almost every weekend. And, for teenagers, we earned
a decent amount of pocket money.

Although my bandmates kindly reminded me, "You
really can't sing well, James," they did encourage me to get
near the mic for speaking parts. From a young age, I had a
very deep voice, and everyone agreed it sounded cool when I
introduced the band or set up a song. It was during those high
school days that I met Omar Hakim, my spiritual brother,
friend for life, and writing partner. He was only fourteen, but
he was already a professional, kick-ass drummer, who went
on to play with Weather Report, Miles Davis, David Bowie,
Dire Straits, Sting, Lionel Richie, Madonna, Michael Jackson,
Bruce Springsteen, Mariah Carey, Jewel, J-Lo, and the Foo
Fighters. We hung out a lot, and through him, I met other
gifted musicians and was able to occasionally attend recording sessions in some of New York's most famous studios.
Many were unforgettable sessions with artists who were, or
would become, international household names.

Altogether, these experiences gradually taught me that as
much as I loved music, I'd never be disciplined enough to be a

great musician. And I had zero desire to be a mediocre musician, or a mediocre anything.

Thankfully, I had another passion.

The Radio Star

Close to the same year we started our band, I met my cousin Gerry Bledsoe, who had just moved to the area from Buffalo to become a disc jockey at our local station, WWRL—which happened to be my favorite station. He was an extremely handsome guy, in his late twenties, who embodied the essence of sophistication and cool. He was "like a son" to my mom— she told us it was she who had named him, and they were very close. It wasn't long before I asked if I could visit him at the radio station, and he agreed.

The day I visited WWRL lives in vivid technicolor in my memory bank. I dressed up in my shiny, blue, double-breasted sharkskin suit and took the train to Woodside. When I got to the station, I announced myself to the receptionist, Barbara, who welcomed me with, "Oh, you're Gerry B's cousin. Come on back."

Once behind the set of double doors, I passed from the lobby into an electronic wonderland. My mouth dropped open. News director Dick London was preparing a newscast, while someone else was pulling the latest stories off the wires. As we entered the control room, I was mesmerized by all the electronics, the cart machines, the "board," and the set of turntables that the disc jockeys used, one to cue up the next record while one was playing on the air. When I went inside the air studio and saw my cousin at work, I was thunderstruck. It was a rush of pure adrenaline just to watch live music radio taking place and Gerry spinning the records, checking the log, and playing commercials. He somehow made it all happen, interspersed with his smooth patter and his deep, rich, seductive voice.

At age fourteen, I was in love with music, and with radio. *This is what I want to do.* Rush was on a similar path in his teens.

> *"I wanted to do radio since I was eight. So when I would run into anybody who was in it, I'd just ask them question after question after question. I asked so many questions, one guy said, 'You know, it sounds to me like you're more interested in how to do it than actually doing it.'*
>
> *"I said, 'What do you mean?'*
>
> *"'Well, at some point, you gotta stop asking questions and start doing things.'*
>
> *"And I said, 'Well, I'm not old enough to start doing things. I'm not old enough to get hired yet.'*
>
> *"'Well, yes, you are, if you really want to, but at some point, you gotta stop asking and you gotta start doing. You can't learn everything about doing something just by asking about it.' Which I knew. It was still some relevant advice, probably from somebody who was tired of all my questions." —RL*

What blows my mind to this day is while I was headed back to the lobby, the production director and host of a gospel music show, Rocky Bridges, walked by, looked at me, and said, "You. Come with me." We went into the station's busy production room, I sat down behind a reel-to-reel tape recorder, and Rocky showed me how to cut and splice tape. Another world of creative expression opened up for me. This was my first time at a radio station and I was learning how to edit recordings and create some of the magic I'd listened to all my life. I don't know why he took me under his wing, but I do believe it was destiny. The rest of the day was a blur.

But I was clear. I wanted to be in the radio business—just like Rush Limbaugh discovered when he was eight years old.

My cousin went on to become one of the most influential Black jocks in the country, let alone in New York City. While I was still in high school and in the band, I pestered my cousin and visited the radio station as often as possible. During those visits, I had the opportunity to meet and learn from the most influential DJs in Black radio, including Gary Byrd and Bobby Jay. I ran errands and did odd jobs for my cousin and a few of the other jocks. I never got paid and didn't care.

When I told my cousin I wanted to be in radio, he gave me an assignment. "OK. Listen to the station for a few days and write down everything you hear." When I brought my hand-written papers to Gerry, he looked at them and said, "Study it. That's a format."

Study it? That's a format? Well, I did study it, and I started to understand the on-air component of radio. But there were still many mysteries to solve.

The Hoax

I was seventeen years old when "the letter" arrived. It was on WWRL AM stationery. Although I hung out there a lot with my cousin and a few of the other DJs, I flew well below the radar of management. So I was awestruck to read that the station wanted to offer me a job. The letter invited me to meet with the program director, Jerry Boulding, on the following Monday at 3:00 p.m.

I was elated, but I couldn't understand why he would be interested in hiring me. My "big show-biz break" had arrived, and I was still a teenager!

On Monday, I arrived at the station fifteen minutes early, presented myself to the receptionist, Barbara, and let her know I had a meeting with the program director. She picked up the phone and called up to the second floor where his office was located. Her smile changed to a look of confusion. Mr. Boulding did not have a scheduled meeting with me that day—or any day for that matter.

I showed her the letter, which was written on official letterhead, and Barbara called upstairs again. In a few minutes, I found myself on the second floor, holding the letter nervously. An assistant I'd never met before took my letter and asked some other staffers about it. Between whispers, they occasionally looked in my direction with expressions of pity. A few minutes later she returned, shaking her head. "I'm sorry, James. Nobody knows who wrote this, and we don't have any job openings."

The letter was a hoax. I was humiliated.

I racked my brain to figure out who would play such a prank on me—and more importantly, why. The hurt ran deep. For the next few years, I'd replay that trip to WWRL in my mind and relive the embarrassment over and over.

But the experience had an additional effect—it fueled my ambition. I was determined to be in the radio business.

Whoever forged that letter, if you're reading this, I want to say, *thank you*. Out of that humiliation came a relentless desire to achieve my first goal in radio, to land a job at WWRL. No matter what.

Fast Forward

After graduating from high school in 1973, I went to Queens College to study communications. I quit the band and worked at Howell's Pharmacy, near my home. Yeah, life was exciting.

The whole college experience just turned me off. I didn't like the attitudes of most of the faculty. Maybe I was the one with the attitude, but this is my book. In those days, there was a program designed as a precursor to affirmative action, which brought a lot of African Americans into the college, and I was constantly asked if I was enrolled through that program. No, I was not. I was there because I deserved to be, and because I was paying tuition.

A friend of my cousin Gerry's helped me land a part-time job in New York City as an associate literary and film agent with the Peter Miller Agency, and I was quick to resign from the drug store. I worked at the agency for about two years. It wasn't exactly the A-list celebrity scene, but it was a different arena of authors and creatives.

During my time at the Peter Miller Agency, I moved in with Gerry, who had become a TV personality with a popular weekend show called *Soul Alive*, which was basically a local version of *Soul Train*. Prior to that, he had played a prominent role in another television series called *Soul at the Center*, a relatively highbrow PBS production filmed at Lincoln Center.

He was also in high demand as a voice-over artist and had his own production company, Voiceiferous. Under Gerry's guidance, I helped write copy and handled some production details. I'd listened to him on the radio since I was fourteen, so I quickly discovered I could easily write and edit scripts to fit his style. I really enjoyed learning how to write copy in someone else's voice, and I got pretty good at it.

As a sophomore at Queens College, I saw a *golden* opportunity. (You knew that play on words was coming, didn't you?) We were introduced to a new technology, something called videotape. The school had access to a few huge videotape players—the size of large suitcases—and a camera that would record onto this new medium. If you've ever programmed a VHS tape machine, you might remember how game changing this technology was. Film and video recording were not accessible for the masses. We were still using film cameras and going to the local drugstore to get our photos developed. Up to this time, recording video required rooms full of equipment and several trained staff. I understood audiotape but couldn't wait to give video production a try.

My fellow students and I were given an assignment. We were to interview someone and edit the final product into a short documentary. My project would showcase the ins and outs of running a successful radio station. My interviewee of choice was the new program director of WWRL, Sonny Taylor, because I was still determined to get into radio. When I called and explained what I hoped to accomplish, he was intrigued with the new technology and agreed to be interviewed. This time, I finally made it to the program director's office. Sonny and I hit it off, and after the interview, I was able to pick up the phone from time to time and call him for advice.

Those Who Can, Do

In my third year of college, one particular communications teacher became a pivotal influence on my career. I believed that the teachers always knew more than the students, and in one particular class, I was trying to resolve something that didn't make sense to me as someone who already had some real-world media experience. I asked a question, and the teacher tried to answer. His response didn't make sense, so I asked a follow-up question. As this continued, he finally rolled his eyes and dismissed me with, "Well, you can question *anything* to a point."

Well, that's why I'm here—to ask questions and learn. I picked up my books and walked out. That was the end of my college career. Looking back, I realized I was learning much more about media and broadcasting in my part-time jobs than I was learning in school—even by listening to the radio with an educated ear. I was writing copy and working behind the scenes on TV and radio productions. I wanted to work in the real world, not learn theory in the classroom. I wanted to innovate, not copy.

Rush knew he wanted to be in radio at age eight. I was in my teens when I had the revelation. Rush dropped out of college in 1971. As his mother described him, "He just didn't seem interested in anything except radio." In that same year, Rush took a job as a DJ at WIXZ, a Top 40 station in McKeesport, Pennsylvania. A few years later, in 1976, I was about to take my first steps in a radio career when Sonny Taylor hired me.

"And, by the way, I mentioned McKeesport because that's where the first radio station that I worked at when I left home was. It's the Pittsburgh market, but it was a suburban station in McKeesport. It was WIXZ, salted rot and mold, played oldies. Well, it was solid rock and gold, WIXZ, 'solid rock and gold,' the jingle. And I called it 'salted rot and mold' 'cause after two years I'd heard every song on the playlist 20,000 times.

"I'm just sitting here listening to Under My Thumb *by the Rolling Stones. That's from, I think, '64-'65. I got fired for playing that song. One of my seven or eight times of being fired was for playing that song too often in McKeesport, Pennsylvania, at WIXZ. I really got fired. I got fired for violating the program format by playing that song too often in the rotation. It was an oldies format. I just liked the song and I got canned for it." —RL*

Because I stayed in contact with Sonny Taylor after the college video assignment, it wasn't long after I left school that he hired me as the marketing and research director for WWRL. This was the best job I could've had as my entry into radio. I learned how to analyze Arbitron ratings and create reports—I even had to hire a math tutor to help me crunch the numbers. As part of my job, I combed through the weekly ratings and issued a series of reports to the program director, sales director, and the general manager.

My performance, along with our station's ratings and ad sales, must have exceeded expectations, because it wasn't long before I was called into a meeting with Mac Allen, the national program director for the Sonderling Broadcast Company, the parent company of WWRL. Mac wanted to do something fresh. He wanted the radio stations under his direction to scientifically research the music that audiences wanted to hear. I embraced the nationwide challenge wholeheartedly, and the creative manner with which I designed our music research program at WWRL would lead me into the big leagues of radio.

My role expanded to take the lead in developing the art and science of music research. I had a small staff of interns who called people and played song segments over the telephone, then asked them to rate the songs on a scale of one to seven. Each call took between five and ten minutes. This way we could track the opinions of our target consumers on a weekly basis to understand which records were gaining or losing appeal. This was a trailblazing approach in deciding which music would air on radio.

One day, I had an idea. Actually, I had a lot of creative ideas on lots of days, but this one was a keeper. *I know how to make our station sound smoother.* Stay tuned as I riff on some music theory. Music comes in many different keys, and the keys of songs have a relative tonal impact with other keys— some more pleasant than others. I wondered if we could figure out the best song to play based on the key that would best compliment the previous song.

We brought in my friend, Omar Hakim, still a teenager, but an incredibly gifted musician who had perfect pitch. He listened to all of the songs on our playlists and used a guitar to figure out the keys in which each song began and ended. We then determined the relative majors and minors of those keys so that I could arrange the playlist into a smoother listening experience. Blending research and musicality was so dope— and nobody else was doing it.

I was innovating, but like all creatives, I was also learning and copying from generous innovators who helped my career and invested in me, personally. As you'll soon discover, these mentors came in all shades of skin, but I would be remiss if I did not take a few lines to acknowledge a few Black mentors whose talent and excellence blazed new trails.

Black Talent

One of my high-school friends, Fountain Jones has been family since very early on in my life. As a teenager, his interest in media was evident. He passed the extremely difficult "First Class License" exam from the FCC, and was already into recording—in fact, he recorded many of the gigs of the band I belonged to. By the time he was in his twenties he was recording segments of the multi-Grammy-award-winning album, "Songs In The Key of Life" for Stevie Wonder. He advanced in his positions with television networks and today is a multi-Emmy-award winner for his work as a technical director. But more important than all of that, he is a wealth of spiritual knowledge who looks at life's work as an opportunity to do spiritual work.

Another of my high school buddies, Fred Buggs is a fixture of New York Radio, having worked both on air and behind the scenes, since soon after leaving high school. Have you ever met one of those people who seems to know everybody in the industry you work in? That's Fred. Not only is he a gifted broadcaster, he's a one-man reference library of all that is important in the radio and music industries. After I began weekday shows on WABC Radio, Fred called to tell me how much he hated them. And how good they were. He hated the political analysis because we are ideological opposites, but he loved the broadcast elements. He remains a true, honest, ever-encouraging friend.

I could write a book about Omar Hakim. We are as close as brothers by blood. Many times over the decades, when he was touring on the other side of the world, I would think of him and the phone would ring, and it was Omar on the line. He was already a professional drummer at age twelve. He has become one of the top musicians in the world, not in just one genre of music but across the board. He plays guitar, keyboards, and has authored a Grammy-winning instrumental. His work ethic is incredible—one of those guys who reads the manuals and spends hours in preparation for everything he touches. That includes playing, recording, writing, composing, arranging, or building out a studio. He is a highly spiritual man with an extremely gracious good nature and even keel.

The biggest mentor in my radio career was my cousin, Gerry Bledsoe, who took me under his wing, taught me how to write copy, and gave me an understanding of the business of radio that was invaluable. More than that, I simply adored Gerry.

Sonny Taylor was one of two great program directors I had the honor of working alongside, with the other being his mentor, Jerry Boulding. They both became my treasured mentors.

At age eighteen, I first met Jerry Boulding because I wanted to learn about ratings and music formatting. He decided to take me to Arbitron headquarters in Maryland and show me how the science worked. That was my first business trip. What a thrill as a young man, and what a game changer for an aspiring professional! We spent the day analyzing the diaries that were sent in for ratings. Why he did this, I'm not sure, except maybe I was one of the few kids who wanted to know the mechanics of the business, as opposed to being on the air.

Sonny Taylor was one of the very few people who called me Jimmy—and could get away with it. He gave me my first job in radio doing market research. I will never forget his voice on the phone. "Jimmy! Jimmy, listen Jimmy, I have a job for you." That job was to analyze the ratings. Thanks to Jerry, I was already familiar with the ratings books. I owe Sonny and Jerry so much.

Gary Byrd was another mentor, and like my older brother, he really taught me how to think on a higher level. He was a fellow college dropout who started his own radio show at age sixteen, and he was a true genius. There is so much I want to thank Gary for—his kindness and generosity to me, and to so many of the younger generation he mentored, even while he was still a young man in the media business. He was, and is, a creative genius in his own right, who was writing songs with Stevie Wonder and also working on educational content for school-aged children. His perspective was a unique combination of DJ and educator. He taught me about business and how to be in charge of my own creative output. I will never be able to express the impact he had on my thinking and my life.

Bobby Jay was a disc jockey who used to walk me through all the music from the '40s and '50s. He taught me who the great influencers and innovators were, how they were significant, and how they impacted music in the decades since. Bobby once called me after I had moved to WABC and was doing my Sunday show. He wanted to tell me how proud he was of me. It took everything I had not to break down and cry. And then I cried, a little.

Those guys at WWRL, Gary, Gerry, Jerry, Sonny, and Bobby, that whole crew looked out for me. As a kid, I was different from most of my peers in school. By the time I hit my twenties, my experimenting years were over—no drinking and no drugs. At parties, the drugs flowed, but these guys kept an eye on me and kept the thugs at bay. They respected the fact I was serious about my career—and life. They always protected me and made me feel special.

I must also include two other guys in radio. One is Darryl Brown, who became the executive vice president and general manager at ABC Networks. The other is Zemira Jones, who was president/general manager of ABC Radio/ESPN Radio and WLS Talk Radio in Chicago. Zemira was a young Black guy running a huge radio station. I'd never seen that before. I didn't know that Black people could actually make it that far up the corporate ladder the way these two had, so I followed their careers. Later, I learned they were following mine, too. I often refer to Zemira Jones as the smartest man in media. He has spent many hours tutoring me, and he still does to this day. He is also a spiritual mentor who reminds me every chance he can that, in his eyes, I have a purpose in life that runs deeper than my radio career.

The highlight of my early career, apart from getting my first paid radio job from Sonny Taylor, came while I was a music researcher at WWRL. I got a call from my boss, the music director, Linda Haynes. "LeBaron Taylor wants to take you out to lunch." I was stunned. Among African Americans, LeBaron Taylor was the biggest name in the record industry. That would be akin to a rookie radio guy getting a call to go to lunch with Clive Davis, the legendary Grammy-Award-winning record producer whose name lives on in the Rock and Roll Hall of Fame. That was the first and only time I met with LeBaron, but I still remember every detail.

We had lunch at the Bombay Palace in upper midtown Manhattan, near CBS, before it became Sony Music. He had heard about my music research and wanted to learn everything he could about how we surveyed listeners, analyzed the results, chose the records—all of it. He understood the implications for the record business and wanted every detail. I cannot overstate enough what an honor it was to have a few private hours with the man who would open the door for so many African American executives in radio and the music industry. As a bonus, he introduced me to Indian cuisine, which remains one of my favorites to this day. Before his death in 2000, LeBaron had been the senior vice president of corporate affairs for Sony Music Worldwide, Sony Music Entertainment, and Sony Software Corporation. An amazing man indeed.

Without these kind mentors, my radio career would not have been the same, and I doubt I would have ever met Rush Limbaugh. And I certainly would not have developed the skills and experience I needed to succeed in the business.

RUSH: "In what is now something of a tradition for my big pre-election issue [2008], Mr. Snerdley and I sat down for a longer version of one of our political free-for-alls that we often have during commercial breaks. I'm sitting here with James Golden, aka Bo Snerdley, who serves a triple role here at the EIB Network as the official program observer, the new official Obama criticizer, and the official call screener. Let me first ask you, because I get this all the time, and even though I have assigned the role, people still want to know, what is the official job of the program observer, and why can't they do it?"

SNERDLEY: "It's a few things, actually. You have to have a very good memory. I remember your profundities—they are many, and they stretch back now over twenty years. So that is number one."

RUSH: "You remember more than I do."

SNERDLEY: "I remember things you said, and I can call them up instantaneously. That's not an easy task. I'm not bragging, but it isn't."

RUSH: "So it's not just sitting there observing. It is listening and associating with things that have happened in the past."

SNERDLEY: "Soaking it in and making sure that you put it in context."

RUSH: "Right. Because I'm so focused on the now, you have a chance to look back and relate the past to the present. [. . .] So how do you officially observe and screen at the same time? Because when you're screening, you're listening to the callers, you have to go through a lot of them to get the good ones that we get. So how do you observe?"

SNERDLEY: "I can't explain that. It's a gift. I'm catching most of what you say while I'm talking to someone else. I can't explain how I do that."

RUSH: "I can attest to this because I look across the glass at you screening calls in there while I'm doing a monologue and I think, 'He can't possibly know what I'm talking about in great detail.' Yet you seldom put up a call that repeats what I just said."

SNERDLEY: "Thank you."

RUSH: "People don't understand the call-screening process and how important it is to a show like this that doesn't take very many. We have never believed—this is not an insult to anybody—that callers are the primary reason people listen. Those who play music—to correlate callers to music—play the hits. You find the best you can.

That's why I'm a benevolent dictator, there is no
right to free speech except for me. I grant it to
those who have earned it by virtue of their ability to contribute to the program. It's your job to
figure that out, and you have five or ten seconds
talking to somebody. If they waver, if they don't
show confidence, you have to move on, you have
to broom them. It's one of the key elements of the
program that few people understand. It can't be
done by everybody. A lot of shows don't screen
much."

SNERDLEY: "And don't screen heavy."

RUSH: "Yeah. They are called 'caller-dependent.' And
it sort of strands the host out there trying to make
something out of people who are perhaps not totally
equipped to call. But you do a superb job at it."

The ABCs of Radio

The discipline of music research for radio was brand new,
and my team put together many components that would later
become the industry standard. I was one of maybe three or
four people in the country conducting this statistical exam-
ination of audience tastes, and that's what brought me to the
attention of the Top 40 radio giant, WABC.

Out of the blue, program director Jay Clark called and we
set up a meeting at his Manhattan office. "I want to talk to you
about becoming the music director for WABC." The station
wasn't doing formal music research, and they'd seen the results
I'd achieved at Sonderling. WABC was the most iconic Top 40

radio station in the world—the most famous call letters in the nation. W-A-Beatles-C is where Beatlemania started on radio. It was the biggest music station, with the richest history. The job of music director was a big freaking deal.

Our meeting went perfectly, and he offered me the job.

A month passed, with no start date and no word from Jay. Three months passed. As I waited and wondered about the ABC gig, WWRL downsized and wanted me to go to WDIA in Memphis to become the music director, and maybe one day, the program director. It didn't take me long to decide that the gig wasn't going to work for me—I wanted to be in New York. Now I was unemployed. New York City was a tough market to break into because everyone wanted to work there. Most people had to prove themselves in smaller markets across the country before they would be considered for gigs in the Big Apple. But as Frank Sinatra famously crooned, I was determined to *make it there* in New York radio.

In 1973, I quit the band. That same year, Rush was fired from WIXZ and moved on to a role with Pittsburgh, Pennsylvania's KQV radio. About a year later, he was fired again, and although he had a job offer in Wisconsin, he decided instead to move back home and live with his parents as he sorted out his career. Once again, as we would later learn, Rush and I shared a determination to chart our own course in the industry, even if it meant enduring painful setbacks.

Rush went on to work Top 40 radio at KUDL in Kansas City, Missouri, for two years, then KFIX. After getting fired for a third time in 1979, he worked with the Kansas City Royals baseball team. But his love for radio never faded.

Meanwhile, with more time on my hands, and expanding experience in TV and radio production, I produced a little documentary with Lionel Richie and the Commodores. I was a one-man band—arranging the meeting, writing the questions, interviewing the talent, editing the tape, and pitching it to the station. In this case, I pitched it to WABC. I called Jay Clark, and he aired the show, but he said the job he had offered me was still going through the corporate bureaucracy.

Finally, six months after our initial meeting, Jay Clark called. His team had conducted a thorough background check on me, and the report came back so clean that no one in management believed it. So they had to start over and do a *second* background check—each involving hours of calls with past employers, peers, record-industry people, and anyone they could find. They couldn't find anything negative, because there wasn't anything negative to find.

In the '50s, payola (record labels paying DJs and program directors to play their music) was a common problem in radio. By the '70s and '80s, it was still thought to be a common practice, particularly in Black radio where the salaries were so much less than in white radio. But in all my dealings with record promoters, I took no payola or side deals. As a music research director, I influenced what went on the air, and many record companies were willing to hand over cash to get their records played. Promoters offered me lots of stuff, but by this time I lived a pretty tame life—I was a vegetarian and didn't do alcohol or drugs. WABC, and thirteen ABC-owned stations, had a lot to lose if their music director was corrupt. The intense vetting was part of the reason for the six-month delay. The other part, I think, was because of the color of my skin. There was absolutely no prejudice from Jay, but rather a problem somewhere within the corporate culture.

Without missing a beat, I took over the entire music department at WABC as music director *and* music research director. I presented my research to a committee where we'd debate the songs to be put on the playlist. That's when I started to hear a lot of static from some employees about Black people and Black music. One guy made a crack about listening to music on a ghetto blaster. Others were skeptical—OK, prejudiced—because my background was in "Black radio." Radio is radio. Good research is good research. And my work was groundbreaking, excellent, and produced results. As with college, I was there because I earned the opportunity. And I let it be known that I wasn't going to tolerate any racial crap.

As a blatant example, shortly after WABC transitioned into a talk station, two new guys from a southern radio station arrived to launch a morning show. In our first meeting, one of these hosts sketched a large circle on a piece of paper, drew lines across it dividing it like a pizza, then put two little dots in each of these slices. "Know what this is?" he asked with a grin. "It's the last thing a Black guy sees when the Klan is about to get him!"

Nobody seemed to know how to react. Except me. "Listen, asshole, you're not down south anymore. I don't know how this kind of racist shit goes down there, but you will not do this here. Otherwise, we're gonna have some issues."

Yeah, that was the kind of stuff still happening in '70s radio. Thankfully, those idiots were actually in the minority.

Talking Heads versus Talking Heads

At first, my research department at WABC consisted of me and a tiny office. Soon, it became such a big deal, the station gave me a huge office on the seventh floor with people working for me morning, noon, and night. We were growing fast. Until we weren't. By 1980, FM radio was growing while AM radio remained ... static. I knew I needed to learn more about the radio business to stay ahead of the curve.

I'm not sure why, but I picked up the ABC phone directory and looked for the network president. I didn't even know his name at the time, but it listed a guy named Ed McLaughlin. He wasn't the president of my station, he ran the entire radio *network*. By some miracle, my call made it through the gauntlet, and I heard, "This is Ed."

"Hi, Ed. I'm an employee at WABC, but I really want to learn more about how the network works."

"Well, come on over," he said.

After I picked myself off the floor, I went across the street to the ABC building, where I was escorted to a huge conference room. A few minutes later, Ed McLaughlin walked in, carrying a stack of network rating books. He shuffled them across the table and greeted me with a warm smile and energetic handshake. Before I knew it, he was explaining how the industry worked on a national level and continued answering all my questions. After almost an hour, we shook hands again, and he said, "Whatever you need in the future, James, just call me."

I had the sense those words were sincere, and history would prove that they were. I did call him from time to time, and he was always generous with his time and talent. Whenever we happened to be in the same gathering, Ed always came over to talk with me or introduce me to people. This was the case in 1987 when Ed introduced me to a new talk radio guy by the name of Rush Limbaugh. Had I not reached out to Ed and developed a great working relationship with him, would I have ever met—and worked with—Rush? I don't know.

ABC was the dominant nationwide radio company at the time, with ABC Networks and the ABC radio group. They had decided it was time to move more of their stations into talk radio, including WABC. It took years, and lots of trial and error, to make the necessary changes. By the time we fully transitioned from music radio to talk radio, we had over a million people per week tuning in, down from six million at its peak. Today, execs would be celebrating those numbers, but we were so used to dominating our market, the ratings were seen as dismal. Sales had declined and, like it or not, radio is all about sales.

During the transition, I stepped into the role of producer. And I loved it. It was during the Tylenol poisonings of 1982 that I realized I was a damn good producer. This was the lead story in all the talk shows and newscasts, and somehow I knew—instinctively—what to do. I knew who to invite on the air as guests, how to frame a story, which politicians to challenge, and what angles to explore. I screened callers and scanned the wires for the right news nuggets to highlight.

I'd always been a voracious news reader. Since I was a kid, I read the *New York Times* every day, front to back, along with the *Daily News*, *New York Post*, and *Long Island Press*. Producing talk radio connected the three Rs: radio, research, and reading. I worked with all the top talent—and because these were live broadcasts, I worked every shift. Yeah, sometimes I pissed off management by expressing my views and found myself working the overnight hours. And there was that time I fell asleep while producing a Yankees game. But I digress.

I approached talk radio like I approached music radio. We needed to give the audience—and the host—a flow that kept everyone engaged. Because of my previous research, I knew where five-minute and seven-minute patterns fell in terms of keeping the rating numbers up. I knew how a segment could deliver a dramatic pause, and which callers could rile up the host to make sure the listeners didn't touch that dial. I wasn't afraid to experiment, but I must also give credit to the wonderful, smart, and generous people who helped me along the way.

I believe God prepares us for what we're put here to do. I had the right combination of experience, instinct, and connections, and my career was rising in the charts. Sometimes when you work in an industry and see how things are really done behind the scenes, it dampens your enthusiasm. But for me, the more I knew about radio, the more I loved it.

"Unfortunately for a lot of people the thing they love the most is their hobby. Something they don't get paid for. But the next thing to do is to realize that you live in a place with boundless opportunity. Don't listen to the noise. Don't listen to the pessimists. Do not seek advice from people who failed at what you want to do.

'Cause they're everywhere. And they don't want to be alone.

"I can't tell you the number of people who tried to talk me out of it. 'Rush, it's vicious, it will eat you up and spit you out. The chances are so slim, it's just a road to misery.' And I decided after a while not to listen to those people and then I decided after a while not to even talk to 'em. I was only gonna find people who had succeeded and try to learn from them.

"I don't care what it is that you want to do, you have to have a well-rounded knowledge and more importantly, the ability to demonstrate that you have it. This is not just broadcasting and radio. You have to be able to communicate what you know. You have to do things that are going to inspire confidence in yourself.

"You have to really like yourself to be confident. And it is confidence that will open up opportunity to you. It's confidence that will allow you to transmit what you know in ways that are persuasive and impressive." —RL

Stepping Up to the Mic

Radio was the friend that introduced me to new ideas and new music. The Beatles; Stones; Stevie Wonder; Chicago; Blood, Sweat and Tears; Earth, Wind and Fire; Herbie Hancock; Jimmy Hendrix; and more. Santana opened my ears to the world of Latin grooves, fused jazz with rock, and brought improvisation back to the mainstream. Talk radio opened my mind to new ideas and perspectives.

Radio has always been my safe place. But it took a long time for me to come to terms with being on the air. Although, in all my years of watching and listening to jocks, I always wondered if I could be excellent behind the microphone.

Being afraid of mediocrity was a lame excuse, and for the first dozen or so years of my career, I hid on the other side of the glass. Several years after I'd started working with Rush, I went on the air for the very first time, co-hosting a talk show for WABC. The program director took a chance and put me on the air on Saturdays, then gave me my own show on Sunday nights. I worked with Rush during the week, then did my own show on the weekends. A quarter of a century later, in 2021, I returned to my New York City radio home, WABC with a weekday drive-time program, in addition to a Saturday morning talk show.

Performing music in the spotlight always scared the crap out of me. I was always afraid of making a mistake and being the subject of ridicule on the stage. I never enjoyed *performance*, because I was so self-conscious about it. But when I speak from the heart, I'm in the zone. I don't get nervous, even in front of a live audience or when broadcasting to millions, because I'm not performing. I'm being me.

In 1982, the music died on WABC AM radio. I produced the very last music show at WABC, which was hosted by two of the most well-known disc jockeys in the world. Then I walked out of Studio 8A and went straight down the hall to Studio 8B to produce our first talk show, *NewsTalk* with Art Athens.

Rush Limbaugh reemerged at Kansas City radio KMBZ AM in 1983, using his real name for the first time. That gig lasted about a year before he was let go, but he quickly found a job at KFBK in what would become his "adopted hometown" of Sacramento, California. Behind that microphone, Rush's voice and career began to resonate. All the way to New York City.

"At no time when I was young and climbing the ladder of success did I ever think I would be doing the same thing for twenty-seven years at the same place. I might have been doing the same thing, but I might have gotten fired twenty-five times in the process. But I haven't been fired in the last twenty-seven years, or twenty-six. No, I haven't been fired in the last thirty. Now it's kind of hard now because I would have to fire myself." —RL

SHOW NOTES

As of this publication, Premiere Networks chose Buck Sexton and Clay Travis to fill the time slot that was home to *The Rush Limbaugh Show* for over thirty years. Longtime listeners will recall Buck was one of our excellent guest hosts, before striking out on his own. Dan Bongino is stepping up onto a larger platform also airing from noon to three. And Erick Erickson is also syndicating a show that will air during that time slot. All are wonderful people and I cheer them on, wishing each all of the success they desire.

That said, I fear no broadcaster will ever fill the void Rush left. As Sean Hannity recently told me, it's up to the rest of us to step up to the plate. I'd add that "the rest of us" includes me and you. Rush's love for radio motivated him through difficult times. My experience mirrored his, in that I knew my calling was to be in broadcasting—in whatever role best suited me at the time.

What interests and passions point to your calling? The things you love, and that bring you joy or desire, are important. If you're following those, I encourage you to never give up. The road won't be easy, but it will be worth it. If you're wondering about what to do with your dreams, you already know the answer.

A Recent Message from a Listener

"I grew up listening to Rush and have listened to him every day since I was sixteen years old. I am now thirty-three and miss him terribly. Although I never met him, I, like so many other Americans, felt as if I lost a family member when Rush died. God bless you Bo! There will never be another Rush Limbaugh!"

A Word from One of Our Amazing Guest Hosts, BRETT WINTERBLE

"Rush Limbaugh is a once in a millennium talent. I learned about the brilliance of a broadcaster performing day after day against all sorts of adversaries, both professional and sometimes even on a personal level. When you consider the amazing work he did in the different parts of his life and over the course of thirty-three years, you have to be struck by the genius. But it was also due in large part to the amazing team behind the scenes. This was truly a family and a family it remains to this day."

I'm 100% deaf and I can only hear bionically. The human ear has thirty-five thousand hair cells each. They determine the frequency and the sensitivity of human hearing. Mine are dead. They laid down and died. Autoimmune, so I have eight manmade biological electrodes or bionic electrodes that try to do what thirty-five thousand hair cells do.

—RUSH LIMBAUGH

6

SILENCE IS NOT GOLDEN

"**W**hat's your question or comment for Rush?"

For more than three decades, that's how I greeted callers to the program. Hundreds of thousands of them. I didn't want to know your name, where you're calling from, or why. I had to find out what you wanted to say, and fast, because you were one of about ninety people I'd talk with in three hours.

If you couldn't immediately tell me what you wanted to talk about, and make it interesting, it would be a short call. "I can't use that one today, thank you for calling." *Click.* Next!

If you got past my first question, I'd ask a top-secret series of questions, because I wanted to know what led you to this call. What's your real point? What's behind the first answer you gave me? Because if Rush drilled down into your comment, he would locate your true agenda—with half his brain tied behind his back just to make it fair—and my ass was on the line for any bad calls.

Here's the profound takeaway for would-be callers, and anyone who wants to use their voice in a positive way. *Before you speak up, you've got to know what you want to say—and why—then frame your words clearly.*

For every single call-screening rule I created—and there were a lot of them—you could break one or two and get on the air if you were that *right* call. Based on what I sensed of Rush's mood that day, the topic of discussion, and the vibe of the caller, I made exceptions. Thankfully, I developed a pretty good sense of who to put in the lineup. And I did this with one ear tied behind my back, because I had another role on the broadcast.

> *"The official program observer, Mr. Snerdley, yeah. Well, yeah, this is a very important program. We have a program observer. We have somebody who observes it and documents it and archives it for history. We don't just let this program go off into the ether. Rush-Limbaugh.com is also the official archivist of the EIB Network. And you could call them program observers. But the actual title goes to Mr. Snerdley, who also is the official screener of calls." —RL*

Of course, several talented staff members were officially observing the program in ways I couldn't. Over the years, I developed the ability to screen callers and listen to Rush at the same time. I somehow remembered things he said years earlier and occasionally offered opinions, questions, and ideas for the show. You may remember the occasional "Mr. Snerdley just reminded me . . ." segue. I sure do, and I miss those moments dearly.

Air Pressure

Everybody and their momma wanted to get on the air with Rush. One politician, a senator from a very big state, called into the show and Rush allowed him on, which was a very rare thing. I paid very close attention to the call, and after their exchange, I noticed the senator forgot to hang up the phone. I listened—only because that was my job, of course—and heard the asshole gloating with his staff about how he had just played Rush.

I didn't blab about it—right away. The next time this politician called to bend Rush's ear about something, I casually mentioned to Rush that the last time this guy was on, we overheard him talking to his staff, and he showed his cards. I may have used the word "snake" to describe him. And somehow or another, the senator never again made it onto the program.

Radio is exhilarating, but it's not always fun and light. As much as we were enjoying the show, there were stressful times. President Clinton was accusing Rush of being a racist. The left had truly become awakened to how damaging the broadcast was to their agenda. The attacks were relentless and personal. Rush willingly took the brunt, and tried to shield the staff, but the stress did get to me. In the late '90s, as I prepared to drive into the New York studio, I'd often throw up because of nerves.

Here we go, into the minefield again. My performance level has to be perfect. I cannot let a bad caller through.

Let me be clear, this was pressure I put on myself; it never came from Rush. I knew Rush was under a lot of stress, and

I didn't want to do anything that would add to it. I, wrongly, took the "zero mistakes" line literally and personally.

My schedule certainly didn't help. When Rush was out, I would compile the "best of" programs and produced most of the guest hosts' shows. Even those shows had to be perfect. Incidentally, a few radio careers were greatly accelerated because I suggested certain people sit in the "prestigious Attila the Hun Chair," as Rush jokingly referred to it, at "the Limbaugh Institute for Advanced Conservative Studies." I never took all my vacation days, and when I did take a few days off, I still watched the news, sent articles and notes to the team, and listened to every minute of the broadcast.

In 1998, about ten years after I joined the broadcast, I left the Rush Limbaugh program. I got an offer to go to Seattle and become vice president of a new company that was exploring a new internet technology called "streaming media." The technology was way ahead of its time and I knew the internet would be a game changer for broadcasting. To me, it was the evolution of everything that I'd been working on. I've been a communications guy all my life, and there was something about interactive communications that felt like I was walking into a radio station for the first time: *I have got to be a part of this!*

But I also finally admitted to myself that I needed a break.

As much as I loved working with Rush, I told him and the EIB family that I had to find out what this tech was all about. And I told them I'd be back. I won't divulge the conversations Rush and I shared about my departure, simply because they are so treasured and sacred to me. Rush threw me a party at the Four Seasons in New York before I left for Seattle. He also presented me with a treasured gift—a signed poster, from a painting that LeRoy Neiman did for him from our fifth anniversary show. It's a large portrait of a young, dark-haired Rush in the brilliant splashes of expressionist color that Neiman was known for.

I enjoyed the new challenge with TalkSpot, part of Worldstream Communications. In the late '90s, when most people were using dial-up modems to get online, we offered internet radio, video, whiteboards, graphics, and chat. I was responsible for ninety-six hours of programming across three different channels: news and politics, lifestyle, and a humor channel. Our hosts were as free as they wanted to be—so opposite of today's cancel culture. After a year in Seattle, I moved to Washington, DC, to focus my work in the political broadcast arena.

I stayed in contact with everyone at EIB and even talked with Rush on the air about certain topics. I listened every day, sent articles, and never felt disassociated. I was still a small part of the DNA of the program, and had a unique connection with Rush, so I suppose it wasn't a surprise to anyone when I slowly got back to helping with certain aspects of operations.

Years before I moved to Seattle, I began writing the "morning updates" for Rush—ninety-second commentaries that were aired every weekday morning on affiliate stations. Diana Allocco, who ran the newsletter, edited them expertly and we'd send the finished result to Rush for the next day's update. Of course, sometimes Rush would ask us to change things, or he'd address a different topic on his own. After leaving EIB, I stopped drafting the morning updates, but by the time I moved to DC, they asked me to start writing them again.

Over the years, I had learned a lot about Rush's unique voice—how he expressed perspectives and ideas. Writing is all auditory for me. I can hear the voice—the inflections and the pauses—in my head, while I'm writing. Reading news stories, I could *hear* what would interest Rush and, to the degree that anyone could, predict what his take on certain stories would be. I couldn't predict what Rush's take would be on political events that were still transpiring, because he had a knack for coming up with brilliant and unconventional insights.

A Change in Rush's Voice

Before I took the Worldstream job, Rush had moved the broadcast studio to Florida. I listened every day and was still the *semi-official* program observer. I noticed things—little details that few others would catch.

In 2001, I began to notice that something was off with Rush's voice. The timing, the pauses, the pitch and tone of his voice was off. At times, he seemed to slur some of his words. Concerned, I called him one morning. "What's going on, Rush? Something sounds different."

"Look, James. I'm sorry, but if I told you what was going on, you wouldn't believe it." He was right.

So I called John Axten, who was the president of the company, and I asked him what was going on. John didn't go into detail, but he told me Rush's hearing was compromised.

"I need to be there with him," I said. "Please get me on the first plane tomorrow."

The next afternoon, I drove my rental car to the new EIB Southern Command Headquarters in Palm Beach. As I pulled up, Rush was in the parking lot walking to his car. Without either of us saying a word, I gave him a big hug. He knew why I was there. *You're not going to go through this by yourself, my friend. I'm here.*

My own media consultancy was gaining clients, and I knew my experience with interactive communications could make my company a leader in the industry. But my career has never been about money. The moment I heard Rush was having challenges, I knew what I had to do. I have never doubted my decision and I've never regretted it. *This is where I need to be.*

There was never a formal discussion with anyone at EIB about whether I should come back or not. It was simply understood and celebrated.

The Show Is Still the Thing

The next day at the studio was the happy day I met two irreplaceable members of the EIB family: Dawn Bachinski and Brian Johnson.

During my three-year absence as call screener, Brian had been hired to complete various installations and upgrades to the EIB Southern Command Headquarters. Brian had worked at his father's engineering firm and came to EIB's attention because his father was well known in the radio industry. After September 11, 2001, Premiere Networks asked if he could be available every weekday to assist Rush. In Brian's words, "I basically dropped everything I was doing with my dad. And that's when Rush said that he lost all his hearing in one ear."

Rush's progressive hearing loss was rapid, and he was expected to become completely deaf, so the team brainstormed ideas that would enable him to stay on the air. Dawn had been a court reporter and stenographer for many years when John Axten called and asked her to come to the studio for a short gig. Kraig Kitchin, Rush's broadcast partner and one of the founders of Premiere Radio, was also there. Here's Dawn's telling of their first meeting.

"I just thought it was a job for the day. They said it was for Rush Limbaugh, who I had never heard of. When I first met them in the studio, Kraig Kitchin told me they had tried out all these stenographers and they didn't work out. Now I'm thinking, *What did I get myself into here?* Rush was on the other side of the glass with Kraig, who said, 'I'm just gonna have a conversation with Rush and could you just type it on this computer?' I thought, *This is the craziest job I've ever had. What is this?!*

"Kraig wrote him a little note to start a dialogue, then Rush started talking. As they continued, Rush read Kraig's words on the screen, and would respond in normal conversation. After about thirty minutes, they said they'd like me to come back the next day. I said, 'OK,' still not realizing the gravity of what was going on.

"Just before I left, Rush gave me a note he had written. It read, 'I can't thank you enough. I know I can do this now.' He had tears in his eyes.

"I wasn't planning on being full-time, but I saw this man, the passion he had for what he was doing, what he was going through, and how he had completely lost his hearing. I really didn't have to think much about it. I knew this is what I was going to do. I was going to make sure, no matter what, I was going to be there every day for Rush."

On October 8, 2001, Rush made the announcement to his listeners.

"If the pattern keeps up, I'll be totally deaf. Hearing aids, the most powerful made, mean nothing. If I take the hearing aid out of my right ear, I cannot hear a thing." —RL

Back Behind the Glass

I remember my first day back, screening and observing. Kraig saw the interaction that Rush and I had across the glass and was wowed by it. He realized how vital it was for me to be there. And it was vital for me, too. When I sat across from Rush in the studio, I felt like I was still a young kid at the beginning of my career. The show was fun again. All the previous pressure I had put on myself was totally gone.

For the next year, I commuted to Florida from my home in Maryland every week and was there for every show. After the program ended on Friday, I flew back to Maryland and arrived home late at night. On Sundays, after watching *Meet the Press*, I drove to the airport and flew back to West Palm Beach. Finally, I realized the commute was crazy, and flying after the attacks of September 11, 2001, had been interesting to say the least. So I moved to Florida.

Hush Rush

During this time, the Democrats continually ramped up their attacks on Rush and other conservative voices. Some in Congress called for the so-called "Fairness Doctrine" to be brought back, after President Ronald Reagan wisely canceled it in a 1987 executive order. Rush called such legislative threatening the "Hush Rush" bill. Publications started taking aim, like *Time* magazine's cover with the headline "Is Rush Limbaugh Good for America?" The Associated Press did one of the most despicable things I've ever seen, when it published parroted accusations made by a group with the misleading name Fairness and Accuracy in Reporting (FAIR). When Rush actually took the time to source every single thing that he said, he gave it to the AP so it could retract its story. It never bothered. This wasn't journalism. This was pure politics.

Even deafness couldn't silence Rush. Through the years, he'd faced every kind of attack, bent on silencing him. One of the first attempts to shut down his voice came in 1994, after the Florida Orange Juice Commission spent a million dollars advertising its product on our program. A throng of feminists decided to boycott the Florida Orange Juice Commission because of the commission's support of the program, and they held a rally to protest the ad campaign at a local grocery store. But word got out, and those protesters were far outnumbered by Rush fans, who also managed to purchase every drop of orange juice from the store. The movement to support Rush and the Florida Orange Juice Commission flowed across the country, as people suddenly developed a taste for the product of the Sunshine State.

This boycott backfired. Those who were against conservative values sought to punish those with different opinions. All it did was generate more support for the program and our sponsors. That's when it became clear that our audience would boycott anyone who tried to boycott Rush. We spoke about it when I interviewed Rush for the *Limbaugh Letter*.

"You remember the orange juice fiasco. Imagine this. Here are the Florida orange growers, who want to sell orange juice. So they sign a year contract to advertise on my program. The National Education Association, the teachers' union, is having their annual convention in New Orleans, before it was destroyed by George Bush sending Hurricane Katrina in there. They issue a statement condemning Florida orange juice growers. This is an education convention! Libs brought all kinds of pressure. A feminist protest was scheduled at a Tampa Publix, I think it was. Hearing this, a bunch of Tampa listeners got a caravan of cars and bought every container of orange juice off the shelves, to demonstrate that liberal pressure groups weren't going to bother the public at whom the advertising was directed. The feminists showed up—there were three of them in a convertible, remember?

"Still, the Florida orange juice growers panicked. In the old days, businesses did not want to get complaint letters or protests. It didn't matter who was behind it, they just didn't want to deal with it. Today, they know that most of these campaigns are organized by five or six politically motivated people writing thousands of letters, who are just trying to harm my program, not even the advertiser. We have been able to educate advertisers, so it doesn't happen much at all. Look, after nineteen years, we finally got General Motors." —RL

The left always got its way . . . until Rush Limbaugh. The mainstream media tried to project their thinking as the mindset of the country. Rush exposed the fact that NBC, CBS, ABC, the *New York Times*, the *Los Angeles Times*, the *Chicago Tribune*, and the *Washington Post* were not the conscience of the American people. Exposing this divide between the few elite and the vast majority of Americans is one of the greatest elements of his legacy. This was the beginning of the end of the media monopoly in America.

In subsequent controversies relating to the support of Rush and his show, Rush decided to do what no one else had done to this point in time; he looked behind the scenes. He found out the people organizing the boycotts were actually a small group of activists—often using computers to magnify their influence by generating thousands of letters directed at companies who supported the show.

Today we have "woke" companies like Atlanta-based Delta Airlines and Coca-Cola, who caved into political agitation from the leftists over Georgia's voting-reform legislation. These companies, and many others, actually supported moving many of their scheduled events *from* Georgia to other states. For example, when Major League Baseball pulled the All-Star Game out of Atlanta, it pulled hundreds of millions of dollars away from local businesses—including a large number of minority-owned businesses.

Cancel culture—threats to boycott companies and destroy careers—has become so extreme we now have comedians like Chris Rock talking about how it's impossible to tell jokes because today's millennials are so sensitive and ready to cancel at the drop of a microphone. Conservatives are losing a high percentage of millennial votes because they fall prey to this mindset, instead of standing up to it. That's why it's necessary to keep talking about how dangerous cancel culture is to every American.

The left was never able to cancel Rush because as he often said, the media didn't build his audience, so they couldn't take his audience away. He didn't depend on social media or advertising to grow his audience; he created his own niche and his own platform. There's a huge lesson there for conservative influencers.

Canceling Free Speech

Canceling opposing views is a step toward an authoritarian state, which is what the left wants. If you don't think the way they do on any number of issues, like transgender women athletes competing against women, liberals say you're a bigot and try to shut you up. If you have the balls to express a different opinion, they will try to cut them off.

In May 2021, a Virginia teacher was placed on leave because he refused to "affirm that a biological boy can be a girl and vice versa" because it was against his religion. A leader in the school district's Minority Student Achievement Advisory Committee (MSAAC) reportedly stated, "If our teachers and staff cannot be open and willing to learn how to be culturally competent then they do not need to be in the classrooms any longer, as they will only hinder the process and most importantly cause irreparable harm to the vulnerable hearts and minds of our students."

What the hell does "culturally competent" mean? I'm not sure, but about a week later, after many parents spoke up, a judge ruled that the teacher must be reinstated. Evidently competence works both ways.

I want people to be who they are. But if I was a female weightlifter and my competitor had more flesh stuffed in her briefs than her bra, I would speak up. Rush discussed this with a caller in 2019.

CALLER: "Well, my comment is straight to the point. I saw the LGBTQ and, you know, transgenders, what happens to the women's soccer team when transgender men start identifying as women and go out to play women's soccer?"

RUSH: "Now, we're not supposed to talk about this out loud."

CALLER: "Sorry. I thought I'd go there."

RUSH: "You have presented me with such a target. Hitting the bull's-eye on this, I could do with both eyes closed. The question is do I take the shot or do I pass on this for peace the rest of the week.

"Snerdley said, 'Take the shot, Rush!'

"Her question is for all of this pomp and circumstance and all the celebration of women champions, what happens, what's gonna happen when a bunch of transgender men enter this arena? Answer is it's already happening. And do you know where it is already happening? Yes indeed. It is happening in wrestling, ladies and gentlemen.

"Oh, by the way, I have a piece. We're not allowed to say 'ladies and gentlemen' anymore. [. . .]

"It's already happening. I'm sure it's happening in soccer somewhere. [. . .] The feminists are supporting this under the theory the more women, the better. And the more women with penises, I guess, the better. Folks, I'm not making this up at all. And it is infuriating some, and those who express their anger and objection to this at the high school and college level are being told to shut up and to stop being discriminatory and bigoted.

"Now, for these guys who decide they want to become women and then get on the women's wrestling team? Folks, I'm just telling you here now that once it starts, it's gonna creep everywhere."

When someone's so-called "rights" infringe on my rights of conscience, religion, and free speech, the issue is no longer about rights, it's about *control*.

Wuhan Weaponized

Look at what we're now learning about the origins of the Wuhan—excuse me, COVID-19—virus. When President Trump first raised the idea that this could be a laboratory inspired virus, he was ridiculed. Those who agreed were shut out of social media. Now, as it turns out, the mainstream press has finally embraced what many of us suspected all along, that the virus could have originated in a lab.

Conservatives also need to get smarter about the media and technology. While we were out buying guns and ammo, the leftists were buying the megabytes. We have guns, but Democrats run the data centers. As of 2020, Amazon controlled at least 33% of the cloud data market, and I'll bet that number will continue to rise. A handful of companies control most of the data storage and web traffic. Remember Parler—the conservative alternative to Twitter? The platform grew impressively, until it was canceled. An entire social media company with millions of users, shut down by the people who control information technology. As of this writing, Parler is back online, but will it be tomorrow?

These gatekeepers are tampering with free speech at every level, yet they enjoy anti-trust protections. Conservatives must mobilize around the First Amendment again and own the tech platform. We can't just be the consumers on the sidelines. Just like Rush brought competition to the media, now conservatives have to bring competition to technology and communication platforms.

You cannot allow yourself to be shut out, and you cannot shut up. And, as Rush demonstrated, we must have our facts straight. We must have a clear message. If Rush taught us anything, he taught us that we have to bear the brunt of being ridiculed and still speak our minds. There is a price to pay.

In February 2020, just as the virus was taking hold in this country, Rush boldly spoke what few were saying, and many were thinking. And these same insights apply today.

> *"The drive-by media hype of this thing as a pandemic, as the Andromeda strain, as, 'Oh, my God, if you get it, you're dead.' Do you know what the—I think the survival rate is 98%. Ninety-eight percent of people [who] get the coronavirus survive. It's a respiratory system virus. It probably is a ChiCom laboratory experiment that is in the process of being weaponized. All superpower nations weaponize bioweapons. They experiment with them. [. . .] The coronavirus is the same. It's really being hyped as a deadly Andromeda strain or Ebola pandemic that, 'Oh, my God, is going*

to wipe out the nation. It's going to wipe out the population of the world.'

"The stock market's down like 900 points right now. The survival rate of this is 98%! [. . .] That's less than the flu, folks. That is a far lower death statistic than any form of influenza, which is an annual thing that everybody gets shots for. There's nothing unusual about the coronavirus. In fact, coronavirus is not something new. There are all kinds of viruses that have that name. Now, do not misunderstand. I'm not trying to get you to let your guard down. [. . .]

"But look, back to the coronavirus for just a second. That is true that the Hong Kong protests strangely subsided as the news of the coronavirus expanded— and I'll tell you, it is a way . . . If you are a totalitarian government and you need to control your population, one of the best ways of doing it is unleashing something they think is a deadly disease and then you, as the dictator, have the 'safety solutions.' You have the ability to round people up from their homes and take 'em to so-called health camps. Be very leery of this, folks. It probably is not what the media's leading you to believe it is." —RL

Speaking Up

It's one thing to be trolled online, it's another to be shouted at in person. When I was at WABC Radio in New York doing my own weekend radio show in the '80s, I spoke out about some of the hateful language coming out of the Nation of Islam.

A few days later, I was out in public and confronted by three members of the group. Honestly, I was a bit intimidated and wondered if the situation would end badly for me. Thankfully it didn't.

Many years later, on Saturday, November 17, 2012, I was heckled at an event for Congressman Louie Gohmert at the Breakers Hotel in Palm Beach. As I ended my speech and prepared to introduce my good friend, Louie, some guy—who clearly was not a Gohmert supporter—started to heckle me. He looked like one of those Antifa types. I let a few things go, but finally, I walked over to him. "Listen. I don't play this shit. I don't show that kind of disrespect to you, you're not going to show that kind of disrespect to me."

Oh, and I was still wearing my lapel microphone, so the audience of several hundred people got to enjoy every syllable in surround sound.

As I got within a few feet of this punk, my six-foot-two, linebacker-sized frame eclipsed him. I ended my impromptu speech with, "I'm not playing. You want to keep heckling me, I'll kick your ass right here." The audience cheered and applauded—and the heckler slinked out of the room.

The videographer later told me she thought the whole scene was some kind of performance art. But it was very real.

What's the point, you ask? First, I just love that story. Sorry. My reactions are usually unanticipated by the left, and sometimes clearly wrong. But I do believe that conservatives have been too passive when someone tries to shut them down in public discourse. Let me be clear—I'm not talking about violence, and I never condone any form of intimidation. The point is we must not allow our voices, values, and views to be silenced.

Caricature Culture

Shutting up is dangerous because people assume that if there's only one voice talking, that voice must be the consensus—and correct—when there's no opposition to it. If a lie is repeated often enough, it's adopted as the truth unless it is challenged. But there's another danger that needs to be addressed. We live in a world of media caricatures. The media often puts the spotlight on people in an effort to define them. If people believe the caricature, and no one offers a contrary point of view, the media lie will become adopted by the public as truth.

While I was in Washington, DC, trying to grow my media and political consultancy, I was often interviewed on FoxNews, MSNBC, and occasionally CNN. I was also in the United States Capitol building all the time. In my dozens of walks through the Capitol lobby, there was one senator—the only one—who came over to say hello, or simply wave to me. That man, who was so nice to me every time he saw me, was Joe Biden. I could write a book about everything I think is wrong about Joe Biden's views, and I also happen to believe the stories about his corruption, but I can't take this away from him—he was a nice guy to me every time I ran into him. And sometimes, being nice goes a long way.

Around the same time, I was speaking at an event in one of the parks next to the Capitol and one of the other speakers was Hillary Clinton. I'd always heard the caricature, that Hillary could not deliver a good speech in person. But you know what? It was a damn good speech. I didn't agree with what she said, but it was still an effective message for her audience. After the speech was over, I noticed that two young ladies were trying to get Hillary's attention, but they seemed a bit shy and intimidated. I was close enough to say something, so I said, "Mrs. Clinton, those two girls in the back are trying to get your attention."

She went over and spoke with them. I had always heard that this woman was the ice queen, not a friendly person, and had no time for anybody. After Hillary finished her conversation, she walked back to me, looked me in the eye, and said, "I just want to thank you for letting me know. I wouldn't have known that they wanted to talk to me. Thank you very much."

Hillary Clinton had no clue who I was. For many years, I believed the caricature—what certain people wanted me to believe about her. The brief encounter changed me, hopefully for the better. I'm not saying that Hillary Clinton isn't a political snake or one of the worst Democrat politicians in the last century and a half, but my experience with her did not match the caricature.

Most of what liberals think about Rush is not true. It comes from a media caricature. This situation with Hillary and my limited interactions with Biden opened a window in my mind that I've tried to keep open. Despite everything I'm told by the media, despite everything I'm programmed to think about people, I try to keep a close eye on how judgmental I allow myself to be. I've learned that when it comes to public figures, the media narrative is very different from reality—for better or for worse. The media and the mob never give us the full story, so unless someone you trust can speak from direct experience, your opinions could fall far short of reality.

What does this have to do with speaking up? Keeping silent about issues and people creates a vacuum for lies. Political opponents are human beings. Most of them anyway. We would do this country—and ourselves—a world of good if we stopped making politics so personal and make it about the issues. Do I sometimes fall into the trap of mocking or labeling people? Yes. I've said things that I didn't intend to be mean-spirited or incorrect, but that have been both. And for that, I would like to publicly apologize and ask forgiveness.

If anyone were to define us based on what they saw on our worst day, they'd be wrong. If anyone were to define us based on what they saw on our best day, they'd be wrong. All of us are flawed, all of us also have good points that other people never see unless we spend time with them. No matter what news platform you read, watch, or listen to, remember—every organization has a worldview, a corporate culture, and an agenda. What they report about issues, and what they choose not to report, presents a distorted view. The same holds true about how people are presented in the media.

Rush Kept Speaking

Beethoven was deaf. Yet through the vibrations he felt and his memory of what notes sounded like, the composer was able to create some of the greatest music the human race has ever heard. Rush, at a crucial point in his career, became totally deaf. Yet through advances in technology, like the cochlear implant, his own inner muscle memory of sounds, and his sheer determination, Rush was able to continue a powerful discourse that resonated for two decades. In fact, Rush spent more of his syndicated radio career deaf than he did with the ability to hear. Despite every reason to quit, he kept speaking.

Rush loved music, but when he got his cochlear implants, they didn't completely replicate the audio experience. He had to listen to songs he already knew so his brain could fill in the blanks of the soundscape. Brian would remix his favorite songs and add compression so that the sound he heard was truer, but still like listening to an old transistor radio. As the years went on, something curious happened. He started listening to new music again. In fact, he often listened to songs during show prep and sometimes even during commercial breaks. Once in a while, he'd even sing along. I sure miss that voice.

It is a remarkable achievement for anyone to overcome challenges and persevere because of their love for their vocation. Through willpower—and of course, if you're a person of faith, with the strength that comes through that faith—you can still achieve astounding things. Whether it's about Rush's career, my career, or the challenges you may face, my charge to you remains: achieve anyway.

It is possible for us to achieve, even under the most challenging circumstances we might face. That's not saying we won't at times experience disappointments and devastating failure. We all know that some hard-fought battles are lost—as with Rush's fight with cancer. But by fighting, he achieved.

By refusing to be silenced, he achieved. The same holds true for us. We may ultimately lose the things we want to hold on to, but *achieving anyway* means that we don't give up. We are can-do people who can persevere. And sometimes, if perseverance is all the legacy we leave, that's enough.

Before you speak up, you've got to know why. And when you know why, speak clearly. Don't be silenced.

SHOW NOTES

As I was finishing this chapter, I spoke at a fundraiser in Louisiana and met a dear friend and golf buddy of Rush's, who told me something that blew my mind and melted my heart. He confided that Rush often talked about me after I went to work with Worldstream and said he would do anything to get me to come back to the show.

Although Rush and I stayed in contact during those years, and even though I was welcomed back to the team with overwhelming warmth, I had no idea he missed me that much. Now I see he didn't want to hold me back from pursuing new challenges. The revelation from his friend came at a time when I really needed it.

A Recent Message from a Listener

"Thank you James Golden! Though, of course, I never met Rush, I loved him with my whole heart. I was a lifer to The Rush Limbaugh Show. And I have figured that Rush will be the single voice I have listened to more than anyone in my lifetime. He connected with me and taught me so many things."

Another Message from a Listener

*"My condolences on the loss of your great friend.
When Rush announced having cancer, I remember
that sad day. It hit me harder than when my doctor
told me I had stage 3 cancer. My day wasn't
complete until I could hear what Rush had to say.
I'm just a service technician. I'm not very articulate,
but I loved Rush from day one and was a dedicated
listener since the early years of the show. And
I always tried to get people to give the show a
chance, even though they were hardcore leftists.
Some callers said that Rush was like the big brother
they never had. I view it a little differently. I feel like
Rush and you were the older brothers I never had."*

Let me tell you who we conservatives are. We love people. When we look out over the United States of America, when we are anywhere, when we see a group of people, such as this or anywhere, we see Americans. We see human beings. We don't see groups. We don't see victims. We don't see people we want to exploit. What we see is potential. [. . .] We believe that person can be the best he or she wants to be if certain things are just removed from their path like onerous taxes, regulations, and too much government.

—RUSH LIMBAUGH

7

RISE OF A BLACK CONSERVATIVE

When I was a teenager, I wanted to be a member of the Black Panthers. They were my heroes—the original ones like Huey Newton, not the pathetic bunch that cropped up in Philadelphia over the last twenty years.

In high school, as an assignment for English class, I wrote and delivered a short speech about how great the Black Panthers were. No joke. And in case my verbal expression didn't make an impression, I closed the presentation by raising my fist high in the air. *Black power!*

Surprised? My English teacher certainly was.

Yeah, I wanted radical change, but not because I hated America. I wanted radical change because I *loved* America, and I hated what was happening to so many people in my neighborhood, and in neighborhoods across our nation.

Recently, I went back and read the Black Panthers manifesto and was amazed. *Oh, my God, this is straight-up, communist bullshit!* But as a teen, I was impressed with their actions. Local chapters set up kitchens in their neighborhoods and fed hungry kids. Instead of begging or blackmailing the government schools to provide breakfast, they stepped up and made it happen. Instead of promising hope and change, they purchased, prepared, and served food.

They were also willing to defend Black people with their own lives. But let me be clear about the context of the 1960s. The FBI was corrupt then, and the FBI is corrupt now. Leftists knew it then, and conservatives should know it now—especially after what's been revealed about the agency's leadership in the political drama of the past five years. During his almost fifty-year directorship over the agency, J. Edgar Hoover violated the Constitution and violated the rights of countless Americans. That corruption has never been driven out.

I wanted the FBI to be held accountable for the harassment and murder of Black activists. I wanted to see justice for the illegal wiretapping of Dr. Martin Luther King, which John Kennedy and Bobby Kennedy were involved with. But I also loved Bobby Kennedy because he had a heart, even though I didn't like all of his politics. He went into Black neighborhoods and talked about how much we should love *everyone* in this country. I cried like a baby when Bobby Kennedy and Dr. King were murdered. Those men had guts. I loved them both because they stood up for what they believed.

Can you see why, as a young person, I admired the Black Panthers? It's the same reason so many young people are swept up into cults of leftism today. Talk is cheap. Action costs something. If the only helpful action people experience comes from a radical group, many people will embrace radicals. And that's one of many reasons why the number of conservative young people has declined so radically since the 1960s.

I was a teenage, conservative Black Panther supporter. Thankfully I quickly grew out of two of the three. But I still respect action over talk—especially when it comes to reviving conservatism.

> "Most people want problems solved, and conservatism is actually about that. It's about solving poverty. It's about solving racism. It's about solving bigotry. But look at what the branding has said of conservatism, that conservatism is racism, that it is bigotry, that it is bias, that it is discrimination. Yet the truth is, we want to solve all those problems. We want to wipe 'em out! We want a colorblind society!" —RL

What's Wrong with the Conservative Brand?

Through the years, Rush often pondered whether it was time to give up the "conservative" label. He finally concluded that we should not shy away from that word, but rather clarify what we are *for*.

There's political theory and then there's real life. We can debate about Keynesian economics and whine about socialist politicians—or we can take a hard look at the problems our fellow Americans face and promote simple solutions.

I saw hardship in the neighborhood I came up in. I still have friends in my old neighborhood and know many people who are barely holding on—they have mortgages, kids in school, elderly parents, and medical conditions, and they face rising crime. They're trying to make ends meet, but so much is against them. What ideas could we conservatives put forward to make people's lives better?

Many years ago, another guy named James wrote a book. Here's a line that comes to mind: "Suppose a brother or a sister is without clothes and daily food. If one of you says to them, 'Go in peace; keep warm and well fed,' but does nothing about their physical needs, what good is it? In the same way, faith by itself, if it is not accompanied by action, is dead."

Yeah, that's in the Bible, in what's known as the Book of James, and it was written two thousand years ago by a disciple of Jesus. But those words still apply to our interactions with fellow humans, and I'd even dare to say it relates to putting our conservative ideas into action.

Communism and socialism have flourished where the elites—in both political parties—have done nothing to improve people's daily lives. The essence of conservatism is love, because it provides solutions. If our arguments, solutions, and actions solve problems, we can rebrand conservatism. Election wins will follow.

Why Aren't There More Black Conservatives?

A few years ago, I was the featured speaker at a political rally. As the politician hosting the event led me and my friend Debi into the packed ballroom, we walked by the poster his staff created to promote the event. The photo on the poster featured a big, black, smiling face, but it wasn't my face. I stopped, recognized that the image was of a professional football player, and lost it. "What?! We all look alike now, is that how it is?"

The politician was mortified. I sputtered for a few more minutes and finally regained composure, while my friend almost fell over laughing. She still has a copy of that poster. I'm not sure what that story has to do with being a Black conservative, but I bet there's a lesson in there somewhere. The real question is, *Why aren't there more Black conservatives?*

> *"We want the country to succeed, and for the country to succeed, its people—its individuals— must succeed. Everyone among us must be pursuing his ambition or her desire, whatever, with excellence. Trying to be the best they can be. Not told, as they are told by the Democrat Party: 'You really can't do that, you don't have what it takes, besides, you're a minority or you're a woman and there are too many people that want to discriminate against you. You can't get anywhere. You need to depend on us.'" —RL*

Rush was always clear about conservatism, and we need to be clear about what it means to be a conservative and communicate it far and wide. That's what my political action committee, New Journey PAC, and radio show are about. But more importantly, that's what I'm about. Trust me, in order to change hearts and minds—and win elections—we Republicans need to do some soul searching and update our tired talking points.

One of the hallmarks of the Rush Limbaugh program was that Rush was not a political activist. The program was not an activist show. We discussed the issues of the day, but Rush felt his audience was intelligent enough to make up their own minds about the issues. I was not an activist until the 2016 election. I knew early on that the Democrats were going to define the election along racial lines. The Republicans failed to be aggressive with the Democrat race-baiting, which had become their signature strategy for running national elections. I decided to form a political action committee so that I and some communications-savvy friends could start to do the job that the Republicans had failed to do: push back on the continued race-baiting of the Democrats.

After I formalized the PAC documents, I went into the studio to tell Rush, right before the show, and said, "Rush, I did something." He looked up at me with interest and asked, "What did you do?"

"I formed a PAC called New Journey."

"Why?" he replied.

"Because, number one, I'm tired of the way the Democrats are always using race. I'm also tired of the way they have attacked people like you and conservatives using race over the years, and this time if they pull that crap, we're going to shove it right back in their face."

Rush smiled and asked, "You need any help?"

I said, "No, Rush, I don't want you to do anything, because if we are called to defend you, I don't want anybody from the press looking into this thing and saying that New Journey PAC was bought and paid for by Rush Limbaugh. This is something that I'm doing. All I need is your blessing." And he gave me his blessing to go ahead with it.

Cultural momentum is against conservative ideology—partly because leaders aren't communicating well and partly because what we've been saying is thoughtless. I'm about a new kind of conservatism that puts our values into action.

Let's Get Real

I'm a raving fan of capitalism. But we conservatives should not accept *crony* capitalism dominating what should be *free* markets. There's a lot of corruption in the highest levels of business and finance. Republicans should be against corruption and be *for* the average American who aspires to participate in the miracle of free enterprise.

> *"I know that it is a myth anymore that big business tycoons and Wall Street people are exclusively Republican. They aren't anymore. The Democrat Party is bankrolled by Wall Street, for example. Take a look at the money Kamala Harris gets, or Plugs, or Obama. The idea that the Republican Party and Wall Street or big business are inseparable, that ended I don't know how long ago. They are tied at the hip with Democrats now, for a host of reasons. And a lot of it is crony capitalism and crony socialism." —RL*

The Great Recession, which started in 2007, was caused by incompetent politicians and greedy executives. No one was held to account, and billions of dollars—taken from you and me—were paid to bail them out. The system didn't change, and because of new layers of government regulation, it's even more difficult to enter the market. If you or I stole a credit card and racked up a few grand, we'd be taken to jail. But countless Wall Street players did far worse and took it to the bank. Are we really OK with this?

Establishment Republican politicians froth about "socialized medicine"—and rightly so—but sit on their hands while people can't afford health care. Other than being *against* socialism, where are our legislative solutions to the problems most people worry about?

To half of the voters in this country, the silence is loud and clear. Politicians destroyed the process of health care—where your doctor could treat you and then send you a bill that was affordable. Insurance used to be needed only for catastrophic illnesses.

President Trump is the lone Republican who really tried to implement some common-sense ideas. He demanded transparency from hospitals about the actual itemized costs of products and services, and now this reform is in place. Of course, the media didn't praise him; he had to do his own PR. Regardless, he offered a solution and worked to see it implemented. Conservatism is at its best when it helps people by solving problems and removing unnecessary obstacles.

Animal Rights Update

Rush used to say that conservatives can never win by being *against* stuff—no matter what the issue. We have to tell people what we are *for*—and how it will benefit their lives and futures. Every single American can and should prosper.

The reason there aren't more Black conservatives is the same reason there aren't more white conservatives—or pick any demographic. Everyone knows what conservatives are *against*. But we have done a dismal job creating and communicating solutions that we are *for*. Republican leaders have also alienated potential friends and allies.

Do you love animals? I've never understood why so many Republicans make fun of people in the animal rights movement. Sure, there are some rabid activists, but generally speaking, they care about life. The same goes with tree-huggers. *See? I just insulted a potential ally.* I've never met a Republican who didn't appreciate nature and wildlife, have you? Am I an "environmentalist"? Maybe so. Rush was—in his own way.

"I did my good deed of the week yesterday. I was playing golf yesterday morning at a course down here that's closing for the summer. It always closes on Mother's Day. It's Seminole. I shot a hell of a round. I shot an 85, so 42-43. But I was plus five on the par threes. If I could have just parred the par threes, I would have shot an 80. I mean, if—if, you know, if is for children. Anyway, as we're heading up to the sixteenth, all of a sudden as I'm walking up, I see something that looks huge in the middle of the fairway with a bird prancing around. I got closer, and it's a turtle, a pretty big turtle. Not a sea turtle, but a pretty big turtle and this bird is just harassing this turtle like you can't believe.

"My caddy said, 'You know what's going on there? That turtle is heading for the sand traps. She's going to lay her eggs, and the bird knows it, and the bird's just waiting to get the eggs.' And I said, 'Well, this isn't going to happen when I'm out here.' So I went over and picked up this turtle, and took it back over to the creek, because the turtle had turned and was aiming for the sand trap. But when we turned it away from the sand trap, it started heading back to where the little stream or creek is in the rough.

"So we figured, 'OK. The turtle has figured out here that the bird wants its eggs and is going to wait to lay them. The turtle was just laboring. You've seen turtles just laboring to move. So the bird finally flew off when the turtle turned around. I picked the turtle up, took it back to within a foot of the creek, and it got scared. Its head was bopping in and out. It was not a snapper turtle. Its nose looked like nasal spray, one of those bottles of nasal spray. But it was a good deed. I picked up that turtle and we took it over there and I hope that it laid its eggs somewhere. She was doing this in broad daylight, folks, so there was plenty of light out there. Normally, these turtles do this at night to prevent other animals and beasts like birds getting in there and doing [interruption]. Yeah, you could say that. You could say I interfered with nature.

"But I didn't interfere with nature because I am nature. I'm as much a part of nature as the stupid bird." —RL

No doubt you can hum the opening music to *The Rush Limbaugh Show*, but do you know the legendary rocker who wrote and recorded the song "My City Was Gone" was a vocal animal rights activist and environmentalist? In the lyric, Chrissie Hynde of the Pretenders bemoans that her "pretty countryside" was paved over "by a government that had no pride." After her publishing company told the EIB network to cease and desist playing the tune, she actually fought them and allowed Rush to use it.

> *"She was on PLJ in New York and they asked her about it. 'I don't care. If Rush wants to use it, fine with me,' which totally confounded her publishing company. So, we got the song back. The reason is that her dad was a huge fan of this program." —RL*

If that's not surprising enough, when President Trump awarded Rush the Presidential Medal of Freedom, Ms. Hynde tweeted:

> "Dear Mr. President, I often think of how much my father, Melville 'Bud' Hynde, who proudly served his country as a Marine on Guadalcanal, would have enjoyed your presidency.
>
> "The other day when you gave that award to Rush Limbaugh, my father would have been so delighted. He loved listening to Rush, which is why I allowed my song 'My City Was Gone' to be used on his radio show. My father and I didn't always

see eye-to-eye. We argued a lot. But isn't that
the American way? The right to disagree without
having your head chopped off?"

Chrissie Hynde is not known for her conservative views, but she shares appreciation for freedom of expression. She was also against the concept of animals—and humans—getting decapitated for their opinions. And she loved her dad.

Instead of a knee-jerk disrespecting of differences, we might want to consider talking with other people about what we have in common.

Common Ground

I grew up in a normal, middle-class environment—with values that used to be part of mainstream American culture. Why did my dad and his generation fight in World War II and the Korean War, knowing they would come back home— if they were fortunate enough to survive—to segregation and being treated as second-class citizens? What motivated these men and women to work hard, feed their families, and educate their children? My dad stayed in the military for most of his life, going from active duty to the Army Reserves, and was very proud of his service.

He and his Black friends loved and served their country, even though, in many agonizing ways, their country didn't love them back. They were *against* injustice, but they were *for* the country that offered opportunity for true justice and a better way of life. They shared the same values that most other Americans held at the time. Even during the Depression, which many of them lived through, it wasn't OK to steal. Today, we have district attorneys and news anchors saying people shouldn't be prosecuted for "minor" thefts. Back then, citizens of this nation were clear about our values. *You don't steal. You work hard. And if you work hard, things will most likely turn out your way.*

There was a social contract, and it happened to be based on conservative values. Decades ago, Black people in America were part of this social contract, too—even though they often got their asses kicked by the cops, suffered injustice in the justice system, and faced segregation in every facet of daily life.

I believe part of what finally energized the civil rights movement was that most white Americans understood that they held the same core values as Black Americans. When they were finally confronted with their own bigotry—and actual institutional bigotry—they realized it wasn't right. Their fellow patriotic citizens, Black Americans, were working hard, feeding their families, fighting wars, and trying to pursue the American dream.

If my parents' generation of Black men and women could find it within themselves to love this country, why is it so difficult today for so many young people of all races to do the same? Rush offered his insights in June 2020.

"Because I don't want to be unnecessarily argumentative or provocative, I will go ahead and let it stand that Black Lives Matter has been hijacked. Ahem. I'm just gonna tell you. Antifa is simply a new name for all

of these left-wing, Democrat Party aligned and spon-
sored protest groups going back to the '60s. You had the
Weathermen. He had the SDS, Students for Democrat
Society. I can't even think of all the names. Antifa is
Occupy Wall Street. It's Black Lives Matter. They're all
the same people and thinking under different names.
They have different organizations for the purposes of
fundraising.

"Membership is actively recruited. But it is the
Democrat Party.

"They are the Democrat Party. What you see on
the streets of New York and all these other blue states,
this is—what's the term, the outgrowth? This is what
you get. This is the Democrat Party. This is what they
sponsor. This is what they inspire. This is what their
policies lead to. Democrat Party policies are conceived
and created in rage and anger. [. . .] The Democrat
Party is the reason for the angst, the reason for the
nervousness, the fear, the anger, trepidation. All of this
can be traced to the Democrat Party and a famously
uttered philosophy of theirs: A crisis is a terrible thing
to waste." —RL

In addition to decades of negative propaganda by the
Democrats, maybe part of the problem is how far we conservatives have gotten off message. With few exceptions, and
until President Trump, our so-called leaders have focused
on esoteric issues while forgetting about the basic values and
desires most people share.

Conservative values are American values. Conservatism in the African American community is not a rarity, and it used to be the mainstream. Let's focus on the values we share, offer solutions to problems, and form new alliances. If helping people experience more of the American dream is our priority, we'll see more Black conservatives, and we'll win elections.

"Alter the Structure"

Why don't Republicans disrupt the political conversation with big ideas—ideas that show what conservatism truly is, in contrast to liberal policies?

I believe at least one policy debate in this country would be turned right-side-up if every Black person in America who owned a gun, or wanted to own one, joined the National Rifle Association. Just consider that idea for a moment.

We can continue to watch those on the left make it more difficult for law-abiding citizens to own guns—which only shifts the balance of power to the bad guys with guns—or we can educate and encourage the exercise of our Second Amendment rights. So, *hell yes*, I think Black people should join the NRA, by the millions! Imagine the conversations at local meetings as new people meet together and realize they have so much in common. Imagine the chaos and shrieking in the Democrat Party! Makes me smile just to think about it.

Moving on, let's talk about the issue of economic freedom and opportunity, and one of the real root causes of poverty. In most states, you have to obtain a license to be an entrepreneur—even to braid someone's hair. It's the law. I'm talking about a cosmetology license. Don't believe me? In

New York State, this means "shaving, trimming, and cutting the hair or beard either by hand or mechanical appliances and the application of antiseptics, powders, oils, clays, lotions or applying tonics to the hair, head, or scalp, and in addition includes providing, for a fee or any consideration or exchange, whether direct or indirect, services for the application of dyes, reactive chemicals, or other preparations to alter the color or to straighten, curl, or alter the structure of the hair of a human being. It is the responsibility of licensees to understand the Appearance Enhancement Law."

If you're a sixteen-year-old who wants to legally "alter the structure of the hair of a human being" you need to wait until you're seventeen years old. Sorry kid. But the good news is, you now have another year to "complete a 1,000 hour approved course of study" and "understand the Appearance Enhancement Law."

If it's this difficult to start a small business that cuts and styles hair, can you fathom how challenging is it to open a grocery store? Or a bank? If Black people wanted to join together and open up their own community bank, federal and state legislation would make it virtually impossible.

Who created all these hurdles—and keeps adding more? Liberal Democrats.

True Social Security

One of the best policy changes that could happen for Americans of all shades is for Social Security to be reformed. President Bush 43 tried to pass a plan to allow people to control their own money. Yeah, another radical conservative idea. He

and Republican congresspersons botched the PR—as usual—
and retreated. What a missed opportunity.

*"Social Security, as you know, is the third rail of
American politics, meaning if you step on it you die. If
you touch it, you get electrocuted, and that's it. So there
are very few people who even talk about, as candidates, talk about Social Security, other than to say it's
necessary. Remember when George W. Bush wanted
to privatize some of it, remember what happened? It
would have made all the sense in the world to do it. It
would have been one of the greatest, in terms of fiscal
responsibility, privatizing. That's actually the wrong
term, privatizing. All the policy was, was allowing
Social Security recipients an opportunity to invest a
portion of their money so that it could grow larger than
Social Security does." —RL*

Here's what generally happens under the Social Security
system. Black guys like me work their whole lives to get to be
sixty-seven years old—or a few years older if we're lucky—and
then we die. All those paycheck deductions we sent to DC stay
there. Yes, spouses get some benefits, but in most cases the
monthly payouts are sent to older white women because they
live the longest. Is that racist? No, it's data.

My dad died at age sixty-seven. He worked his whole life
and collected Social Security for less than two years. In Peru,
they allow some of the funds to be invested privately, and
people are able to keep wealth *inside* their family, which can

now be passed down through the generations. Democrats do not want this because it would mess with their power structure, which is based on dependency. What an opportunity for Republicans and conservatives of all parties to help people—and win more elections.

We don't need reparations. Let Black families keep the money they earned so they can pass it on to their children and grandchildren. There's your damned reparations.

Cult of Personality

Years ago, I did an interview in which one of my comments was twisted beyond recognition. Here was my point, and I still stand behind it. *In some specific ways, life was better for many Blacks seventy years ago than it is today.*

Why? Because back then, two-parent families were the norm. In fact, Black people, proportionally, had the highest rate of two-parent families of any major group in the country. We had the lowest rate of abortion. In some cases, the *quality* of education was better, despite the evil of segregation. Howard University, for example, didn't have a reputation as a party school, but as a serious institution whose Black students were earning degrees in law and medicine.

In New York City alone, one-fourth of all public schools have been labeled as "failing." If that statistic doesn't shock you, this represents over one hundred thousand children in over three hundred schools. I guaran-damn-tee you that those failing schools serve mostly minorities—and are in districts controlled by liberal Democrats. Yet decade after decade, the children in these communities are allowed to squander their youth in failing schools and emerge uneducated and unprepared to meet the challenges of an increasingly competitive world. In July 2021, the Democrat governor of Oregon signed Senate Bill 774 into law, which eliminated requiring proficiency in reading, writing, or math in order to graduate. A governor's spokesperson told the media that the change would help "Black, Latino, Latinx, Indigenous, Asian, Pacific Islander, Tribal, and students of color."

Society calls it child abuse when a parent smacks their kid on the ass for getting out of line. But why don't we consider it abusive to let children go to school for twelve years and not learn how to read, write, speak the English language, and compete in the workplace? Rush discussed this in the summer of 2020.

> "It's a way to further segregation by making really attractive, decent places unaffordable for the people you don't want living nearby. And who's doing this? White liberals with their plantation mentality. [. . .]
>
> "Segregation's been maintained, performance among poor minorities is getting worse because they are going to inferior schools, which are being kept open on purpose. It is a crying shame. [. . .] If you want to talk about losing the country—and it's not final yet, of course, but this is where we've lost so much ground is in the education system. A lot of people, 'Nah, it's the media, Rush. If we had control of the media, we could fix it.' The media is a crucial element of it, too, I know, but education largely dominates." —RL

Look at the cheating scandal in the Atlanta public schools. Teachers and administrators didn't teach the kids, so they decided to change the answers and inflate test scores to save their own skins. Almost two hundred teachers were implicated, and many received felony convictions. And this was all before COVID-19. Can you even imagine what happened last year in terms of the quality of education for millions of kids?

> *"Take a look at all the constituency groups that for fifty years have been depending on the Democrat Party to improve their lives. And you tell me if you find any. They're still complaining, still griping about the same problems. Their problems don't get fixed by government. And those lives have been poisoned. Those lives have been cut short by false promises, from government representatives who said 'Don't worry about it, we'll take care of you. Just vote for us.'"* —RL

Who will stand up for these children by demanding accountability? Democrats won't. To paraphrase the song "Cult of Personality" by Living Colour, Democrats smugly crow, "I exploit voters, yet they love me." Thankfully, Rush inspired countless parents and grandparents to take action and be part of solutions.

> CALLER: "I just wanted to comment on what you said a while ago, that conservatives are sending their kids to Christian schools, private schools, homeschooling them. I decided not to do that.

I decided to send my kids to public school and try to make a difference in the school. And now I'm PTA president. So I just want to encourage parents to get back involved. You know, try to take back public schools."

RUSH: "Well, that's admirable of you."

CALLER: "It's even given me further strength and helped to build my résumé to run for office and city council, so I like to encourage people out there, conservatives. Don't stop listening to Rush—you gotta have that—but get out and do something about it. [. . .] I'm volunteering, and so are my kids, and this is what I think conservatives need to do. This has become a personal mission of mine."

Who will stand up for these children by pointing out the obvious failures of Democrat policies? *We* must.

"What the Hell Do You Have to Lose?"

Leading up to the 2016 election, Democrats who paid attention feared that Donald Trump would persuade a growing number of Black and minority voters, and he did. Trump outperformed any Republican we'd seen since Richard Nixon, who received about 30% of the Black vote, back when Black people were still unafraid to vote for Republicans. But more importantly, Democrats were worried that Black young men were gravitating toward Trump, and they were. Trump was part of the American culture, and even part of rap culture.

Candidate Trump addressed the problems in urban communities, offered solutions, and had the courage to ask, "What the hell do you have to lose?" That question didn't come out of nowhere. It may or may not have been in a report that the current CEO of New Journey PAC, Autry Pruitt, may or may not have presented to the Trump campaign in 2015.

Regardless, the message was clear and effective. "You're living in poverty, your schools are no good, you have no jobs, 58% of your youth is unemployed—what the hell do you have to lose?" What the hell do Republicans have to lose by talking straight to fellow Americans?

There are plenty of RINOs (Republicans in name only) in public office. As former president Trump told me on my radio show in June 2021, the first official Juneteenth holiday, to be exact, "The RINOs in many ways are worse than the left." He continued, "You wouldn't have the vaccine for years if I didn't have the type of personality I have, which is, you know, not necessarily a good personality, but I get things done."

I quickly added, "It's a great personality *because* you get things done." What if conservatives were branded with the label of "We get things done"?

What Rush Did Right

Some people wonder if Rush and I ever sat down and really talked about race. Well, we talked about race often in connection with the news stories of the day. But here's the thing: the middle-class kid from Missouri and this middle-class kid from Queens, New York, pretty much saw issues eye-to-eye. We both agreed, without even having to speak to each other about it, that we believed in meritocracy, not color-tocracy, and that people should be able to advance based on their competence, their desire, and their ambition. We both agreed that the government had no right to single out people for special consideration—or *no* consideration—based on color. The government at every level is supposed to be a color-blind operator. We were both tired of the Democrats using race as a political weapon to divide people.

What did Rush do right in changing hearts and minds of minorities over three decades? He did not pander. He was himself. Rush always treated his listeners with respect. He didn't try to soften or alter his message based on whom he spoke with—on or off the air. He didn't stress overusing the latest leftist labels, such as "people of color."

On the radio, when he talked about politics, he asked Black Americans to question why leaders in Democrat-controlled cities were making the same complaints after fifty years in power. He didn't try to water down his message.

By the way, we always had a significant number of Black people call the show. (Yes, I can tell the color of someone's skin over the phone. It's one of my superpowers.) Some of them agreed, some disagreed, but most told me they respected the way that Rush spoke to them without pandering.

Equal Right to Criticize

This leads me to a question for my Black liberal friends. We talk about equality as the objective. Well, doesn't being equal also mean that you're equal when being criticized? When someone criticizes you, it's not necessarily about your race.

Equality is when you can stand up and take criticism because your idea may be flawed. When liberals imply that criticizing Black people is off limits, that's blatant racism. And this applies to any group. Once you start declaring certain people's ideas as "off limits" from criticism, you are guilty of a very destructive form of bigotry.

Now by all this, I don't mean to diminish racism or the fact that there are real incidents of racism that happen every day. But racism is a two-way street. There are also plenty of racists of all colors. People discriminate. Some people use their powers of discrimination wisely and some do not. But this notion that Black people can't be criticized is disturbing.

Very few human beings have come along in the course of human history who were infallible. In fact, most Christians will tell you that there's only been one. But most of us suffer from the blurry lens of our own experience—and what we've been told about other people.

In 2019, I founded New Journey PAC to help move the Black vote by education and demonstration of conservative values. Here's something our CEO, Autry Pruitt, and I found out quickly: establishment Republicans lie. OK, not all of them, but I'm not new to this game, and some stereotypes are true. They told us, "Oh, this is so needed for our party and I want to help." But the help, and the check, never arrived. Here's a story about an honest Republican.

Autry and I sat down with a major party donor, who had recently put a few million dollars into the campaign of a candidate running against a Black liberal. We told him, "You're gonna need some help in this race because this district has a lot of Black voters—and unless you're messaging to those voters, your gal is gonna lose."

This white conservative, who happens to be a billionaire, looked at us and said, "I don't care about that Black shit." Then he proceeded to talk about his love life for the next fifteen minutes.

That billionaire was the most sincere donor we had met to that point. He told us what he thought—to our faces—and didn't promise support then fail to follow through, like so many others. He was honest.

A few weeks later, we heard a campaign speech from his chosen candidate, who opened with the line "We've got to call a spade a spade." I wish I was joking, but it's true. Millions of dollars were poured into this race, most of it going through the usual suspects of consultancies, friends of friends, and establishment "experts." The conservative candidate lost. She could have won and would have been an excellent public servant—as long as she fired her lousy speechwriter. The same sad story is repeated in every election cycle, in every state, county, and city.

Is it racist, divisive, or disingenuous to target certain demographics in political ads? As someone who is actively involved in political campaigns across the nation, my view is that the donkey has already left the barn on that question. Sadly, we live in a fragmented society. In order to reach people, you have to go where they are. If people are living in various bubbles, you've got to find a way to penetrate those bubbles.

For decades, people have been told that Republicans are horrid, evil people who want civil rights erased and a host of other lies. What's the point of doing a general advertisement that does not address the concerns of people who mistrust you? Many Black people distrust Republicans. Unless you talk to Black people directly about the things that concern them, you will not be able to reach them with the facts. It doesn't mean you pander to them. Again, one of the many things Rush did right was not pander based on race.

Rank and file conservatives are some of the most beautiful, salt-of-the-earth people I've ever known. In Waco, Texas, I spoke at a Tea Party Patriots event, and the gathering was incredible. They didn't hug and high-five me because I'm Black. They loved me because they knew we shared the same values. We were instant allies. The grassroots conservatives in this country don't care about this racial animus stuff. They are busy working, running their lives, running their businesses. They're trying to raise their families, they go to church, they are deeply spiritual people, and they want a fair shake in this system. They also genuinely want *every* American to get a fair shake.

Again, I'm not looking for racial quotas and virtue-signaling photo-ops. I want to see conservative ideology in action, winning more people's hearts and minds—regardless of the color of skin that covers them.

Thankfully, there are many exceptions to the examples of clueless conservatives. We've seen how clear communication about common-sense ideas can win elections.

Who Runs the Hood?

New conservatives also face opposition from the left in the media. In a very recent election, our PAC put out a television ad in a highly contested Senate race. A few days after the election, we received a refund from the giant media conglomerate, with notification that our ad did not air. There was no reason given or apology offered. This is the reality of what we're up against—and why we can't sit back or use the same tired tactics.

New Journey doesn't put our money in our own pockets like some PACs do; we put the *action* in political action committee. Our first ad was called "Who runs the hood?" Residents are well aware of the problems in their communities, but they are rarely reminded about the failings of their leaders. We question the status quo because we care about people.

Many Black conservatives don't message to Black communities. They message to white donors and tell them what they want to hear about Black people, how Black people should be more like [insert the name of a Black person they like], or how we should pick ourselves up by our bootstraps. We're not interested in that, because we want to help solve problems. We're trying to reach Black people and help them understand that continuing to vote for liberal Democrats keeps them in oppressed political conditions—failing schools, dismal economic opportunity, and higher rates of crime. We're messaging for better education and for school choice.

One of the biggest civil rights marches since the 1960s was held in Florida in 2016, and it was not covered by the drive-by media. Over ten thousand people—mostly Black and Hispanic women—came together in Tallahassee to support school choice. Martin Luther King III spoke in support of the cause. We made the issue about the parents' right to send their

kids to the best possible schools. Who could be against that?
Democrats and the Tallahassee mayor, Andrew Gillum.

When Republican Ron DeSantis ran for governor against
Andrew Gillum, Democrat Gillum promised to get rid of
school choice in Florida. Why? Because that would be the best
policy for the children in Florida? No. Because that's what the
Democrat establishment and teachers' union wanted.

> *"A couple interesting stories here, too, related to
> the elections in Georgia and Florida. In Florida, an
> analysis of exit poll data shows that Ron DeSantis, the
> Republican and winner, got a far greater percentage
> of the African American vote and Hispanic vote than
> anybody can believe.*
>
> *"Why did it happen? Why did it happen? Because,
> folks, you know the conventional wisdom is that as
> America's demography changes, so goes the white
> majority and the Republican Party. As more Ameri-
> cans become people of color, as more Americans are
> constituted by illegal immigrants, as more Americans
> become Hispanic and African American, why, that's
> it! That's it! Republicans are finished and white Chris-
> tian males are finished, that's it. So if that's true, why
> did DeSantis win with a larger percentage of African
> Americans than anybody can believe? There's a very
> simple policy-related answer.*
>
> *"According to exit poll data, it was related to an
> issue. You know what the issue was? School choice!
> DeSantis was for it! Andrew Gillum was against it!*

Parents are parents, they want good education for their kids. They want to have the choice of sending their kids to the best schools they can!

"It doesn't matter what their race is. It doesn't matter what their political affiliations are. And Andrew Gillum wanted to take away school choice from a bunch of people, and they voted for DeSantis who was for it, African Americans did. People's heads are swimming down here because this wasn't supposed to happen. White candidates are supposed to lose as the percentage of minorities in any given voting population rises. There's no way a Republican's supposed to get an increased number of African American votes, but it's happening all over. Could happen in Georgia, too." —RL

Ron DeSantis won the 2018 race by just forty thousand votes. What you probably don't know is that the votes of one hundred thousand Black women tipped the election in his favor—more accurately, *in favor of the children of Florida*. Eighteen percent of Black women voted for DeSantis, which was double the amount who voted for the Republican in the previous election. Black "school choice moms" made the difference, along with 44% of Latinos. Who knew there were so many conservative people of color? I did, along with anyone who was engaged with people in these cities.

When conservatives present solutions to problems, we can win elections. When we do so with a motivation of love for our fellow citizens, we will win lots of elections.

Education to Counteract Indoctrination

Please hear me, politicians and think-tank operatives: We as conservatives have so much opportunity to turn the tide in this country. But I'm not even talking about *political* momentum. We have an opportunity to help solve problems that ordinary people of all colors face. Election wins will follow as a consequence, not as the goal. The goal is to help improve the lives of fellow citizens.

We have to demonstrate with deeds—not words—that conservatives love people. We need to be in every single blue city in America, helping our liberal-oppressed neighbors "see the light." But we can't roll in with a prescribed program of help, but must begin by listening.

"We want everybody to be as content and happy as they can be. We want everybody, as many people as possible, realizing their human potential." —RL

SHOW NOTES

Let's be clear about our values and beliefs, but let's also communicate the truth about conservatism: it's all about love. Conservatism is love in action.

I wanted to be a Black Panther when I was a teenager, then became part of a thirty-plus-year phenomenon that revived conservatism. What caused the change in me? In reality, there was no change. I have always cared about people, and I have always been about solutions.

I've always been a conservative, and sometimes, I still wear a black beret.

A Recent Message from a Listener

"Hi Mr. Snerdley. I am a twenty-nine-year-old woman from Canada who listened to Rush faithfully for the past several years but was made aware of Rush many years ago by my father, who was also a longtime listener. I grew to love hearing Rush's voice and his wisdom every day and often sought his opinion on political issues or occurrences that I could just not wrap my head around. He had a way about him that was enlightening and entertaining, and he made perfect sense and was so reasonable, unlike so many these days. I miss him so very much. To be completely honest, I didn't realize what a big part of my life he was until he was gone."

A Word from One of Our Amazing Guest Hosts, MARK BELLINGHAM

"I still remember the first time I guest hosted, in the late '90s, and I was unbelievably sick. So I dragged myself in to do the program, filled myself with as many ibuprofens as I possibly could and survived the whole thing. People thought it was really good. In retrospect, it was terrible. When I came in to do the program, of course I wouldn't see Rush, I'm doing the program on days that he's off. The thing I noticed over the years was the incredible loyalty that the staff had to Rush. I mean, many people were with him for decades. I think of people like James Golden/Bo Snerdley, Mike Maimone, his broadcast engineer, and the late Kit Carson. These people were there forever, and they always had Rush's back. They knew they were changing communication forever."

Success is nothing like I thought
it was gonna be. And if I dwell
on it, I could allow myself to be
disappointed by it, which would be
silly. Certain things I wouldn't trade,
don't misunderstand, but it's not
what I thought it was gonna be.
It did not bring certain things that I
thought it would bring.

—RUSH LIMBAUGH

8

TRUTH DETECTOR

In thirty-three years of Rush on the radio, there's been a lot said about the man, and plenty of controversies. Through it all, Rush was always Rush, and there was much about this man that the spotlight never revealed or changed. From the day Rush first arrived at WABC, through decades of explosive growth, to the last day I was with him, he was always the same man. In case you've wondered if radio is a high-paying industry, it is—for the very few who find national success.

But like a lot of media jobs, if you're working behind the scenes, there's not a heck of a lot of money. You're in the broadcasting business because you love it. A couple months after I met Rush, before I worked for the show, I still wasn't making much dough. And I found myself in debt to the point that I had to screen my own calls—from bill collectors.

Sometimes I'd talk with those collection agencies while I was at work, unaware that others could hear me. One morning, months before I was on his staff, Rush called me on the intercom. "James, can you come back to my office?" As I entered his tiny office, he asked me to shut the door. "You

181

know, James," he said, "I'm not trying to get in your personal business, but I couldn't help but overhear your phone call and just want to ask you, is everything OK?"

I was embarrassed, but I fessed up. "Things are good but I'm having, you know, money problems here and there."

But he persisted. "How much are you in debt for?" Finally, I reluctantly told him I was about five thousand dollars in the hole. "Look, I've been there," he said. "Don't panic over it, things will work out. You're gonna be OK."

His encouragement meant a lot, but in the late '80s, five thousand dollars was a lot of money to me. Five thousand dollars is *still* a lot of money. I walked back to my office, relieved the embarrassing session was over. The next day, I was working in the newsroom and Rush called me on the intercom. Deja vu. I went to his office, shut the door, and wondered, *What in the world does he want to talk about now?*

"Here," he said, as he handed me a small envelope. "This is for you. This is not a loan, this is a gift. I'm doing this because you're a good guy and good guys deserve to have good things happen to them once in a while. Please, don't tell anybody about this."

I felt both mortified and blessed. Back at my desk, I opened the envelope, which contained a personal check for five thousand dollars. I couldn't stop the tears. I wasn't yet working for Rush and he, for sure, wasn't trying to buy my friendship because we were already friends. At the time, he was not making millionaire money either. Rush was simply generous in his heart and soul. That's a moment I'll never forget. Since that day, I've tried to show the same kind of generosity to people in need, because his gift affected me so deeply. I hope Rush would be OK with me sharing this story. Although he asked me not to tell anyone, it is one of thousands of stories that need to be told.

For over three decades, and until this very day, I've heard accusations against Rush Limbaugh from his political detractors—people who never met him, didn't listen to the program, and never took ten minutes to read the show transcripts. As a Black guy, a proud African American, it always infuriated me to hear my friend called a racist. Rush didn't have a racist bone in his body. He wanted his staff to be excellent, so he hired excellent people. It just so happened we had a very diverse staff: gay, straight, Black, white, Asian, it didn't matter, as long as you were good at your job.

Rush Limbaugh had one of the most generous hearts of anyone I have ever met in my life.

Now let's move on and try to clear up some other distortions.

The Mayor of Realville

Rush was always a sports fan, and he aspired to host sports television, which in a way was a throwback to his youth when he used to call baseball games at home on his toy broadcast setup, with only his mom as the audience. As with most of his interests, he quickly became an expert—and the subject of football was no different. He could talk football with you all day long, down to details on individual players, what was going on with the drafts, you name it. Add to that his position as the most listened-to broadcaster in the country, which allowed him to meet not only players, but many of the coaches. In 2003, his platform also opened the door for a gig with ESPN on the *Sunday NFL Countdown* show.

Everything was going well until that discussion about quarterback Donovan McNabb. Here's what Rush said on that fateful ESPN show in October.

> *"Sorry to say this, I don't think he's been that good from the get-go . . . I think what we've had here is a little social concern in the NFL. The media has been very desirous that a Black quarterback do well. There is a little hope invested in McNabb, and he got a lot of credit for the performance of this team that he didn't deserve. The defense carried this team." —RL*

In a couple days, the knives were out for Rush.

> *"Nothing happened that day or the next day, but two days later all hell broke loose. So really all I said about McNabb was that I thought he was overrated. What I said about the media was that I think they, as a bunch of social liberal do-gooders, are still interested in a Black quarterback doing well, and so they're willing to overlook the fact that he might not be as good as they want him to be, and, therefore, when they're wondering what's wrong and why they're tearing their hair out, the answer is right in front of their face. That's what it was. It was a comment primarily about the media." —RL*

Rush thought the media wanted Black quarterbacks to succeed because they were Black. On the surface, what's wrong with that—both Rush's perspective and the media's? Nothing in my view. But Rush was focused on the fact that the media was hiding—not being honest about their motivation. But man, did that motivation become clear in the days that followed.

Years later, when President Obama first came into office, the *Wall Street Journal* asked Rush to describe what he wanted from the Obama presidency, and Rush said, "I hope he fails." That became a huge issue because the liberals gasped at a white guy saying he wanted a Black man to fail. The difference—in both the ESPN and President Obama controversies—was that the media had a racially motivated agenda, and Rush was looking at statistics and agendas.

What Rush said about McNabb was straightforward, yet he was accused of all kinds of other twisted lies that tried to paint him as a racist. It was a made-up controversy, but it did what those controversies are designed to do: cast the Republican or the conservative as a bigot, when in fact, there was nothing bigoted about Rush's opinion.

Rush resigned from the ESPN show a few days later.

If Rush had said that McNabb was in the NFL only because of his race, that would have been another matter. As I mentioned about my college career, some people openly wondered if the only reason I was in college was because of an affirmative action program. That characterization was wrong, and it upset me deeply.

"The real problem was—and I've had a couple people who are big-time sportscasters on the networks tell me this—'They were laying in wait for you, Rush. They were just offended to no end that you were coming into their world, the world of sports, and they were going to get you somehow. They were going to try to get you no matter what, because they resented the fact that you were entering sports, and you're not a sports guy, and you haven't paid your dues, and you're not a journalist and all that.' What you said you saw happen on HBO's Inside the NFL *is a classic example. HBO is a very liberal-oriented network, anyway.* Inside the NFL *has its share of liberal producers and so forth—and a liberal host, who is obsessed with race, Bob Costas—and then of course they have got that babe in there, Wanda Sykes, who is this Black comedian. She can run around and say whatever she wants like a rapper, and of course nobody says a word. They just laugh at that and she's protected because she is a minority. Therefore, like all minorities they can say what they want because they 'don't have the power to be racists or bigots' or what have you." —RL*

In today's world, if a white guy has a view about anything with a racial context, it's bad. But the left can say anything they want, and it's good, simply because they are presumed—by themselves—to have a higher moral platform. But we need to look beyond the endless controversies and see the real agenda. The left wants to silence our voices. Just look at Colin

Kaepernick as he cashes his checks from Nike. Question his performance—or his views—and you're a racist.

I must also mention one other controversy that happened around the same time as this ESPN story, and it only added fuel to the fire. I'm of course referring to Rush's addiction to prescription medications. I was there, I saw what unfolded, and I witnessed the excruciating pain he went through. I will simply remind everyone that Rush was honest about his realization and his decision to get professional help.

In 2007, I sat down with Rush to interview him for a special edition of the *Limbaugh Letter*. Although Rush was always honest with me, I was surprised and humbled by his transparency in this conversation.

RUSH: "I have always had a performer's ego. My situation is not unique, I mean you grow up wanting to be liked. You start changing yourself to meet what you think the expectations are of the people you want to like you. So I ended up subordinating who I really was, trying to be what I thought other people wanted me to be, and of course, it never works.

"I took the rejections that I got in junior and high school deeply, painfully, and personally, and they stayed with me throughout a lot of my life, and I never dealt with the pain that it was causing. I just suppressed it. I kept trying to find ways of medicating it, not with substances—I never heard of one pain pill by brand name until 1996.

But I was medicating it with kissing people's rear ends, just trying to suck up to people who didn't like me, trying to make them like me. That added up to little self-respect. And as I mentioned, judging myself on how little money I had.

"I was just obsessed with finding the negatives. I took that first pain pill and I had never experienced euphoria like that, other than that one time in high school. And I said, 'Oh, man!' That became the way to medicate the pain.

"The five-week rehab process explained all of this to me and it taught me a number of things about how to deal with what I think is rejection. It probably really isn't. It taught me that everybody is like I was, that everybody is self-conscious, that everybody is trying to be what they think somebody else is. The mistake I was making was assuming everybody else was well-adjusted and strong and confident and I was the only one who was messed up. When in fact everybody is messed up. Some people are just better covering it with their acting ability than others are.

"But this process was interesting. One of the counselors said, 'It's amazing in your career you have learned how to do this. You are the most criticized person I know and you don't care. And why? Because you know it's not true. Yet when people in your personal life say things about you, or reject you, or act toward you in ways that you know are wrong, you take it personally and you start down a cycle. Why don't you learn to ignore the people that are wrong? Why do you give them that kind of power over you? You have got to stop surrendering the power of your feelings to all of these people who couldn't care less about you.' That little concept was huge.

"Why should I give people the power to hurt my feelings? They don't have the power. My feelings don't belong to them. One of the things they teach you is to pretend you are wearing a suit of armor—the idea of boundaries—and if people say or do things, if it's true let it in and process it, deal with it; if it's not, let it bounce off, it's irrelevant, it's not worth your time. Besides, who are they? You are giving all these people way too much power and in the process you are letting them determine how you think about yourself. [...]

"I see all of these stories about how more and more Americans are getting hooked on these pills. I got hooked on mine medically, but I still got hooked, I was still an addict. And the process of rehab was the absolute best five weeks of my adult life, in terms of understanding me and why those pills meant so much. I wish I had learned it when I was twenty, but it is what it is. [...]

"We had homework. The first week I was in denial, I couldn't believe I was there. The second week I really got into it. One of the exercises in the second week, the counselor said, 'I want you to write a memo to your dad. Dear Dad, what you taught me about women. Dear Mom, what you taught me about men. And I want you to write a memo to Risk.' And I said, 'To Risk?' 'Yes, to the concept of Risk. I want you to write a memo to Risk.'

"So I turned them in the next day. On Friday he chose the memo that I had written to Risk to discuss. We had a little group of three people. I had written, 'Dear Risk, I guess I don't know you very well because I don't think I have taken very many. I have always had a fallback position with anything that I have done.'

"The counselor said, 'Do you realize how full of crap you are?' And I was taken aback. 'What do you mean?'

"He says, 'The thing that we learned last week about you'—the first week they dragged everything about my childhood and early years out of me, and they dug deep, they made you remember things that you have forgotten. 'We learned the thing that you fear most, and that you expect to happen, is to be rejected by people you love, by people you like. You expect to be rejected. And what do you do every day? You put yourself out in front of the whole country begging them to tell you that you are worthless. Do you realize what an emotional risk you are taking? Do you realize when you engage in something like that, you need something to handle the fallout? No wonder these pills meant so much to you, because they were able to get you out of the situation. They were giving you a phony feeling that everything was hunky-dory.'

"It was enlightening, eye-opening stuff, and it made me think about myself in ways that I hadn't before. As I have said on the air, I think this stuff would be invaluable to everybody, whether they have an addiction problem or not. It was that valuable for—I don't want to call it self-esteem, because it's much more than that. Growing up, the whole concept of pain is something that is to be hidden and you are not supposed to deal with it at all—and yet it's a reality of life. People don't deal with it properly, they find ways to medicate it physically and emotionally, emotionally being the worst. But it was just totally enlightening, and then to be with other people and listen to some of these stories." [...]

JAMES: "And the end result of all of that process is that you come out, you are happy. Is this stretch of time, since you came out, the longest period that you have been consistently happy?"

RUSH: "Without question. I mean genuinely so, yeah. Look, life was not miserable. I internalized all of this stuff. I don't think anybody knew it. This is just the baggage I was walking around suppressing and dealing with. I thought success in this radio show would launch me into a certain club of successful people in media. It's just the opposite; they hate my guts because I am not liberal. Well, who wants to be hated? I didn't understand that at first."

He spoke about it often, and I will tell you he was determined not to let himself, his family, his friends, or his audience down again. In 2009, he was interviewed on *The Today Show* and shared these words.

"You know, I actually thank God for my addiction, because I learned more about myself in rehab than I would have ever learned otherwise. There was a time where I desperately cared what people thought of me. Desperately. Not professionally. I always somehow knew that that didn't matter. But personally. When you're worried about what people think, you stop being who you are." —RL

When Rush took time off for treatment, we received thousands and thousands of calls and emails from listeners offering their encouragement. After he returned to the airwaves, and in the midst of incredible scrutiny, he put what he had learned into practice and refused to let the mob cancel his voice.

"Somebody wanted to know if I was a hypocrite about my use of painkillers and the fact that it was wrong or that I have ostensibly said in the past that people who use drugs ought to be punished for it. And

my answer was, no, it's not hypocritical because my behavior doesn't determine the value of right and wrong. Nobody's does. I mean right and wrong, there are absolutes of right and wrong. And there are people who waver from right and do wrong, and I'm one of them. We all are. Various stages, various levels. It doesn't change what right and wrong are." —RL

All of us face challenges. Rush faced personal and professional challenges. He overcame the challenges. And that's all I'm going to say about it.

Butting Heads

Rush was a huge Pittsburgh Steelers fan, as anybody who listened to the show knows. As for me, I proved to myself that I am totally capable of being in a monogamous relationship by one simple fact: I've been committed to one football team all my life—the Dallas Cowboys. (Although football and I drifted apart after all the Colin Kaepernick crap.)

Rush and Kathryn knew I was a passionate football fan and one year, Kathryn arranged a very special surprise, which just blew me away. They offered to let me use their box at MetLife Stadium on January 1, 2012, to entertain my friends at one of the biggest games of the year, between the Cowboys and the New York Giants. The winner would advance into post-season play. Kathryn thought of all the details, right down to the limo that would pick me up and return me to my hotel. It was a glorious gift, one of the many acts of generosity they performed for me and for many others.

I invited some of my friends, old bandmates, dear friends from Washington, DC, like Connie Hair, and family members—including my mother. I arrived at the stadium via limousine, and our party of twenty-six people enjoyed the game with gourmet catering. The experience was beyond measure, even though my beloved Cowboys lost—and I never heard the end of it from Mike Allocco, the Editrix's husband, who used to play for the Giants. To top it all off, before I left for the game, Rush and Kathryn presented me with two official Dallas Cowboy jerseys. A photo of me and my mother from that night is one of my favorites.

Years earlier, in the fall of 2009, it *somehow* became known that Rush was interested in becoming a partner in buying the St. Louis Rams NFL team. Pandemonium erupted. The usual suspects like Jesse Jackson and Al Sharpton threw penalty flags and snorted. The liberal sports media was enraged. And again—somehow—supposedly racist statements Rush had made started making headlines. Some of those lies still circulate to this day.

Eventually, he withdrew from the partnership. Another goal blocked. I suspected he was hurt by this, but he never expressed any personal feelings about it to me. Again, this was the early days of the cancel culture at work, and Rush was the guinea pig for almost thirty years. Today we see that this cancel culture has leaked from the lab and is now an epidemic.

When Jay-Z wanted to buy into a sports team, you didn't hear anyone on the left cry foul. Mister Beyoncé Z's past dealings and statements are never brought up. Who has looked into the lives of the other owners, whether they be NFL, the

National Thug Association—I'm sorry, the National Basketball Association—or Major League Baseball. The scrutiny is pointed in only one direction.

Speaking of entertainers, why are mainstream media companies, owned by liberals, not held to account for polluting young minds? Why is an ultra-misogynistic culture still celebrated in the age of the "me too" movement? Why are Black kids fed messages glorifying violence and "f— the police"? Democrats whine about gun violence, while their friends at the record companies blast murder and misogyny into Black kids' brains. These are not Republicans producing this garbage—it's a Black celebrity class and they are elevated as heroes. Jay-Z is reportedly a billionaire. He's a former drug dealer whose music empire spewed hatred. Yet Mr. Z was a regular guest at the White House, feted by Barack and Michelle Obama. In 2016, Rush pointed out this hypocrisy by Hillary Clinton.

> *"Here comes a Hillary Clinton political rally in Philadelphia on Friday night. Jay-Z and Beyoncé attend. And the lyrics of the songs they're singing include the word 'Bi-itch,' the N-word, the C-word and the F-bomb. The lyrics! [. . .] We're talking Jay-Z and Beyoncé here, and they're celebrated as great artists and so forth. Hillary Clinton comes out—Trump's right—and hugs them. And they're using these lyrics. And it's degrading to women. It objectifies women by another woman, and by the top male rap artist in the country or R&B. How would you classify Jay-Z? Is he a rap artist or R&B? What would you say he is, just*

an entrepreneur crossing many venues? [interruption]
Huge celebrity. *OK. So it comes out and he sings about*
his own wife in words like this, and Hillary comes and
hugs them both and thanks them." —RL

The left's standard is clear. It's OK to inflict mental and moral harm on Black people, if it's Black liberals doing the deed. By the way, that's also systemically racist.

Double Standards

Why are those on the left celebrated for trash-talking our nation, while someone who defends American exceptionalism has his career and dreams burned down by the mob? I ask this question not only about Rush, but about you and me. Don't be naive. It's open season on free speech, and on those who are bold enough to share their opinions.

If you are going to defeat the cancel culture, you have to be willing to take some arrows. The left has no shame. They will use anyone with any affliction and use that person as a political cudgel against Republicans or conservatives. And that's always the core issue, for those who step back and look at the source, as Rush always did.

For the left, *the agenda is the thing,* and if you're with their agenda, any sin is expunged.

Here's a quote from Joe Biden, during a time he was wondering about "orderly integration" of schools. "Unless we do something about this, my children are going to grow up in a jungle, the jungle being a racial jungle with tensions having built so high that it is going to explode at some point."

Look at the 1984 college yearbook photo of Governor Ralph Northam of Virginia. We're not sure if he's in blackface or the guy in the Klan outfit. *Nothing to see here, and I rather like the governor's mansion. Oh, look, a burning cross!* I guarantee you if Governor DeSantis of Florida was ever found to have done anything remotely like that, the press would be "deeply disturbed," and deeply disturb the governor until he resigned. But always remember, it's not really about race, it's about the leftist agenda.

In June 2021, Florida congressman Byron Donalds wanted to join the Congressional Black Caucus. The Congressional Black Caucus wouldn't let him join their club, and this has been the case with other Black representatives, because it's not about his skin color, it's about his conservative values. Just like Rush rightly added the word "liberal" to the NAACP, I'll also state the obvious and call out the Congressional *Liberal* Black Caucus. To me, leaders of the caucus are segregationists—ideological segregationists.

Do you see the theme from Rush's "scandals" and our world today? The left thrives on using emotional arguments to inflame and divide the American people in order to reach their political objectives. As I write about this, I confess that I am tempted to use the same tactics, and I have sunk to that level on a few occasions. But we must stand up, speak up, and put forth candidates and ideas that help the citizens of this country.

The people I'm calling into question are those who knowingly manipulate stories for political power, and I don't care if they're Republicans or Democrats. The vast majority of American citizens—including rank-and-file liberals, who share most of the same values as conservatives—don't care about these fake controversies. They are too busy with their day-to-day lives. They want their kids educated. They want to live in communities without crime. They want people of every race to excel. That's why new conservatives must speak up from a motivation of love and shared values. That's how we build consensus, win elections, and improve life for all Americans.

Doctor of Democracy

In the presidential campaign season of 2007, it became apparent that Barack Obama was picking up strength against Hillary Clinton. By the way, I must acknowledge something a dear Canadian friend told me at the time about Barack vs. Hillary. "Hillary will never win. They'll put the Black guy ahead of the white woman any day." I told her she was full of it, but sure enough, she was right.

Early in 2008, Rush launched "Operation Chaos"—also known as "Rush the Vote"—to help draw out the primary and weaken both candidates in the general election. One tactic was to encourage Republicans to vote in Democrat primaries where this was allowed. By the way, this may have been the only time Rush asked his listeners to take specific action to realize a political outcome.

The strategy quickly made waves, with victories and setbacks. Rush rallied the troops on a weekly—and sometimes daily—basis. By May 2008, some listeners were getting nervous. Here's Rush, channeling General George Patton, from May 5, 2008.

"*Ladies and gentlemen, I want to start the hour here by restating the origins of Operation Chaos and the goal, because I am continuing to receive mail, email from people, you, who listen in this audience, who are getting panicked and paranoid that Mrs. Clinton is going to end up winning this whole thing and that it will be my fault and that if that happens, you are never, ever, going to listen to this program again.*

"*May we go back, ladies and gentlemen, and restate the purpose of Operation Chaos. It is important for all of you operatives to know that I cannot handle and will not tolerate dissension in the ranks, and I will not tolerate less than a positive, energetic attitude as we approach another battle, two more battles tomorrow. The purpose of Operation Chaos was to politically bloody up Barack Obama when we started this. We started this right before the Texas and Ohio primaries and cauci.*

"*The Republican Party and Senator McCain had made it clear, had made it plain they were not going to be critical of Barack Obama. At the time Obama was sailing to what appeared to be a surefire victory. Operation Chaos was formed for the express purpose of keeping the Democrat primary system alive as long as possible, and who better to bloody up Obama politically than the Clintons? He has to be bloodied up, he has to be taken off that game of messiah that he was on. This has worked.*

"Operation Chaos has exceeded all objectives. The purpose of Operation Chaos was not to see to it that either one of these two is the nominee. We at Operation Chaos, your commanding officers, do not think we have that kind of power over this race. That's not the objective. The Democrat primary is going to turn out however it turns out, and it's going to turn out on the basis of the superdelegates and how they wish to go.

"Now, I have advised and addressed superdelegates on this program on numerous occasions last week, telling them that they should not fear what they are fearing, and that is going ahead and nominating Obama because if they take it away from him, even though he's losing all these primaries, they will forever lose the Black vote. They will not.

"They have done far more damage to Black people in this country with fifty years of liberal Democrat policies, than taking the nomination away from Obama, and Blacks continue to vote Democrat. They stay with the Democrat Party. That's not a fear that the superdelegates need to have.

"So please understand the purpose of Operation Chaos. We don't have a crystal ball here. We have no idea who the nominee is going to be. We really don't. I mean, the conventional wisdom is it's Obama's. OK, fine. The purpose has been to keep this—and it's worked, you have to admit. Obama has now been taken off of his game big time and he hasn't gotten it back. The drive-bys are circling the wagons trying to get him back

*on his game. I saw his speech last night in Indianapolis,
I watched it. It's not the same Obama. It wasn't a bad
speech, but it wasn't the same Obama. There was nothing lofty in it, there was none of this messianic stuff,
nothing about the future and hope and change. He
got issue-specific and spent most of his time criticizing
Senator McCain, who in turn has said he will not turn
around and criticize Senator Obama. [. . .]*

*"What this tells me as your commanding officer
is that had Operation Chaos not been implemented,
this would have been over long ago and we'd be dealing with a far different Obama than we are today, an
Obama that has not been damaged, an Obama that
has not been brought down to earth, an Obama that
would not have been seen as just an average, run-of-
the-mill politician.*

*"Operation Chaos has as its objective exactly
what's happened here. It is not in our battle plan—
sort of like Operation Desert Storm was not to take
out Saddam—Operation Chaos is not to determine
who wins the Democrat primary. It is to see to it that it
extends as long as possible, that the superdelegates have
to make the choice, in the process committing political murder, and that hopefully this goes on through
the Democrat convention in August, the 25th through
the 28th, with the Republican convention following the
very next week.*

*"Now, last night, before Mrs. Clinton took to the
stage, took to the podium in Indianapolis at their*

Jefferson-Jackson Dinner, they received news, and I am told this from inside sources, that Mrs. Clinton's people told her that her internals show her losing Indiana. They told her this just before she took the stage and made the speech last night. They don't think, according to the internal polls in the Clinton campaign, that she has it in Indiana. Which tells me, when I heard this last night—and I trust the source, by the way. I don't think I'm being played here. I trust the source. It simply told me last night that if Mrs. Clinton's own internals show her losing Indiana, it's time to give her a push today.

"So the orders were issued in our first hour from here at headquarters, all of you who have registered Democrat, and you Republicans who have registered Democrat, vote Hillary to keep this going. Don't worry about who wins the nomination. It's not the point now. It is not something over which we have any control, but we can influence how long this thing gets dragged out.

"Snerdley, I know what you're laughing about in there. I'm not giving her a pep talk. Snerdley thinks I'm giving her a pep talk. Have you forgotten who we're dealing with here? We are dealing with the Clintons. This is the thing that she has lived for, it's the reason she put up with all of that excrement daily being married to that lug head that she's married to. This is the payoff. She's going to say, 'Congratulations, Obama, you've run a really great race and I'm heading back to the kitchen to bake cookies.' Do you think that's going to happen?" —RL

Needless to say, Operation Chaos was hugely disruptive to the media, the political establishment of both parties, and most of all, to the status quo. A strikingly similar story was told in the 2011 film *The Ides of March*, which George Clooney directed and co-starred in. I believe they stole the idea of the film from Rush's real-life campaign.

Rush and his listeners weren't the only ones questioning the drive-by media's infatuation with Barack Obama. Cue the bumper music.

"Obama the Magic Negro"

Yeah, let's talk about one of my all-time favorite songs, "Barack the Magic Negro," which also happened to be the most *acclaimed* parody song ever played on the broadcast. And by acclaimed, I mean that leftists went apeshit over the tune.

But here's what most people still don't know about the Magic Negro song. During the Democrat-primary drama, there was a March 2007 column in the *Los Angeles Times* with the title "Obama the 'Magic Negro.'" Who wrote this offensive piece? David Ehrenstein, a Black writer.

Paul Shanklin, our "parody czar," who contributed so many hilarious parodies through the years, decided to write a song, using quotes and points from the article, along with quotes from Joe Biden and Al Sharpton. I still laugh every time I hear the song, set to the music of "Puff the Magic Dragon." There were the usual accusations that Rush was racist, but this tune hit so hard that Black employees at some of our radio affiliates demanded we stop playing the parody or they would resign.

We never stopped playing the parody and I hope they resigned.

Did any of the people who were triggered by the song know anything about the *LA Times* editorial? Here's a line from the article: "The only mud that momentarily stuck was criticism (white and Black alike) concerning Obama's alleged 'inauthenticity,' as compared to such sterling examples of 'genuine' Blackness as Al Sharpton and Snoop Dogg." And who could forget the *columnist's* insight about Obama: "He's there to assuage white 'guilt.'"

Outrage about the parody exploded like a nuclear bomb, and I loved every single minute of it.

The op-ed, and similar comments, expressed the same vile, racial ideology that's used to attack Black conservatives. We're called "Uncle Toms." We're not Black like them because we don't fall in line with all the liberal BS. We think for ourselves, and might vote for ourselves, therefore we should be canceled. "Barack the Magic Negro" is one of the most educational parodies that has ever happened in radio, and I'm so glad that it happened on *The Rush Limbaugh Show*.

People have forgotten how much animus there was toward Barack Obama from the civil rights establishment. In the beginning of the campaign, Jesse Jackson accused Obama of "acting white" and murmured, "I want to cut his nuts off." Barack had a white mother, his father was from Africa. They weren't part of the civil rights movement. He didn't have American slave blood in his lineage. He didn't have civil rights blood in his lineage. He was an interloper, according to entrenched "Black leaders."

Even Joe Biden, then a candidate, said, "I mean, you've got the first sort of mainstream African American who is articulate and bright and clean and a nice-looking guy. I mean, that's a story-book, man."

Jesse Jackson was quick to not only absolve Joe but to translate his true motivation. "It was a gaffe. It was not an intentional racially pejorative statement. It could be interpreted that way, but that's not what he meant." Soon-to-be president Obama echoed the requisite forgiveness. I can only imagine what *the Rev-rund Sharp-ton* must have thought of Biden's comments. Sharpton had been speaking out for decades when Biden complimented Obama as the *first, articulate, clean* African American.

Sorry, Al. I'd like to dedicate this song to you.

Barack the Magic Negro lives in DC
The *LA Times*, they called him that
'Cause he's not authentic like me.
Yeah, the guy from the LA paper
Said he makes guilty whites feel good.
They'll vote for him, and not for me
'Cause he's not from the hood.
See, real Black men, like Snoop Dog,
Or me, or Farrakhan
Have talked the talk, and walked the walk.
Not come in late and won!
Oh, Barack the Magic Negro, lives in DC
The *LA Times*, they called him that
'Cause he's Black, but not authentically.

Does the Media Matter?

If you happen to be a hoarder, check what used to be your dining room for a copy of the *New York Times Magazine* from Sunday, February 12, 1995. The cover headline reads "Look Who's the 'Opinion Elite' Now" and features a photo of David Brock, Laura Ingraham, Lisa Schiffren, Adam Bellow, and a very svelte-looking James Golden—questionably credited as "producer, 'Rush Limbaugh.'"

David Brock broke the story of Bill Clinton's "trooper-gate" sexual escapades, allegedly enabled by some Arkansas State Troopers. And during the early Clinton years, he broke several stories that revealed the inner workings of the Clinton machine. But somewhere along the way, something happened to David Brock. Something sad, in my view. In 2004, he founded Media Matters, with the aim of "monitoring conservative misinformation." In 2010, George Soros gave one million dollars to the organization, and one could suspect that much of its funding still comes from George Soros–backed groups.

Why do I bring Media Matters into the picture? It has consistently misrepresented Rush Limbaugh's statements since its founding. The drive-by media was only too happy to use Media Matters' so-called reporting as accurate and disseminate the unsupported lies when it fit their agenda.

Rush called this out in 2007, after Hillary Clinton claimed she help start Media Matters.

> *"Let me tell you one thing about what's going on with Media Matters. I don't want to leave it here that*

somebody is lying. Mrs. Clinton says she helped start it. Media Matters says, 'No, she didn't. She's just a supporter.' They have nonprofit status, which prohibits them from being involved in politics, if you can believe this.

"They have nonprofit status at Media Matters, which prohibits them from being involved in politics. So, if they admit that Hillary Clinton was the driving force behind founding them, if they admit that they are coordinating in any way with her, or her other entities and campaign people, if they admit that they are in any way doing her bidding, then they've got a serious IRS issue. That's why they gotta maintain their nonprofit status." —RL

For thirty-plus years, the media has consistently distorted Rush's words and tried to cancel him. But the American media has been biased since paper and ink were imported to this continent, and those who bought ink by the barrel were biased toward the British monarchy—which still sits on the throne, watching daily episodes of the Royal Jerry Springer show. Thankfully, the revolutionists and like-minded citizens didn't have this misplaced allegiance.

From day one, the press has been partisan and tried to exploit division for their own gain. If you think that has changed, consider the COVID-19 "controversy" during the 2020 presidential election. President Trump, and anyone—including scientists and medical doctors—who had the gall to hypothesize that the COVID-19 virus might have escaped from the Wuhan, China, research facility (The Wuhan Institute of Virology) were labeled as conspiracy kooks. Social media channels were canceled and dissenting opinion was squashed in ways that would make China's Xi Jinping smile.

On June 10, 2021, Amazon's the *Washington Post* ran a headline that is so mind-exploding it's almost hilarious: "The Media Called the Lab Leak Story a Conspiracy Theory, Now It's Prompted Corrections and Serious News Reporting." Are you kidding me? The same "news reporting" that demeaned people from all walks of life for asking a logical question runs an article that admits there should have been "corrections" and a need for "serious news reporting."

You can't make this stuff up. Unless you're a so-called journalist.

America's Truth Detector

During the Clinton administration, Rush used to play Bill Clinton's words, then with fact and precision, he would deconstruct everything that Clinton said, and more importantly, detail what the policies really were. That's why "Hillary-Care" (the predecessor of Obamacare) never became law. When Hillary did rallies, fans of the show were there with signs protesting the proposals. Rush never asked people to be activists. And he never asked listeners to attend events, except for maybe Dan's Bake Sale. Our audience simply took action based on the facts presented. I doubt Bill Clinton was a listener, but he couldn't help introducing himself when he saw Rush at a New York restaurant. Here's Rush's telling of the time they met in 2007.

"... and all of a sudden, I become aware of a looming presence at the table. I'm seated at a booth, a half-moon kind of booth, and I'm facing the entrance to the restaurant, toward the back. This looming presence, I look up, and, golly, if it isn't former president Bill Clinton.

"He's got a big smile on his face, and I look up, and I imagine I was somewhat startled. I looked up, and I couldn't hear what he was saying because of the noise in there. So I'm turning my head, my left ear to him so I could hear a little bit more, and he said, [impression] 'You're looking great. You're tan, fit, you look very good out there.'

"I reached out my hand, 'Mr. President, it's a pleasure to meet you.' We shook hands and so forth, and he hung around for I guess two or three minutes, maybe five. I lost track of time. Then he and his party went and sat at a table behind me and to the left.

The woman I'm with is sitting there saying, 'Whoa! Does this happen to you all the time?'

"'Ah, yeah, constantly. I can't go anywhere.'

"So about ten minutes later I become aware again of another looming presence at my table, and I look up, and it's former president Bill Clinton—the second time he has stopped at my table. The first time he stopped while walking in. The second time he actually left his table, came to my table, and he's got another guy standing with him, and the guy looks familiar, but I can't place him. And I can't hear the introduction. So I'm shaking *hands and so forth, and this man is going on and on and on about how excited he is to meet me. He wanted to meet me, and the former president brought him over. When the former president told him I was there, he said, 'I have to meet Mr. Limbaugh.' It turns out it was the mayor of Los Angeles, Antonio Villaraigosa, and so we chatted for a while, and while I'm chatting . . . Now, this is hilarious.*

"While I'm chatting with Villaraigosa, I kind of slid to the right in my half-moon booth, and as I did that, that created some distance between me and my guest. I'm talking with Villaraigosa, and when I'm talking to somebody in a very loud place like this, I have to devote full attention. I had to turn my head to my left, away from the action behind me, to hear what the mayor was saying. At some point during the conversation with the mayor, I looked to my left, and the former president was intently chatting up the woman that I was sitting with. He had leaned down, and his elbows and arms were on the railing of the booth, and they were in intense conversation. [. . .]

"And by the way, all this was like two old friends getting together. There was no tension about any of this. It was a good time, and I enjoyed it. I enjoyed it— especially [laughing] when I looked over and I saw the former president intently chatting up the woman that I was with. [. . .]

"What was that, Mr. Snerdley? There is no 'rest of the story.' What kind of rest of the story do you think

there would be? There is no rest of the story. No, no, no,
no, no.

"I don't believe in coincidences with the Clintons.
I just don't. Of all places he chooses to go to dinner, the
Kobe Club the same night I'm there?" —RL

Bill Clinton tried to silence Rush, and our listeners. President Obama did the same thing—calling out Rush by name several times, during his presidency and even in 2020. What Rush did so well was actually demonstrate, using the leftists' own words, what their intentions were for the American people. That's how he saw his role in the interplay between politicians of both parties, government policies, and how it was communicated to the American people.

Rush Limbaugh wasn't divisive. He defended the American people against the tyranny of the left, and for that they called him divisive. He engaged Democrats and Republicans on the intellectual battlefield and could prevail. His audience knew that accusations of being a racist or a bigot were contrived because they actually listened to the show. So when politicians attacked Rush, listeners rallied. I've never seen another media figure who had a deeper bond with his audience. He talked about that bond many times—on and off the air—and said the only person who could screw up that trust would be him, not his critics.

SHOW NOTES

When your words are broadcast fifteen hours a week, for fifty weeks a year, for thirty-three years, maybe you'd agree that a perfect verbal track record is simply not possible. When Rush got something wrong, he didn't hide it. He'd lead off the show with, "I got something wrong, let me correct the record." He did not want to be a guy who got things wrong, and I saw that determination firsthand.

In an earlier chapter I wrote about the dangers of believing a caricature of someone. Although the left tried to paint a hateful picture of Rush, his true character prevailed. I hope this portrait of my friend makes his character a bit clearer.

A Recent Message from a Listener

"Hi James! I am fifteen. As a listener, I always felt close to Rush in a way most listeners feel—they looked up to him as a father or grandfather. I will never be able to show my appreciation enough for what all of you have done. I'm tearing up as I write this. Thanks for being so loyal to Rush and us."

A Word from One of Our Amazing Guest Hosts, ERICK ERICKSON

"The very first time I ever filled in for Rush Limbaugh, they flew me up to New York City. I'm in there. It's Maimone, it's Kit Carson, it is Bo Snerdley himself. I'm looking out and the light goes on and I'm like *What on earth have I just done?* And I freak out. There's silence there for just a second and then I start. And it gets a little natural until halfway through the show and I look. And there's Snerdley, flailing his arms, pointing toward me, pounding his fist on the desk, and I'm like *I've just lost the opportunity to ever do this again*. I had no idea what I had done.

"During the break I say, 'I'm very sorry. What did I do?' And Kit Carson looked at me and asked, 'What do you mean?' I said, 'Well, I mean, Snerdley, he's in there . . .'

"And Kit answered, 'Oh, that's just James talking to a caller.' I was fine.

"I learned more from Rush though by not being able to fill in for him when I didn't support Trump in 2016. Very deviated from where the audience was, and Rush reached out regularly to see how I was doing. He called me and said, 'Look, you've got to build a relationship with your audience.' One thing Rush always told me is find something you can laugh at with your audience.

"And it worked. My audience is now bigger than it ever was, even before jumping into syndication. It was one of the largest local talk shows in the country, in large part because Rush was a great mentor, he gave great advice and I listened. Around October of last year, before Rush passed away, he reached out to me. He wanted to know how the radio was going. I was doing two shows at the time and he knew I was not good with business and wanted to give me some advice on the radio business and how it works. Then he just told me, 'You need to get up every day and make sure that behind the microphone is where you want to be. And if it is, you need to keep doing it. Don't ever not do it.' And I would never had gotten behind the microphone had he not told me that I needed to do it. Everybody in talk radio owes their career to Rush, but I really do owe my career to Rush. Thank you Rush."

I'm like Snerdley. I marvel every time I see these kinds of things right in front of my eyes.

—RUSH LIMBAUGH

9

LIFE IS SHOW PREP

It's far enough along in this book that I can let you in on a secret about me, right? Despite my professional drive and sometimes tough persona, most of my friends know that underneath the gruff exterior I am pretty soft-hearted. Rush knew this, along with the entire EIB family.

"Snerdley brought in a little bird. He has pet birds, and this is a parrotlet, the tiniest parrot that there is, and he's named the bird Stumpy. It's the cutest little thing in there, and apparently he has two other birds, and he mated the two other birds, and Stumpy got caught in the nesting material. [. . .] To save Stumpy's life, they amputated his right leg, it looks like. So Stumpy's running around with one leg. Well, he's hopping around with one leg.

"Snerdley brought him in today because it's bleed-ing a little bit and he wanted to watch him. And he's got him in this little cage and I was in there looking at this little bird, and Snerdley started talking about how

amazing it is to watch these animals do everything they can to live, and it got me to thinking. [. . .] Life exists to live, in whatever form that it takes place, be it animal, a human being, a plant, or what have you. That's the great thing or the mystery about life is how its whole purpose is to sustain itself." —RL

While I'm at it, I might as well confess that I've cried during the writing of this book, more times than I can count. Putting some of my life, career, and friendship with Rush Limbaugh in print has been very tough and emotional. I guess you could describe me that way, too: tough and emotional.

On the day Rush described in the moment from 2007 noted above, I may have yelled at a kooky caller, but I know I got teary-eyed worrying about Stumpy, my fledgling parrotlet. I was worried the little guy wouldn't make it, because he got caught in nesting material when he was hatched. His bird-mom tried to free him, and in the process he lost both legs and half a wing.

The Blur

I do a lot of soul searching. Some of the introspection is good and helpful. But some of it is simply overthinking, which can lead to depression. Most of the time, my schedule is too full for that. If I'm honest, that's one reason I've worked so hard my entire life: to stay busy. And I am very good at staying busy.

In 1992, while I was still working in an *extremely* full-time capacity with Rush, John Mainelli, program director at

WABC, who remains a dear friend and one of the best managers of people I have ever worked for, gave me a shot on the air with co-host Joel Santisteban for a Saturday night talk show. *The James and Joel Show* was born, and it was successful for about six years.

From the first moment the engineer pointed at me to begin the program, I was in "the zone." Especially after so many years of doubting whether I could be better than mediocre on the air. I wasn't nervous, there were no butterflies in the stomach, it felt natural. The patter just flowed. Joel and I had a blast together and the program turned into an ensemble show. We had people helping us do funny news bits, we were playing scenes from movies, and commenting on the news and gossip of the day. As you'd expect, I got into trouble a few times. Once, if you can believe it, for offering my opinion on the unshaven armpits of certain women.

The show did very well, and we were always in the top five in the ratings, and sometimes number one in our target demographic. After a couple years, my role expanded, and I was given my own talk show on Sunday nights. It was just me—*The James Golden Show*—and I was able to bring all of my personality into that program. That, too, felt natural, and the show also did exceedingly well in the ratings.

For almost seven years, I worked seven days a week, on three different radio shows—and on Rush's television show for four of those years. And this schedule mirrored my love life.

One of my best friends, who's more like family, refused to let me make excuses for my attitudes and behaviors. We discussed my issues with womanizing and my own spiritual dilemmas, and she helped me work my way through it. One of her insights involved the painful and unjust workplace experiences many women have in the broadcast field. I admit, I had a mindset of, "We all have problems in our career, everybody who's in broadcasting has to face the same challenges." She made me realize that wasn't true. At all.

Women do have a tougher go of it, not just in media, but in other career fields because of many men's prevailing, wrong, and destructive attitudes. I came to recognize that I was one of those men. You can talk the talk about respect and equal opportunity, but if your actions don't line up, you're part of the problem. It took a few years of talking with her before the light bulb went off in my dim wits. And it also exposed my attitudes toward women in general. I decided to apologize to the women I dated—for my dishonesty and for not respecting them in the way they deserved.

As one of my ex-girlfriends told me, "You know, James, you're a really good friend but you were a *lousy* boyfriend." Months and years zoomed by in a blur. I don't remember much because I was always preparing and working and juggling. Every day bled into the next and they were all workdays. Looking back, I see I was just trying to survive.

"Every time I'm looking at Snerdley's little bird in there—and you could put it in the palm of your hand, it is that tiny—but that bird, it doesn't know anything other than it's trying to live. Every living organism has this. It has this innate will to live. [. . .] You can learn

a whole lot about nature and instinct if you just watch.
[...] I'm like Snerdley. I marvel every time I see these
kinds of things right in front of my eyes.

"When you see an animal give birth or a bird
hatch from an egg and you watch the miracle of life
actually happen right before your very eyes, how you
cannot have a profound, almost sanctified respect for
it is beyond me. [...] The farthest star in the universe
from us eight-something-billion light-years away. Now,
that's a size that we humans cannot comprehend. And
how anybody can hear that, go outside at night and
look at the stars in the sky, how can anybody believe
it's just coincidence or an accident is beyond me. I have
the same reaction when I look at Snerdley's little bird
in there. In fact, when I first saw Snerdley it was during
the break. I walked in there and he had Stumpy in the
palm of his hand and Stumpy was just clinging to his
shirt and so forth. Just the cutest little bird, my heart
melts, folks, it just does, especially since the bird's hurt
in there, and Snerdley says he hopes he lives." —RL

Thankfully, Stumpy survived. And so did I.

Vegetarianism and Other Religions

When I was about twelve years old, my family and I went to
Alabama to visit my grandparents and great-grandparents on
my mother's side. One of my cousins killed a chicken in front
of my siblings and me. *Chop!* The head was off but the body
kept going. *Much like a later version of me in the 1990s.* I was

shocked. Later, I sat outside with Granny, my great-grand-mother, as she plucked and cleaned the bird. I have to admit it was pretty gross to witness.

The next day, we all sat down for Sunday dinner. As was my habit, I grabbed the drumstick from the big platter of fried chicken and started to devour it. Someone complimented Granny about how fresh and delicious the chicken was. Then another voice mentioned this was the chicken my cousin had killed the day before. I dropped the drumstick and never touched it the rest of the meal. Until that moment I'd never put it all together. In my poor little city-fied brain, the chicken I was eating came from the grocery store. It could not possibly have been the poor animal I had witnessed getting executed the previous day. That was the moment. It was over between me and chicken.

Over the next three or four years, I started reading more about the spiritual connections of life, which is one of the reasons that I am pro-life—and a vegetarian—and believe new conservatives can have an alliance with people who revere various kinds of living creatures. By the way, I'm not asking anyone to agree with me about their food choices. Eat whatever you want. I still like the smell of bacon. Who doesn't? On occasion I watch hunting shows and foodie shows about cooking meat. But, my point is that I believe all life has a soul. There is some connection to the creator inside every-thing alive. What separates us is the level of consciousness we possess. Living things fight to stay alive. So I arrived at the conclusion that I would only eat things with the lowest level of consciousness possible. This meant either liberals or plants, and the obvious choice for my taste was plants.

I decided to not eat any meat, fish, or eggs, and this was decades before vegetarianism was mainstream. My mother, who was a saint, was also an unbelievably great cook. She adapted to my diet and created amazing dishes. My mother gave me so much—gardening skills, music appreciation, a love of poetry and the arts, and certainly she was the driving force behind my own spirituality.

When I was fourteen, I was asked to share a sermon at our church, Grace Methodist Church, and my words were received very well. Looking back, I believed I was being groomed to become a minister by members of my church. But that trajectory veered off course when I was fifteen and started reading books about Eastern philosophy, karma, Buddhism, Jainism, and Sikhism. I studied the Koran and Islam, and also wanted to know about Hinduism, and I was still reading the Bible on a consistent basis.

At seventeen, I continued to enjoy going to church with my family, but my concept of spirituality was expanding. I still called myself a Christian, but I appreciated other sincere approaches to God. In 2004, when Mel Gibson's *The Passion of the Christ* was available on DVD, I tried to watch it, but the scenes were too upsetting. I eventually made it through the whole film, but the visuals affected my heart greatly—in ways I can't put into words.

I believe our mission is to lead a good life, to be good, to do good, to live every day by the Golden Rule—or at least try. The entire purpose of life, I believe, is to try to perfect ourselves spiritually. That is no small undertaking—it is a lifelong pursuit. Because most of us fail every day. We are all in need of forgiveness and mercy. I'm acutely aware of this because of the life I've lived.

The Topic of Cancer

In 2011, I went to see a urologist because I started having to go to the bathroom very frequently. I had the usual exam, and the doctor found that the prostate was enlarged. "We should probably do a biopsy on this," he said. We did the *snip-snip*, and in a couple of days I received the dreaded request for a visit with the doc. In his office, I heard him say, "James, you have cancer."

My first reaction was, *Huh. I wonder what blessing God has in store for me through this.*

A few seconds later, my second reaction was, *Oh shit. He just said "cancer."*

As I researched treatment options for prostate cancer, two main paths emerged: radiation and removal. I went to see a radiologist, who had bad things to say about the folks that do prostate removal. The prostate removal doctor talked trash about the radiation guys. *Damn, what the hell am I gonna do?*

I called a doctor friend who had worked with two former U.S. presidents, General Richard Tubb. He was kind enough to listen to my questions and refer me to a physician at the National Institutes of Health in Maryland, who was a renowned expert on prostate cancer, Dr. Peter Pinto. After a reassuring phone call with the doctor, I scheduled two days of testing for the following week. Because I'd be near DC, I asked my decades-old friend Connie, who worked as chief of staff for Congressman Louie Gohmert—who has also become a very dear friend—if she would go with me. She took off work and drove me to and from the initial appointments. Of course, when I told Rush, Dawn, and Brian about the diagnosis, I felt their deep concerns. The recent death of our beloved chief of staff, Kit Carson, was still weighing heavily on all of our hearts.

Journey to the Center of the James: Rated PG-13

If you don't have the stomach for details about my prostate cancer treatment, which is a new treatment protocol, or don't care to read about what me and my behind went through, please skip to the next section. You've been warned.

Checking in to the NIH is like checking in to the CIA. Connie kept me laughing the whole time as we went through the gauntlet of checkpoints on the sprawling campus. I was scheduled for an MRI, which was normally a pretty routine procedure. We went in through the front door, but the doctors, as I was about the learn, preferred the back door.

Once I was changed into my hospital gown and in the MRI room, I was asked to lay on my stomach on the MRI table. A few minutes later, a technician waltzed in carrying what looked like a very large, white . . . cucumber, but with all kinds of tubes and wires attached to it. With the calm voice of a plumber talking about clearing a drain, he said, "I'm just going to lubricate this and insert it."

Before I could respond or object, the deed was done and I was slid into the MRI machine. The next thing I knew the plumber mentioned, "Now we're going to inflate the balloon." *What?! There's a balloon in there?* Thankfully, MRIs don't record thoughts.

"OK, James, do *not* move. If you move, we have to start this all over again." Not moving sounded like a good option, so I did my best for the next fifty minutes. I later learned the balloon was used to push various organs and tissues out of the way so they can get a worm's-eye view of the prostate. Day one was successful, from the doctor's perspective anyway.

I was told the next day involved surgery. Connie drove me and stayed at the NIH the entire day, and we kept each other laughing, *almost* the entire time. Apparently, details about my surgery were given on a need-to-know basis, because after I changed into my flowing gown, I was informed, "There will be no anesthesia."

After being wheeled into the operating room, I spied an even bigger probe, which I named Moby Dick, complete with even more tubes and wires—and a video camera! Then I realized why the operating theater had so many big TV screens. Here I was in the starring role, but this just wasn't the television debut I dreamed of.

After the great whale was at home in my colon, I heard the familiar voice of my cancer specialist. "This is going to hurt a little bit, James." Here's some free medical insight: when doctors tell you that something will hurt, believe them. The next thing I felt—because, no anesthesia—was a needle violating my prostate. A week earlier, I had no idea where my prostate was. At that moment I knew the precise location, *because there's a needle in it and it hurts like hell!* I screamed. But it was over in a few seconds. Then came the second jolt from the needle. Yeah. I screamed again.

Don't get mad at me, dear reader. I told you this would get ugly.

I learned the process is called a "fusion biopsy." This process involved comparing the previous day's MRI with the live images of my prostate.

But the fun wasn't over. I was then instructed to move my hips to various other positions so the probe could snip samples of the prostate. This time I muffled the scream. They removed the device, and I breathed a long sigh of relief. Then I heard a soft, high-pitched woman's voice. "No, don't move yet. We have to clean you up."

Oh. My. God.

After yet another first for me and my posterior region, they rolled me into the recovery room, where Connie was waiting. She took one look at my face and her usual smile was gone. "Oh, James. What happened to you?!"

James the Guinea Pig

A few days later, and after I was back in Florida, my doctor called. "You do have cancer, but it's only on a very cellular level. This is not something that requires your prostate to come out. This is not something that requires you to have radiation." He explained that most men have a form of prostate cancer at some point in their life, and many go to their graves without realizing it. "It's a very slow growing cancer, but when it gets aggressive, then you really have to act." I would be tested every year to monitor the situation.

Four years later, I got the call. "Mr. Golden, the cancer has turned aggressive. You need to get back here right way." And I did. Once again, Connie was there to help.

They did a full body scan to see if cancer had metastasized elsewhere, then we started talking about treatment options with my patient care coordinator. About an hour after this consultation, the doctor would then tell me, based on the scan, whether or not cancer has spread. Every possible scenario blared through my brain—and mostly the worst cases. *How much time do I have left? A month? A year? Do I need to get my affairs in order?*

After my patient care coordinator read me details about what I could expect during the next few days, she looked up and saw that I was a nervous wreck. She put the clipboard down, walked over to me, and asked me to stand up. "I can see how nervous you are. I am your patient care coordinator. I cannot tell you what the doctor is going to say, but I can tell you this, you need a hug." After a much-needed embrace, she added, "We love you. We are going to take very good care of you and everything is going to be OK."

At that moment, all the anxiety vanished. I was ready to hear the doctor's report. He told me, "It is very close, but the cancer hasn't broken out and we're going to be able to treat you." That was the good news. The bad news was that I would need radiation treatment for forty-four straight days, plus other tests and treatments, which could last at least six months. I would need to move to Maryland to be near the NIH.

I wanted to continue working, but how was I going to screen calls from Maryland? Rush, Julie Talbott, and Kraig

Kitchin—along with the Premiere Broadcasting engineering staff—came to the rescue. They found me office space in an iHeart radio facility in Maryland, not far from the NIH campus. The engineers devised a "go box" with a bunch of equipment that connected me to the New York and Florida studios, and patched me into the phone lines.

The day before I left Florida, Dawn came into my office with a huge gift basket overflowing with dozens of cards, books, and all kinds of goodies to keep my spirits up. Rush, Brian, and Dawn had all contributed to make that huge gift basket, which was incredibly personalized and unique.

Connie offered to let me stay at her place in Virginia. Every day, she made sure I was up by 5:00 a.m., had the coffee brewing, and made me a protein shake with a full complement of nutrients and vitamins. She also made another shake for me to take to work with me. During more than six weeks of radiation, I experienced only four *very* rough days when I could barely get out of bed. In contrast, many other patients were totally wiped out after the first week or two. I never missed a day of work and, overall, emerged from the radiation feeling pretty good.

The doctors and nurses who monitored me every day finally asked me what I was doing because I wasn't handling the treatment like most of the other patients. I was awake, bubbly, and full of energy. I attribute all that to Connie, the amazing staff at the NIH, and the EIB family.

After almost five months my intense regimen at the NIH was over and I was put on hormonal drugs for two years. Yes, I've had every side effect in the book, and I'm still dealing with fallout from radiation. But everything was cool on my last exam. Thank God.

If you, or a loved one, is going through a scary medical situation, I'd like to offer you some encouragement. I know there's pain—physical, mental, and emotional—sometimes worse than you ever thought you'd have to bear. And I don't know if "everything's going to be OK." But I do know some good things can happen to you as a part of the process. And in more and more cases, whether it's cancer or other diseases, doctors working as God's agents can work miracles.

The culture of *care* that I found at the NIH was phenomenal. If that culture could be replicated in every aspect of the American health care system, nobody in this country would be bitching. Period. Nobody. The cultural DNA of that organization is amazing.

I discussed this with Supreme Court justice Clarence Thomas and his wife when I had dinner at their house a few years ago. After telling them about the experience, and my utter shock (as a conservative) at the excellence of the program, he looked at me and said, "This is your story and you have to tell it in one hundred percent truth. Never mind what the political outcome is, this is your story. Don't shade it."

I've often remembered my first reaction to the news that I had cancer. *I wonder what blessing God has in store for me through this?*

In hindsight—pun intended—I believe God allowed me to go through prostate cancer so I could get past my own partisanship and become an advocate for people who put the *care* in health care. Maybe this is my legacy. Maybe someone reading this—perhaps you—will understand that it's time to move beyond the games and into solutions. Health care is not a political issue.

> *"You know, I have a philosophy, there's good that happens in everything. It may not reveal itself immediately, and even in the most dire circumstances, if you just wait, if you just remain open to things, the good in it will reveal itself. And that has happened to me as well." —RL*

Everybody Dies

When the musician Prince died in 2016, I called one of my musician friends, who was also a mentor, Edwin Birdsong. "Did you hear Prince died?" I asked. "Everybody dies," he said. His reaction seemed a bit harsh, but was it? Everybody does die. Some deaths simply affect us more than others.

In February 2021, my world was rocked by three deaths in one week. On Monday the 15th, Stumpy died. I had a feeling that day, almost a premonition. "This is just the start of it." Little did I know.

On Wednesday, Rush passed. Three days later, my mom. I've had some bad weeks in my life, but that week was the worst. And in some ways, it's been a blur since then. But I'm getting better. Being on the radio has helped. But most of all, good friends have helped—longtime friends, new ones, and those whom I hadn't heard from in years, who reached out after Rush's passing.

I meditate every day. I have God-time every day and that's my anchor. What keeps me moored is the belief that although we are here for a short time, each of us has a destiny. Mine happens to involve radio.

Open Line Saturdays

I hadn't been in front of a microphone since 1998. I didn't miss being an on-air voice. But a couple of months after Rush's passing, WABC offered me a Saturday morning show. I accepted. Even after more than twenty years, when that mic went live, there were no butterflies. It was as if I was back home where I belonged. As I write this, my broadcast team—led my by my incredible agent Jim Robinson, my business partner Lisa Cathie, and my longtime friend Scott Hogenson—helped me negotiate a new position with WABC for a weekday afternoon drive-time show, which began in August, and I will keep my Saturday morning program.

I prepared for that show all week, but as much as you prepare, when you're doing a live show, you still have to be spontaneous. People say I have a knack for interacting with callers on the air. That comes from thirty years of dealing with callers *off* the air—and working with the greatest broadcaster of all time. For me, the show is the most beautiful experience every week, and when it's over, I'm exhausted. This reminds me of Rush and how I relate to him on so many levels. Like him, once the show is over, it's time to focus on the next one.

Being on the air is like playing live music. You can practice and practice, but when you're on stage, you have to let it all go. With Rush, I worked with the greatest there will ever be. Before meeting Rush, I had already spent nearly twenty years working with amazing broadcasters. I had also worked with less-than-amazing broadcasters, some of whom I couldn't believe were able to hold their on-air jobs. In Top 40 radio, as well as in "Black" radio, I had worked with some of the most renowned radio personalities. So when Rush came along, I recognized how special and unique he was. He had the cadence of a Top 40 disc jockey, the authority of a newscaster, the coolness of an FM announcer, and the humor of the best morning or afternoon hosts in the business. His keen sense of performance and timing could have provided him a career on the stage. But most important of all, I saw in him a passion for excellence that I had never experienced before. If I were a musician, it would be akin to spending most of my adult life working with someone as remarkable and unique as Duke Ellington, or Stevie Wonder, whom I once had the pleasure of meeting.

I was an employee, but we worked together as peers. He knew I was in awe of his talent, because I told him so. But he knew I was just as passionate about excellence in radio as he was, so the professional respect was mutual. There were occasions when Rush felt his show was not up to his own standards, and he would not be happy about it. But I would tell him, "Rush, the shows you think are your worst are still far and above better than most people's shows on their best day." He appreciated hearing that. It wasn't me sucking up. I knew it was true. He respected my experience in the business, and he listened to my opinions. Every so often, we talked shop and he would ask my opinion about his performance. For example, if his voice sounded hoarse or tired, I would tell him. He could accept constructive feedback from me because he knew I was a student of the business, just as he was.

SHOW NOTES

This is a spiritual conclusion that I've come to at this point in my life. No matter what trials and tribulations we have, if we all stood together and everybody tossed all their "stuff" into the air—their experiences, accomplishments, and heartbreaks—and we were able to grab somebody else's "stuff," it wouldn't be long before we'd want our own life back, the good and the bad. We are who we are supposed to be. I've never felt like I needed to be famous; I just want to be the best me. When I feel down, it's mainly because I know I've fallen short of the person I was created to be.

I never became a minister, but I had the honor of speaking with a pretty big radio congregation. Rush often spoke about the indescribable connection he felt with listeners during the show. He said, "I can see you. It's strange, but I know you're there. I know you're there in great numbers and I know that you understand everything I say." I can relate completely. And I'm as thrilled to communicate with my fellow New Yorkers and people from all over the country who listen to WABC as I was to have a moment to speak with Rush's twenty-seven million listeners.

There's a reason you love the people you do, and there's a reason you love the work you do. Maybe it's destiny. Even during the very hard times, keep going. Persevere and trust. Achieve anyway. That's the essence of life.

A Recent Message from a Listener

"Super Mega Dittos, James. I found The Rush Limbaugh Show in 1989, when I was still in college, and heard the name Bo Snerdley thousands of times since then. Rush Limbaugh was like a best friend we never met, riding in the car with us for years."

A Word from One of Our Amazing Guest Hosts, MARY MATALIN

"[Rush] was the smartest man that I ever knew, but he always was seeking and explaining virtue, and the essence of a representative republic—and freedom is virtue. It takes virtuous people and virtue requires, and freedom requires, constant vigilance. And he, I think, in the span of history, he will be understood by fair people, by fair historians, which there aren't very many, as a pivotal, transformational Socratic-type person. [. . .] I think his legacy will be, he guided us from the industrial age to the information age—very, very tricky—while maintaining the principles that got us to the position that we could continue to progress constructively and humanely and globally. [. . .] He lived his best life and that's a legacy in and of itself."

We all grow up wanting to be loved.
None of us are raised to be hated. And
I was the same way. I mean, many of
us will alter our own personalities to
be accepted by people. We'll try to
figure out what people want us to be
and then be that so that we'll be liked.
In the process of doing that, we deny
who we really are.

—RUSH LIMBAUGH

10

THE DIVIDED STATE
OF AMERICA

Before I met Rush, I had the honor of working with the late Alan Colmes, producing his radio talk show. His show was liberal leaning, even before he went on to co-host the Fox News program *Hannity & Colmes*. Alan became a friend, and I miss him dearly. But our first night working together at WABC radio did *not* begin well.

During the first hour of the show, Alan ordered some food from a local deli. When his order arrived at the reception desk on the first floor, I heard Alan's voice through the IFB (our internal intercom), making a demand for me to leave the studio and go downstairs to pick up his food delivery.

By now you know me well enough to imagine what came next—I politely agreed and asked if I could buy him a Snapple, right? Not exactly. "Go get your fucking food yourself! I'm here to produce your show, I'm not your house slave." We traded more unprintable banter from opposite sides of the glass for a few minutes before somehow, someone relented.

I honestly don't remember who finally went downstairs for the food, but I do know we did a great show that night. Within days, we were on great terms with each other—professionally and personally. We became very close friends and stayed in contact when he hosted *Hannity & Combs*. I was even a guest on their show when they first started.

Here's my point. Yes, there's a point. People make mistakes. I did in how I reacted to Alan that night. I knew he couldn't leave the studio in the middle of a broadcast, and deep down I knew he wasn't trying to be rude. But still, it's always OK to set boundaries and be honest. That's how people grow. That's how we learn who you can trust and who you can't, no matter whether you're liberal or conservative, agree or disagree, on any particular issue.

There are Democrats I trust, almost completely, even though we are at opposite ends of political issues. I grew up with some of them, and they are among my best long-term friends. Others are family members. So while I do trust some Democrats, I need to clarify they are non-elected Democrats only. And, while we're at it, I'll tell you this. There are some Republicans whom I wouldn't trust to get my lunch. It's not about the politics. It's about the person.

I'm sad to say that, thanks largely to politics, this country is still embroiled in strife. We have elected members of Congress who are blatant racists—many of whom are Black. They condone violent conflict and confrontations with their supposed ideological "enemies" in public spaces like restaurants, or even outside opponents' homes.

Today we see racism in reverse. Instead of *not* treating and viewing people a certain way based on their race, Democrats tell us to focus on skin color more than ever. The left is trying to silence open and honest opinion about race, activism, and policy. And they've made frighteningly fast progress.

Rather than flinch from far-left shouting points, we must hold to our values, and when we disagree, we must do so with civility.

Declarations of Disagreement

"America as founded" was a phrase Rush used often. Those words didn't sit well with me, and they still don't. When I heard America as founded, I heard something different from what he intended. My reaction was, *That may have worked well for white folks back then, but it certainly wasn't working for the Black folks.*

I finally understood what he meant, because I asked him about it one day. Profound, right? But I make the point because asking questions seems to be a lost art these days. Rush was referring to the founding *ideals*, including the idea that this country could change—culturally and constitutionally—and that our republic *needed* to change from where it was, as founded. On this, and so much more, we wholeheartedly agreed.

He always respected my views, which is one of the reasons why I loved him so much. On the air or off, when he asked, "What do you think, Mr. Snerdley?" he meant it.

One day on air, Rush smiled at me and announced to his audience in a hushed tone, "You know . . . Snerdley doesn't celebrate the Fourth of July." Weeks earlier, we had discussed the Fourth of July holiday. "I don't celebrate Independence Day," I declared. "That's white people's independence day." Rush made it clear that he totally understood my perspective.

Make no mistake, my view of the holiday carries *no* disrespect for the United States—unlike those liberals who use the Fourth of July to trash our nation and falsely claim that Black people "still aren't free." As the son of an Army veteran, I proudly observe Veterans Day and Memorial Day, and support the men and women of our military.

I love this country and I celebrate its creation. I love history and I love the history of my people in America. By that, I mean not only every citizen, but African American people who are my people, and Irish Americans who are my people, and other descendants of Thomas Jefferson who are my people. Yes, DNA and genealogy suggests I'm related to that hypocrite on the two-dollar bill, dammit. OK, we're probably both hypocrites, but I will get back on topic.

Let's be honest, in 1776, and for many decades later, Black people were still enslaved, in chains, and subject to slavery, which was enabled by the Democrat Party. But the founding of this country represented *real* hope and change.

The United States of America was the first nation in history to bring this kind of government to the world, and as a result, the destiny of the world changed for the better. I knew Rush's heart, and never, ever questioned it. Period— end of that story! And in all my years with him I never heard him say anything that I would remotely consider to be hateful. And, because of the relationship we had with each other,

I never hesitated to bring up issues and questions. As a result, I believe we both walked away from our conversations with a better understanding of the issues and a deeper appreciation of each other's perspectives.

On more than one occasion, he worried whether the country could ever recover from the resulting racial strife— especially because of the way Democrats continually exploited the situation. Every nation on earth has its own issues and problematic history. But leftists in America have chosen to exploit these issues to keep the people of this country divided and down. Or at least they try. It's dishonest and they know it.

Let me be very clear about something. I *never* seek to minimize the evils of slavery—especially the way it was practiced in America and the Caribbean nations. Chattel slavery was unlike the slavery that was practiced at other points in history because it separated people from their families, their culture, their own language, and their entire historical identity. People became total commodities, not even recognized as members of the human race.

I also believe history can be used as a bludgeon. For instance, in the twentieth century, Chairman Mao's policies were directly responsible for millions of deaths in China, in addition to the oppression of millions of other Chinese citizens—and oppression continues there. In the former U.S.S.R., Joseph Stalin, our ally in World War II, was responsible for millions of deaths, including the starvation of millions of people in the Ukraine. The conditions in Eastern Europe and other nations under Soviet domination brought untold misery and oppression to millions more. Germany, under the evil leadership of Adolf Hitler and his Third Reich, along with the other Axis powers, was responsible for the Holocaust and a war that could have taken anywhere from fifty million to eighty million lives. It's amazing that we still don't know the final human cost of that war.

Yet not one of these nations is looking backward—condemning the current population or government for their historical sins. In Japan, the atrocities committed during World War II in China and elsewhere are not even acknowledged in most school books. Yet the Japanese government wants America to apologize for Hiroshima and Nagasaki, even though both cities are flourishing today. These nations and most others that have committed these atrocities are focused on their *future*.

Yes, in America we have a responsibility to teach history accurately and without fear of acknowledging how evil slavery was. But that should not define present-day America. We are the nation that has devoted more resources—including the lives of our citizens in the Civil War—to secure more freedom, for more people, than any other nation in human history. We should be cognizant of our past but proud of who we are, and struggle to bring the ideals of our founding to fruition, to, in the words of our Constitution, create "a more perfect union."

I believe those on the left are actually afraid of people coming together in honest, loving conversation—resolving differences respectfully, or at least agreeing to disagree. And new conservatives must be careful to avoid the temptation to withdraw from conversations.

Differences or Divisions?

The move into politics on *The Rush Limbaugh Show* solidi-
fied after the Republicans won control of the United States
Congress in 1994, two years after President Clinton was first
elected.

Rush told the incoming members of Congress not to get
corrupted by Washington, DC. He made mention of Cokie
Roberts, who was with ABC at the time, and warned these
freshmen not to be fooled by friendly overtures by the media.
"These people are not your friends," he said. "They will do
everything they can to undermine you."

Rush was right, of course, because that battle has since
escalated. The mainstream media have revealed their bias
and corruption while social media has jumped into outright
censorship. Rush was aware of this from the beginning, and
the show became more serious over the years.

The left blamed Rush for being divisive in the '90s and
still blames him today. What really happened was that he
pioneered competition in the media. Please do not underes-
timate how vital this distinction is. Part of Rush Limbaugh's
amazing legacy is that he single-handedly changed the direction of American media—and not just on radio. Before the
Rush Limbaugh program, most conservatives assumed the rest
of the country was overwhelmingly liberal because that's what
the liberal media projected. The newspapers were liberal, the
three broadcast news outlets—ABC, NBC, and CBS—spewed
the same worldview, and this was echoed by the *New York
Times*, the *Chicago Tribune*, and the *Washington Post*. There

was no Fox News, and when CNN came along, it parroted the same liberalism—but it did so twenty-four hours a day.

Rush was the first national media figure of consequence to openly, and daily, call liberals and liberalism out for being a destructive force in the American body politic. And he did so by creating a bond with his audience, the likes of which never existed before. In the decades before Rush, theorists and futurists had predicted that a more "interactive" level of mass media communication would emerge. But none of those theories detailed how it would happen.

Rush used the tools of the day and innovated. His enduring love of technology made him an early adopter of Apple's computer offerings. He embraced email, gave his email address on the air, and used his email dialogues with listeners to instant message with them during the program—live. In addition, he had facsimiles pouring in from all over the country—all day and all night. His show became a clearing house for national news and discussions on the trajectory of the "culture." A significant amount of the material was sent to Rush's attention by the listening audience, in addition to his massive show prep efforts.

In the second and third decade of the Rush Limbaugh program, there was definitely a noticeable shift in attitude. We in the studio went from laughing at what we viewed as political nonsense or impossibilities, to realizing, *Holy crap! This is serious. These liberal ideas could actually happen!* This is when Rush shifted the focus away from a lot of satire, parodies, and humor to a more serious consideration of the ideas that were being pursued by the left. Of course, the parodies and humor never disappeared. But the political tone in

America was undoubtedly growing more serious, and Rush wanted to be at the forefront of the discussion.

President Clinton insinuated that Rush was reckless, a racist, and a purveyor of hatred. Even left-wing Chris Matthews said Rush shouldn't stand for being called a racist, and of course, Rush didn't. He demanded an apology, just as he had demanded an apology when Clinton tried to blame him for the Oklahoma City bombing. Yes, we've always been a divided nation, but the era of toxic politics began with "nice guy" Bill Clinton.

Certainly the 1987 Supreme Court confirmation hearings for Justice Robert Bork was a polarizing moment that more conservatives should have paid attention to. Ted Kennedy— *the Swimmer*—took the floor of the Senate, smeared Justice Bork, and declared that if he were confirmed, Black people would be put back in chains. The smear worked because Republicans didn't stand up for Robert Bork.

Joe Biden has made a lot of noise about rooting out "domestic terrorism." Every time the left uses that term, I get a shiver because I know what they really mean. They don't mean right-wing whack jobs wearing Viking horns at the Capitol. They're talking about anyone who disagrees with them politically. Including me. And you.

They say conservatives want to prevent people from voting. Of course that's not the case. But in doing so, the left subtly ties us in with white supremacists who tried to keep Blacks from voting—also known in the nineteenth and twentieth centuries as Democrats. It's another attempt to demonize an entire sector of the population that has legitimate concerns. The same goes with the term "nationalism."

Nationalism

"As I said in my address to the Joint Session of Congress, according to the intelligence community, terrorism from white supremacy is the most lethal threat to the homeland today. Not ISIS, not Al-Qaeda, *white supremacists.*"

—PRESIDENT JOE BIDEN, JUNE 2021

With the simple addition of the word "white," the term *nationalism* has become another N-word. There is nothing wrong with nationalism, but the press and liberals don't think so. Nationalism simply means I care about the needs of my country first, before foreign powers. Yes, I study history and am well aware that back in the 1930s, a bunch of Germans formed the National Socialist German Workers' Party and shortened the name of their fascist club to "Nazis."

I'm an American nationalist. Like most citizens, I want our elected leaders to do what is in the best interest of *our* country every day.

While we're on the subject, let's talk about the Stars and Stripes. Some leftists get triggered at the sight of our nation's flag. So do I, but in the opposite way—*I happen to love it.*

Not so much with the Confederate flag. Years ago, I was house hunting in a neighborhood and saw a big Confederate flag flying in front of someone's house. *Oh, hell no. I'm not moving into this neighborhood.* To me, that flag was intended to send a message. Sure, maybe the homeowners were massive

Dukes of Hazzard fans. But I wasn't going to buy a home on that street. You can, of course, have a different opinion, but that's my take, and in this case, I probably speak for a high percentage of Black people.

Liberals love to bark about conservatives and their "dog whistles." You know, they believe phrases like "law and order" and "America first" are racist. Well, if those are dog whistles, the Confederate flag is an air horn to me. I know, from many conversations with those who honor the Confederate flag, that many of these people are not racist and intend no harm from displaying it. But because of some brutal realities in our society, may I respectfully suggest that flying the Red, White, and Blue sends a much more unifying message that cannot be mistaken for anything negative. Unless, of course, you're a liberal.

There is nothing wrong with being a nationalist. There is nothing wrong with wanting to place the interests of our country first. But we've seen politicians and media megaphones add the word "white" and now we hear about the alarming rise of *white nationalists*. The message is clear: nationalism is bad—because America is bad.

Was Rush divisive? No. In today's politics, *divisive* is simply a term the left uses for nonconformists. Remember that when you hear people disparage the United States and those of us who unashamedly love our country.

A Young Nation

All my life I've heard people talk about America through a prism of blame. *America is at fault, we are oppressors, our country was founded on slavery!* And despite all of the changes this nation has witnessed from its founding until now, somehow we are still oppressive, racist, bigoted, and unjust. But when I look at America today, I see something different.

The United States is still a very young nation. And we have been able to do great things in an incredibly short period of time. Let me put this into perspective. In thousands of years of *recorded* human history—let's use a number of ten thousand years—our nation has been in existence only about 2% of that time.

Compared to any other era, look what we Americans have accomplished. Our nation has brought more freedom, personal liberty, and economic prosperity to more people on this earth than any other nation in the history of mankind. We are the light of the world, not the oppressors of the world.

What did the world look like before America? Go back about nine hundred years, and in 1184, the Inquisition began in Europe. This oppression took place for over six hundred years until 1826, when the last person was executed in the name of this so-called purging.

Look at what else was happening in the world while America was part of the horrible institution of chattel slavery. Not only Blacks were enslaved in many parts of the world. People in homogenous societies were enslaved by other people. In Europe, millions lived as serfs under feudalism. There were similarly horrific living conditions for untold millions of common folks in Asia and Africa, while the elites prospered.

Chattel slavery was probably the most heinous crime against humanity, and there was a moral obligation to dispel it. That is what America eventually did. The lives that were lost in the American Civil War still outnumber any other war this nation fought. Republican president Abraham Lincoln knew slavery was a sin that could not go unpunished, as he noted in his second inaugural address in March 1865.

> "Fondly do we hope, fervently do we pray, that this mighty scourge of war may speedily pass away. Yet, if God wills that it continue until all the wealth piled by the bondsman's two hundred and fifty years of unrequited toil shall be sunk, and until every drop of blood drawn with the lash shall be paid by another drawn with the sword as was said three thousand years ago, so still it must be said 'the judgments of the Lord are true and righteous altogether.'"
>
> —PRESIDENT ABRAHAM LINCOLN

And as the war ended, Lincoln hoped for peace.

> "With malice toward none, with charity for all, with firmness in the right as God gives us to see the right, let us strive on to finish the work we are in to bind up the nation's wounds, to care for him who shall have borne the battle, and for his widow and his orphan— to do all which may achieve and cherish a just and lasting peace among ourselves and with all nations."
>
> —PRESIDENT ABRAHAM LINCOLN

While arguments still rage about the Confederacy, flags, and statues, what cannot be argued is that America was the first nation to articulate in its founding documents that our rights are granted to us by God—not by men, not by a monarch, and not by a government. In our constitution are the mechanisms to change and right wrongs.

It is true that America was born with the sin of slavery. It is also true that in our founding documents, Black people were characterized as being three-fifths of a human being. The reason for that was political, and the rationale for that hideous characterization is often not taught or understood. It was a political compromise that weakened the power of the states that practiced slavery. Had those states claimed every Black person as an "equal" human being, they would have had more representation in Congress because we are a representative republic based on the population of individual states. Northern states might never have gained the political power to challenge slavery as "quickly" as they did. Our constitution was ratified in 1789. Seventy-two years later—a relatively short time—the Civil War began.

Our founders—many of whom were flawed individuals—knew slavery was evil and wrong. This quote from my distant relative, Thomas Jefferson, as shown on the Jefferson Memorial, indicates that clearly.

"Can the liberties of a nation be secure when we have removed a conviction that these liberties are the gift of God? Indeed, I tremble for my country when I reflect that God is just, that His justice cannot sleep forever. Commerce between master and slave is despotism. Nothing is more certainly written in the book of fate

than that these people are to be free. Establish the law
for educating the common people. This it is the business of the state to effect and on a general plan."

—THOMAS JEFFERSON

The mistake some people make, many of them conservatives, is that they don't want to talk about slavery. Slavery
didn't just happen during a distant past, four hundred years
ago. People who were enslaved in America were still living
in the 1930s. My own great-grandmother, whom I loved and
adored, was married to an ex-slave, Frank Kerley. If you want
to understand some of the dysfunction of our present society, understand that we are not so far removed from this
dysfunction of chattel slavery, and we are still working toward
correcting that.

But contrast this with what the rest of the world has done.
Can you name the first Black president of any European
nation? The United States grew into an economic and military
superpower and a leader in human rights because, despite our
history, we incorporated in our founding documents the idea
that liberties and freedoms were granted by God.

American Exceptionalism

Rush was unapologetic about American exceptionalism, and I
am, too. Here's his take on the subject from 2013, which holds
true today.

RUSH: "I want to play an audio sound bite for you.
It's Barack Obama during his speech to the

nation on Tuesday night, and here he is with just a really sad, quasi-definition of American exceptionalism."

PRESIDENT OBAMA: "America is not the world's policeman. Terrible things happen across the globe, and it is beyond our means to right every wrong. But when, with modest effort and risk, we can stop children from being gassed to death and thereby make our own children safer over the long run, I believe we should act. That's what makes America different. That's what makes us exceptional."

RUSH: "No. No. Here's a guy who wants to be selective in his morality. We're not the world's policeman—*except we are*—when he wants us to be. 'Terrible things happen across the globe, and it's beyond our means to fix them—*except when I think they should be*—and with modest effort and risk we're gonna do something. It isn't gonna be very big. We're not gonna offend anybody, and there's not a whole lot of risk, otherwise I wouldn't do it because I'm risk-averse.

"'When children are being gassed'—never mind RU-486 and abortion, 'cause that's, you know, my buddies. That's what makes America great. 'That's what makes us exceptional.' No. What makes us exceptional is what we used to have in situations like this: that was a moral authority. We had the moral authority because of what we stood for, and we stood for what I just explained. We stood for the absolute primacy of the individual.

"We stood for the concepts that are in our Declaration of Independence: right to life, liberty, pursuit of happiness. We stood for that, and we were the beacon for it, and to this day that is why the oppressed of the world still seek to come into this country."

Conservative Exceptionalism

As new conservatives, we should be people who show their love by proposing solutions to help people. Our communication style is crucial; it can either alienate people and turn them into adversaries or it can help to create allies.

I'll never agree with the left on almost everything they want. I want them politically defeated and I don't want their policies to succeed. That sounds very much like what Rush said about Obama: "I hope he fails." They are my *political* adversaries. I want to defeat them in elections. But they are not my mortal enemies. I do not want to see people harassed or threatened because of their beliefs, whether they're on the left or the right. It's not healthy and it's not morally correct.

My political strategy all comes down to a surprisingly simple premise: do unto others as you would have them do unto you. You wouldn't want somebody disturbing the sanctity of your home by protesting on your sidewalk, so don't do it to them. You wouldn't want somebody lying about you in the media, so don't do it to them. You wouldn't want somebody telling you that because you love somebody, you're wrong and your life is wrong, so don't do it to them.

Frankly, if the small-but-vocal kook contingent—who think they are conservative—would stop the stupid crap, more people would understand the true nature of conservative ideology. If we also provide solutions for the pressing problems people face, they will shout less and listen more.

Last summer, I spoke to a group of die-hard Republicans and Rush fans in Baton Rouge, Louisiana. I told them they cannot just continue to bad-mouth Obamacare and think they've done their job. I excoriated the Republicans for not coming up with a workable solution after all these years. People are afraid to be sick because it might drive them into bankruptcy. This is the reality for Americans of all races and political affiliations, and it is not the way Americans want to live. It's a concern that crosses political lines. I received a rousing applause, and the experience gave me hope.

We're never going to all think alike. We are never going to be a unified, homogenous society because that is not what America ever was. If you look inside somewhat homogenous societies, you will find that they have divisions, too, because that is part of our nature. The human struggle has always been a struggle of survival against nature and other human beings.

What America did that was unique in the world was profound. We gave people from all over the world a home where they could prosper and enjoy freedom—including religious and economic freedom. If you were born poor, you could thrive and acquire wealth. In other societies where there was a strong aristocracy, even if you gained wealth, you were still looked down upon. But not in America. That's a meritocracy. That's a good thing.

Meritocracy has always been resisted by oppressors, and there have been ugly oppressions in the United States. I have never denied this fact. But in the vast majority of cases, hard work, excellence, and honesty are rewarded in this country. Meritocracy is still the best solution to oppression.

Rush articulated this honestly and with compassion in 2007 with a caller named Derek, who was Black. With just a few edits for brevity, here's part of their conversation.

CALLER: "Well, Rush, this is my point. When my dad turned eighteen, he wasn't allowed to vote. You see what I'm saying? We've only had the vote since 1964, you know what I mean? And a lot of times when people say, when you say, 'Get over it,' it's like, hold on, we've only been able to vote . . ."

RUSH: "The point is I'm not saying you should forget about it and get over it. But recognize progress. Recognize that there are great strides that have taken place and will continue to take place, and understand that everybody in life has certain kinds of obstacles. There are any number of people who are discriminated against because of various aspects of their existence. And we all face them. My point is that rather than sit around and tell people to continue to wallow in the past and think that that creates some sort of an entitlement, that is not a service to people. That is keeping them down and keeping them in a place where they're never going to realize their full potential.

"There are countless millions of examples throughout this country of Black Americans who have overcome all of this, who are realizing their dreams, who are doing it by their own hard work and their initiative. The market is there for achievement and for excellence and accomplishment. I want every individual to be the best they can be. I want every individual to understand the potential that resides inside them, because I want a great country. I cringe when I see anybody, any group or any individual being told that they don't have a chance to become anything because of X, when this country disproves it each and every day.

"Derek, there are certain undeniable facts. There are Asians that have immigrated to this country who are running rings around Native Americans born here, white, Black, what have you, because they don't have any of these reference points of discrimination and history. In fact, if they wanted to, they could. They could go back and say we were imprisoned and we were mistreated building the railroads. They don't do that. They just come here and they run rings around everybody. Achievement orientation,

becoming better than you think that you can be,
any of these things, these are great human characteristics. Human, not white, not Asian, not
Black. They're in all of us.

"But when somebody, or especially a group
of people, is told by a political party for fifty years
that they don't have a chance unless they vote a
certain way, I react the same way as when I hear
that people suffering incurable diseases only have
a chance if Democrats are elected. It offends me,
it enrages me, and for those of you in Rio Linda,
it makes me mad.

"All I'm saying is that the desire I have for
every human being to use the opportunity of life,
to maximize their enjoyment and the opportunity to achieve. This is how we define ourselves,
it's in all of us, and when it's denied because of
a political party desiring to get a bloc of votes
from people by keeping them dependent, I am
offended, I am outraged at that. That, to me, is
human bondage, Derek, and it is still going on.

"If there's a plantation in this country today,
it's owned and operated by white liberals."

CALLER: "I do agree with you, and like I said before,
there's no place in the world I'd rather be, you
know what I mean, because my opportunities for
success are not going to be greater anyplace else.
I don't want anybody to hand anything to me,
never, ever, ever in life. I want to earn everything

I get and that's what I teach my son. But I also teach my son the historical perspective of the things that his forefathers went through."

RUSH: "Just don't turn him into somebody who hates. Because that will paralyze him. Hate doesn't do anybody any good. It doesn't. It's not a motivator. It doesn't inspire. It just enrages and angers and paralyzes."

Divide and Conquer

We have *always* been a divided nation. And before the United States was a nation, the people who lived here—decades and millennia earlier—were fiercely divided. In our current political and social climate, how did the divisions get so bitter? And what should we do about it?

"Liberals do not believe that a majority of people have the ability to realize the American dream on their own. Liberals have general contempt for the average American and average human being. Liberals have a condescending contempt for the abilities, the intelligence, the ambition, and desire of average human beings.

"They must hold that view in order to be liberal, because liberalism is assuming people are helpless and hopeless and then growing government and all kinds of state power structures to 'assist' people in their incompetence, and in the process you actually make your philosophy a self-fulfilling prediction. You disable the

competitive nature; you disable the entrepreneurial spirit; you disable the American dream; and you force people to focus on government and whatever benefits they can get as a means of getting by.

"Conservatives have the ultimate faith in the individual. Conservatives believe that the individual, rugged individualism is what defines excellence and its pursuit is what made this country what it is. We believe that people can be better than they even know themselves or think themselves capable of being. We want to do everything we can to educate and inspire and motivate people along those lines." —RL

The "village" is not supposed to parent a child. It used to be that the village shared the same values, most of which had a common underpinning in religious beliefs. Those days are gone.

The idea that we the people must conform with "correct" thinking and behaviors goes to the heart of liberal ideology. . . and fascism . . . and socialism.

Rush talked a lot about rugged individualism, how individuals and their individual effort are part of what made America. It's part of American exceptionalism, this idea that an individual can strike out on their own and, through their own ambition, succeed and prosper and help enable others to prosper. The concept of rugged individualism has been called a social devolution by the left. They see it as the weak being persecuted because someone else has become stronger, because the left wants us to have a *communal* society. Except for celebrities or Democrat leaders—those elites are applauded for their unique voice and sizable paychecks. After all, *someone has to be in charge of the commune, right?*

Innovators are individualists. America has usually rewarded its innovators. But this cultural cornerstone is being chiseled away by those on the left as they mindlessly attack individualism. I mentioned my concern to Rush in 2009 during an *obscene profit break.*

"Snerdley says, 'You better explain why the individual is so important. You know, a lot of people, you got a whole bunch of brand-new tuner-inners out there, Rush, and a lot of these people think the individual is just a greedy SOB, and the individual, a bunch of individuals are what got the country in trouble.'

"I said to Snerdley during the top-of-the-hour break, 'If I have to explain this, it's over.' I mean, it depresses me to have to try to explain this, why is the individual important? If you have to explain why the individual is important in the United States of America, then you have to explain freedom, and if you have to explain that, I'm at a loss. I guess I'll just ask you a question. [. . .]

"Why is it you are free? To me, that answers it. I mean are you free because you are a member of a group? Or are you free because you are your own soul, endowed by your creator, God, certain inalienable rights: life, liberty, pursuit of happiness. From where does your freedom come? Do you not have freedom until you join a club? Do you not have freedom until

you join a union? Do you not have freedom until you are part of the disabled? Do you not have freedom until you are a minority? Where does your freedom come from? [...]

"This country was not built on group politics. The country was not built on group identities. The country was built on rugged individualism. Rugged individualism is portrayed, unfortunately, as selfishness. But it is not selfishness. Rugged individualism is self-interest, and self-interest is good. If we were all acting in our own self-interest ... What are your self-interests? Let's say you're a father, a husband. What is your self-interest?

"Well, if you take it responsibly, the responsibility of being a husband and father, your self-interest is improving the life that your family lives. You want economic opportunity for them. You want social stability for them. You want a relatively crime-free existence. You want some security. You want to see to it that your kids don't go off on the wrong path. All of these things are the things that you work for. And you rely on yourself to provide them. Of course you have support groups, the church and friends and so forth. It doesn't mean that you are solitary, doesn't mean that you're isolated. But it means that you accept responsibility for your life and what happens to you is your responsibility, and that you have, in this country, all of the ability and opportunity in the world to make the most of it. Or, you can slough it off, and you cannot make the most of yourself.

"But then you're not acting in your own self-interest. Then you're letting everybody down. When you don't seek your best, when you don't try to be the best you can be, you're letting everybody down, you're letting the country down. Obama even said this. When talking about the dropout rate, he said, 'You people dropping out, you're not helping your country. You're harming your country.' That's the same thing: self-interest. [...]

"Even I, ladies and gentlemen, you listen to me, and you see whatever you see, but you see me as successful, it may make you mad, may make you furious, but nevertheless you see me successful. But you don't know the thirty-five, thirty-seven years that I've spent in this business since I was sixteen (minus five that I worked for the Kansas City Royals baseball team), you don't know the seven times I got fired, and you don't know how many people in this business told me to quit and told me to give it up, that it's not a fair business, even if you're good, there are too many idiots above you, too many jealous people above you that don't want you to get anywhere because you're better than them." —RL

Is Individualism Divisive?

We can stand up for what we think and believe without hating the person who opposes our view. This standard cuts both ways, but if we wait for "them" to stop being hateful, we'll never start being new conservatives.

Ask me to consider your opinion, and I will. Demand I change my view—along with my corresponding actions—and I probably will not. That's conformity.

There are certain things the right and the left will never agree upon, like "the right to choose." Women from the left view the right to choose as no one having the right to tell them what to do with their bodies. Women on the right agree that no one should tell you what to do with your body, but we're not talking about *your* body. We're talking about the body of a little somebody who happens to be growing in your body. That individual has rights, too.

An Alternative to "Uniting the Country"

The Republican Party was born in 1854, out of opposition to the Democrat Party and the Democrats' policies to expand slavery across the country. The establishment of this alternative political group and its stance to abolish slavery certainly didn't unite the nation.

In 1860, Abraham Lincoln, the first Republican president, was elected. Representatives from many Southern states threatened to secede if this "divisive" man was elected. This was before threatening to go to Canada was in vogue, I suppose. Six weeks later, South Carolina seceded from the Union. Within a few more weeks, five other Southern states also announced they had left the United States. On March 4, 1861, President Lincoln took office, and in April, the Civil War began.

Doing the right thing does not always bring unity—not right away at least.

Leading up to the 1994 congressional elections, Bill Clinton was president and both the House and Senate were controlled by Democrats, as they had been for forty years. Newt Gingrich and a band of Republicans put forth concrete ideas, in a document they called the "Contract with America."

In case you were born after 1994, the Republicans won both legislative houses and made huge gains in state and local elections.

You can't compromise, or conform, on certain issues. There's no "I'm against slavery, but let's find some middle ground, OK? How about only three days a week of slavery?" The same holds true for many issues of our day, on which we don't agree.

Don't fall for the platitudes. When you hear a politician or do-gooder talk about "uniting America," don't believe them. Unify means "conform" to the left, and "compromise" to so-called Republicans. That's the opposite of what makes this nation great.

What if Abraham Lincoln wasn't so "divisive" and simply got along with Southern slaveholders? What if Dr. Martin Luther King Jr. sought compromise on segregation? I suppose neither would have been murdered. But I can't imagine what life in this country would be like without their courage.

SHOW NOTES

We've always been a divided country, and we probably always will be. Let's stop trying to unite every person in the country and, instead, put forth solutions because they're the right thing to do. More and more people will rally around good ideas and good candidates. Most of all, stop apologizing for what you believe and face the fact that if you speak up and get involved, some people won't like you.

As I speak up in my new season on the radio, Rush's example, transparency, and wisdom continue to be a great help.

> *"A personal story. We all grow up wanting to be loved. None of us are raised to be hated. And I was the same way. I mean, many of us will alter our own personalities to be accepted by people. We'll try to figure out what people want us to be and then be that so that we'll be liked. In the process of doing that, we deny who we really are. Now, when I was growing up nobody hated me and nobody thought that I hated anybody else.*
>
> *"Six months after my national radio show started, 20% of the country hated me just because of my values, just because of my conservatism. [. . .] This went on for three years. I had to learn—which was a tough psychological thing for me—I had to learn how to take being hated as a measure of success. Nobody's raised for that." —RL*

A Recent Message from a Listener and Radio Host

"James, I was a career cop in West Virginia assigned to the Charleston Metro Drug Unit when my boss, a Democrat by the way, called me on the radio to tell me to listen to this guy on WCHS. It was Rush. The boss said, 'I don't know who this guy is, he's a nut, but he's right!' I was hooked.

"That was 1989. Fast forward nine years and I had moved to Florida's Space Coast. The first thing I did upon arrival was find our local station that carried Rush. Rush was, well, Rush. The rest of the lineup left something to be desired. I decided to write the local station owner. I told him I was disappointed that there was no local talk radio that mirrored the quality of discussion I had in little Charleston, WV. I also told him I knew nothing about radio, but did not want to complain without offering to be part of the solution. We met a week or so later.

"After an hour, we left the conference room like longtime friends and I was invited to come in and be part of a late-night local talk show to feel my way around. In the winter of 2001 I became a full-time employee of the station. By spring I was the morning drive talk host. He'd asked my goals before hiring me and I said, 'to be the voice of local talk radio in this market for the next twenty-five years.'

"In January of 2004, Clear Channel hired me away and I have been the program director and morning host of WMMB ever since (outside the 1.5 years in Modesto, CA, at our stations there in the same role). That twenty-five years is quickly approaching.

"It's thanks to Rush and all of you that made the EIB happen that I landed my third career that I absolutely love. I've been in radio longer than I was a cop. So, a sincere *thank you* to you and the rest of the EIB crew. You are all appreciated by so many more than you know. We can never repay you for that professionalism and the example you all set."

—Bill Mick, Program Director/Host, iHeartMedia

A Recent Message from a Listener

"Having Rush on the radio each day, because of his eternal optimism, helped me get through one of the darkest periods of my life. I sure do miss Rush. After nearly three months since his passing, I still feel this gaping hole in my daily life because I can't tune in to listen to him."

The EIB Network now has an "official Obama criticizer." When Obama needs to be criticized, our official criticizer, Bo Snerdley, will do so.

—RUSH LIMBAUGH

11

LET'S GO THERE

Barack Obama emerged as a political force in the 2008 presidential primary, but his campaign wasn't a bed of roses. He was initially considered a long shot, having spent less than one term as a United States senator. And those who weren't paying attention then may not believe that Barack Obama was criticized by other African American Democrats for not being "authentic" enough. Because his father was Kenyan, his childhood was spent in nations other than our own, and his mother was Caucasian, some of the "race purists" in his party said he had no roots in the civil rights struggle in America. The more extreme critics pointed out he lacked slave ancestry— and therefore couldn't connect with the real struggles of Black Americans.

All of this was made-to-order for *The Rush Limbaugh Show*. After Barack Obama won the election, Rush, of course, wasn't concerned about criticizing the first Black president. And I got a chance to be involved with occasional on-air commentary, as "the official Obama criticizer," who was "certified

Black enough to criticize" the president because I possessed slave blood in my ancestry. From my perspective, this exposed liberal racist hypocrisy in a glorious manner.

The commentary followed a familiar pattern. After being introduced by Rush, I would first offer my statement, critical of an Obama policy. The initial statement, read in the King's English, was then followed by a translation for those in the hood.

"This is Bo Snerdley, official Barack Obama criticizer for the EIB Network, certified Black enough to criticize, with a heavy dose of pure, unadulterated, organic slave blood. I have a statement:

"President Obama, your weekend media blitz to again try and reverse your sagging fortunes implementing your socialist health care takeover failed. The only ones buying it are those who are already in so deep, they can't see out. Nobody else wants in. And you've changed messages so many times, you are quickly losing all credibility. It has become apparent that you view speechmaking and television appearances as a substitute for real governance.

"Given the state of our economy and our weakening defense posture, perhaps it is time for you to spend a little less time on television and a little more time coming to terms with the magnitude of failure that your leadership is causing. It hasn't been a year yet, you have no major achievement and you're racking up a string of disasters. Our economy is still in the tank. Our enemies, thanks to your ineffective foreign policy decisions, think we have become a weakened nation and some are openly gloating about it.

"Respectfully, sir, shape up or you will soon replace Jimmy Carter as the worst president in the last hundred years."

Despite my unassailable genetic and genealogical qualifications for the role, the translation for the hood was tricky. I'm a pretty hip guy *(OK, maybe back in the '80s)*, but admittedly, I didn't know all the latest street-speak used in "the hood." So, to prepare, I'd watch an episode of *The Wire* on TV. It had all the best slang and it was so dope! I listened to the Black guys on *The Wire* to make sure I could connect, lingo-a-lingo. Here's an example:

"And now, a translation for our EIB brothers and sisters in the 'hood.

"What'up B? Yo dog, it's been a minute, check it out, yo, you got some issues yo. Loved ya in September, and yo bro we still don't see no jobs out here, yo. Ain't that much hope and what be changing ain't changing like you said was gonna change.

"Bush is gone yo, but you and your crews still raise him up every time somebody starts aksin questions, 'where da jobs?' When you not on TV speechifying, you, and Michelle and the kiddies, are out livin' large, man. We see da pictures, man. Y'all been to Paris, got dinner up in New York, man, London, Harry Potter tours and all that stuff. But check it out, man, out here in the hood, man, nobody's chillin, everybody's illin, ain't nobody got the dough for no kinda vacations, yo.

"You know how bad it is, 'Bama, man? People starting to sell their bling, man. What's up with that? Nobody can see what that stimulatin' money is stimulatin' man, that's just emulatin' unemployment. Oh, check this out, my mayness, tell your crew something some. Stop whining about this race stuff man, you H-B-I-C now, yo. You da Head Black in Charge. You in charge of everything. You runnin the show. You are the man. OK? So just bring it.

"Y'all don't have to come with this race stuff no more, you up in there, man. You up in the House. Bring it. OK? Tell your crew to stop making excuses. Now we see dem boys up on Wall Street, you know they kinda coming out rollin' again, but we don't see a hit. There's another tip, yo, you making the Russians happy, but you makin' the brothers yappy, OK? Ain't nobody got no spending money out here, yo. OK?

"You worried about health care? That's not the deal, man, it's the jobs. The healthy jobs takes care of the healthy health care homie. So lemme run this on you, man, step off the TV, we awready know what you look like, we know you're in charge, start extending, stop the grinning, get busy, get some jobs up here goin' or we gonna break you off that hope and change thing next time election rolls out, yo. I'm tellin you, you got that? You feelin' me?

"That concludes this statement."

My honorary title of official Obama criticizer said a lot about Democrats in 2008, and it says even more about liberals today. Here's some of my conversation with Rush about this, which we put together for the fifteenth anniversary issue of the *Limbaugh Letter*.

RUSH: "What about the Obama criticizer thing?
       That was an idea we came up with here because
       at the time, based on race, no one could criticize
       Obama for anything: couldn't say he's liberal,

couldn't say his middle name, couldn't talk about his wife, couldn't talk about his preacher. So, I decided we have got to be able to criticize the guy, and who better to do it than with you? You have done a superb job. What kind of reaction do you get from people?"

SNERDLEY: "I don't get a lot of reaction outside of the show. I do get some from family and friends, but they won't say much about it—because what can they say? A lot of my friends and my family are liberals, and that's just the way it is. My conservative friends love it and think it's funny. So do some of the liberals, but they won't say too much about it because they are invested in Obama. And the reason they are invested in Obama has nothing to do with politics. That is what I figured out. So, whether it is criticism that you offer during the course of the program on Obama, or other criticism, a lot of my Black friends won't say anything about it except, 'We can't talk about politics until after the election,' because they really get ticked when I lay out the case."

RUSH: "Yeah, but it's raw talent. Do they have no appreciation for the talent?"

SNERDLEY: "They can't admit it's funny because they think it's hurtful to Obama. That doesn't bother me one bit; it means it's effective."

RUSH: "It's supposed to be hurtful to Obama."

SNERDLEY: "Exactly."

RUSH: "We are trying to be. You're the criticizer, for crying out loud. We are trying to inform people about the problems we would face if this guy happens to win."

SNERDLEY: "But see, it's not political, Rush. I have learned that what Obama is to a segment of the liberal population has nothing to do with politics. It has everything to do with psychology, self-esteem, race esteem, and culture. They can't tell you what his policies are. They cannot tell you what his tax policies are. They can't tell you what his policies are in education. It's an investment in 'hope.' And it's an investment in that, well, he is not George Bush, he is not a Republican. The Republican brand is not acceptable because of all the demonization over the years. But they are investing all kinds of things in Obama that he is not; hence, the Messiah. They think that if Obama is elevated to become the president of the United States, the world changes somehow. [. . .] I understand where some of that anger is coming from. Hell, if you lived in some of these neighborhoods, you'd be mad, too."

RUSH: "And if your kids went to some of the schools they have to go to—"

SNERDLEY: "If your kids went to these crappy-ass schools that have been crappy ever since you were born, you should be mad."

RUSH: "Yeah, but why not blame the people actually responsible for this?"

SNERDLEY: "Because it's branding. You can't. Because the people that they think are responsible for it are Republicans. It makes no sense. It's not logical. It is, again, not political. It is psychological. It's the same message that you hear over and over again. You can watch almost any media show. Once in a while I happen to watch reruns of *Law and Order*, and it's just inundated with the liberal mindset, as is everything else in mainstream press. So, you grow up with this stuff, this brand of Republican is seen as the enemy. And you never look to the mindset as actually being the cause of your problems.

"Let me go back to your first question here about what does the program observer do: remember things that you say. But I also do something else. I also research what you say, and I find out some amazing things when I do that. For instance, you were the first one who for me actually explained conservatism in a way that made sense as a political brand. What is conservatism? Barry Goldwater was the enemy when I was a kid. I was one of these little kids marching around the living room talking about 'LBJ, LBJ.' Why? Because back then it was perceived that LBJ was the guy who was going to deliver. My parents thought this, and this came through to me—LBJ was the guy who was going to deliver us from whatever this racial thing was. I wasn't clear on exactly what it was. All I knew was that somehow we weren't free and LBJ was going to save us from that and he was good."

RUSH: "You were too young to know this, but your parents weren't: it was Bobby Kennedy and JFK who had bugged Dr. King."

SNERDLEY: "We didn't know it at the time."

RUSH: "Bull Connor was a Democrat. All those segregationists in the South were Democrats."

SNERDLEY: "Didn't know it at the time. Did not know it, and many Democrats still don't know it. Many Black Democrats, if they knew the history of the Democrat Party, would run from it immediately. But they don't know that history. That history is not taught in school. Nothing else is, either."

RUSH: [Laughs]

SNERDLEY: "But you make conservatism something that people can understand. One of the things you said, and I couldn't believe the first time you said this, was that the Democrat Party was intent on systematically enslaving people politically."

My reaction was, *I don't know whether I can go there.*

Let's Go There

The political world was going *insane in the membrane* in the '90s and *crazy* in the 2000s. Scrolling social media or watching cable news seems like a portal to some depressing dystopian world. Despite the fact that humans can now communicate instantaneously across the world, some themes dominating the national conversation seem to be taking us backward, and deeper into hatred. Today we have the 1619 Project, systemic racism, critical race theory, white privilege, voter suppression, Black Lives Matter, defund the police, and anti-racism.

Most liberal theories and historical perspectives are so flawed it's hard to understand why they keep gaining traction in society, schools, and politics.

I think one reason for this is that the intellectual and theoretical arguments often put forth by conservatives are not perceived as addressing the real-life issues people struggle with. Liberals have spent the better part of a century claiming they understand the problems of the lower and middle classes. They have successfully demonized the Republican and conservative brand as being uncaring, insensitive, out-of-touch bigots who hate minorities, migrants, the elderly, school children, single mothers, the environment, science, gays, poor people, and foreigners. According to progressives and liberals, Republicans want to introduce legislation that would cause Medicare to "wither on the vine." They want to rob hungry, helpless children of their school breakfasts and lunches. They want to take Social Security away from Grammy and then push her—in her wheelchair—over a cliff. (These are all themes Democrats actually ran in campaign advertisements.)

Republicans supposedly want to "restrict your right to vote," as opposed to providing measures that would support election integrity. They want to "ignore science," as opposed to protecting constitutionally guaranteed individual freedom and liberties. Democrat perspectives are regurgitated every day in the mainstream press, using Democrat talking points and narratives, which are taught in schools at all levels. Unless people actively seek out facts, read, watch alternative news sources, or listen to talk radio, they may never hear a dissenting voice that's different from what is put forward in mass communication outlets.

When everyday Americans have a pressing issue—be it unemployment, crime, health care, money, or education—any proposed solution can sound like a good solution. And when bad ideas are the only ideas you hear, you'll probably pick some bad ideas to believe in. Communism was a really bad idea and resulted in the oppression and death of millions of people. But it was accepted as a solution in countries with huge problems that impacted the lives of everyday people. Today, President Biden and "the squad" are following the same little red book.

We conservatives can find plenty to laugh at when leftist Democrats offer what we consider to be "hair-brained" solutions. But often, we don't cry or rage at some of the problems everyday people face. If we are going to speak to a larger audience, and to grow our political base, we cannot be satisfied with just destroying liberal arguments. We have to present Americans from every walk of life with winning ideas that help solve pressing problems—based on a constitutionally sound framework.

As some of these leftist themes emerged, Rush spoke out. And as they continue, I feel compelled to *go there* and shed some light on these subjects, along with some memories and quotes from El Rushbo. Let's start with a little history.

The 1619 Project

I was open to the idea of the 1619 Project because I believe the way history is taught in public schools is seriously flawed. But then I read the article that started all the fuss.

The project's originally stated goal in Nikole Hannah-Jones's 2019 editorial in the *New York Times* was to "reframe the country's history" and bring racism and slavery into our historical narrative. One of her assertions was that this country's actual founding was in 1619 when the first slaves were brought to Virginia. For this, she won a Pulitzer Prize in 2020. But her version of history is, and was, biased and incorrect. The *New York Times* even made corrections to her article but did so without the usual notices.

The article and the debate around it are a mess. In our public schools, there's probably too little taught about the evil of slavery, *and* too little taught about the greatness of the United States.

Stating that America really began in 1619 also misses the point, because the United States was founded in 1776. And if you really want to go back to the history of the Americas, go back to the 1500s and St. Augustine, Florida, which is the oldest city in America. Historians are rediscovering what a true melting pot this city was from its beginning. Various cultures and races—including Blacks—lived together freely and peacefully in St. Augustine.

We have a very American-centric history taught in our schools, when in fact, the American story is part of a larger world story that is very rarely put into context. But I don't agree with putting the horror of slavery into a narrow perspective meant to victimize Black Americans. The project's narrative is that white people are evil and that white men are the worst of the bunch. That's an ignorant perspective that completely ignores world history and American history. As we've discussed, white male leaders and citizens gave their lives to try to right the wrong of slavery. And the very fact that a Black professor like Hannah-Jones is in a position of influence—along with an ever-growing number of her peers—negates her argument. If we're going to try to argue with the way history is taught, we at least ought to be intellectually and factually honest.

Rush made comments from time to time about our nation's "original sin" of slavery—wondering if we would ever truly be able to overcome it as a country. He and I spoke about the issue openly, and we were on the same page.

> *"So, the* New York Times *is suggesting that that's the date that America really began, 1619, when slaves first came, and therefore the* New York Times *points out that everything that's happened since then has happened on the backs of slaves. Whatever America is, whatever America has accomplished, whatever America has achieved has been illegitimate, has been tainted, is unjust, is immoral, because it's built on the backs of slaves."* —RL

Whenever Democrats face a crisis, the first thing they do is pull out the Black pawn and say, "What you're doing is ... racist!" If you want to lower taxes on corporations, it's racist. If you don't want to raise the minimum wage—which raises unemployment, by the way—it's racist. No matter what the policy argument is, one of the first things Democrats usually do is call it racist. And the result is a culture of perceived victimhood.

Black people used to have the lowest rate of abortion in America in the 1950s and now have the highest rate. No one talks about those Black babies harvested by Planned Parenthood—which was founded by eugenicist Margaret Sanger. She believed the human race could be improved by selective breeding. Let's just say if she bred turkeys, she'd produce ones with only white meat.

Colin Kaepernick is the perfect example of the "I'm-the-victim" mentality. Here's a multimillionaire who ascended to the highest ranks of competitive sports. Because sports is intended to be merit based, his performance on the field was scrutinized by the numbers, and the numbers weren't looking great. So, what does he do? He kneels down and says, "America bad, America racist." Then he gets another bunch of idiot, multi-millionaire, mostly Black players, to kneel down with him. What they're experiencing in America wouldn't be possible anywhere else in the world, yet still they say, "America bad."

This deviates from the American values and common sense summed up by one of the greatest basketball players who will ever live, Michael Jordan. As he said: "Republicans buy sneakers, too."

"We don't want to tell anybody how to live. That's up to you. If you want to make the best of yourself, feel free. If you want to ruin your life, we'll try to stop it,

but it's a waste. We look over the country as it is today, we see so much waste, human potential that's been destroyed by fifty years of a welfare state. By a failed war on poverty." —RL

The 1619 Project is a distraction. As always, proponents will seek to gain personal power and profit. Regardless, let's offer an alternative.

Black Lives Matter?

When I was about seventeen, my dear friend Fountain got a new Dodge Charger, a beautiful, yellow muscle car his mom bought him for graduating high school with honors. Every time we were in that car, the cops would pull us over. Every time. Why? Because we were two young Black guys driving a new car. *Driving while Black* is real. After a half-dozen of these stops, Fountain's mother *got real* at the police station and demanded to know why this injustice kept happening. She knew, and they knew, and it kept happening.

As a driver in Nassau County, I was pulled over more times than I can count, and I can count pretty high. I don't have any hard feelings about it anymore, although I was pissed at the time. As I got older, I decided I was not going to be bitter about it. But I do understand why Black people get upset by crap like that. Because it happens and it's wrong.

Most white people have not experienced profiling, so it's difficult to understand when Black people are bitching. Let's be real. And don't tell me I'm stereotyping, OK? Most white people have the experience and attitude of, "Oh, the police-man, he's our neighbor. And he's really nice."

To this I say, *Well, they ain't stopping you or your kids for no reason. If they were stopping your kids, you'd be pissed off too. OK?*

So let's talk about police, Derek Chauvin, and George Floyd. Again, I've heard knee-jerk reactions from some conservatives trying to justify that death. Yes, we should support our police, and we are all innocent until proven guilty. But George Floyd was murdered. Rush and I discussed it, agreed, and he spoke out clearly about the case.

> *"This Minneapolis situation and George Floyd. I mean it. I hope these cops are dealt with good and hard. I've seen the video like everybody else, and it makes me so mad I can't see straight. [. . .] What policy is there anywhere that mandates that kind of treatment of a suspect or prisoner who is totally under control? [. . .] I understand people are out there calling it murder. It makes me so mad, I can't see straight." —RL*

I respect and honor law enforcement. Cops head into situations and neighborhoods that nobody else would want to go into. I believe that almost all people who wear badges serve because they want to help their communities. But some of those good cops know about the rogue ones and haven't spoken out. In the same way, Black communities have to stop protecting criminals.

If you draw a weapon on police and you get shot, too fucking bad. You don't pull weapons on police because they have the legal authority to kill you under those circumstances. And most of the time, not all of the time, the civilian in question has a criminal record. *Gasp!* Sorry, but it's true. And if that criminal wasn't killed by the police, he'd be the last guy you'd want walking around your neighborhood. Much of the BLM outrage is hypocritical. People in the community think, *I don't want him near my children, thank you.* But when thugs get killed by the police they become heroes and martyrs. No, many were criminals—and stupid ones at that for pulling a gun on a cop.

If Black people in America are tired of having Black people shot by police, they should teach their children not to be criminals. Also, remind your children that police have guns and they will kill you if they think they're threatened. When a thug confronts an officer with an attitude of *fuck the police*, they might just say, "F-you, I have a gun." You cannot encourage or tolerate disrespectful interaction with police officers and have a peaceful and prosperous community.

If constituents are repeatedly told that police are evil, racist, and responsible for every problem in their life, some people will commit violence against police. As of the summer of 2021, thirty-six police officers had been shot. And that's just in the city of Chicago. After all the protests, riots, and cries to defund the police throughout 2020, acts of violence against police—and ordinary citizens—have increased greatly in many cities.

Juan Williams wrote a very brave column in June 2021. He admitted that he was afraid for his life because of the recent surge of homicides by Black men against other Black men. He cited this statistic: "Eighty-nine percent of Blacks who were murdered in 2019 were killed by other Black people, according to the FBI." If Black lives did matter, Black Lives Matter would be up in arms about that statistic. And they would hold rallies at every Planned Parenthood center across America, where Black lives are being terminated before they start. How can Black lives matter when they won't address the main driver of Black deaths outside of the womb, which is young Black men killing other young Black men? Look what happens in Chicago every single weekend. Guns are not the problem—the root issue is a fundamental lack of respect for life, which has permeated our culture.

Rush spoke often, on and off the air, about what BLM really is.

> *"Black Lives Matter, by the way, is simply the rebirth of Occupy Wall Street under racial auspices. It is a manufactured left-wing agitator group made to look like an organic, neighborhood, community-organized group. It is bought and paid for. It has a mission, which is to agitate and attack." —RL*

BLM exaggerates, distorts, and manipulates certain events, mixes in large doses of white liberal guilt, and ignores the larger cultural crisis. Why? Because it's an effective way for their leaders to gain power and money—enabled by the media and the Democrat Party. And many of their leaders have cashed in.

Although I take great exception to elected politicians profiting off their positions, you might be surprised to know that I don't see anything wrong with *honest* capitalism, even in the case of these hypocritical figureheads. I simply wish they would encourage other Black Americans to be enterprising, to prosper, to move into safe neighborhoods—and to stop blaming white people.

To a large degree, BLM and "defund the police" are funded by leftists, not by people in mostly Black communities. In 2020 in Minneapolis, an anti-police nonprofit organization received $500,000 from a George Soros–linked group. As Rush always illuminated, we must follow the money—the strings are being tensioned by rich liberals.

> *"Look how quickly, look how quickly the political movement behind all this has been able to effect this kind of change. They've turned a bunch of white, millennial young people into people that hate law enforcement on the basis that—it's white supremacy, it's white privilege or what have you. Nothing could be further from the truth. But that's how successful they have been in their political efforts." —RL*

Democrat policies of releasing violent offenders from jail makes policing even more difficult and makes communities less safe for the people the Democrats pretend to care about. The same goes for policies that eliminate prosecution for stealing less than $950 worth of merchandise. When you tell people they won't be prosecuted for stealing a certain amount, many people will steal almost that amount, and some will do it every day. *Shocker!* Maybe they'll even steal a calculator so they can make sure they're within the "legal" limit of larceny.

As usual, there's a big difference between what Black leaders are spouting and what ordinary citizens of all colors want. Conservative candidates have a huge opportunity to be a voice for reason and solutions, if we will take the time to talk with people.

Critical Race Theory

Here's my summation of critical race theory: this is just more anti-white, racist propaganda. It's designed to make white people feel guilty about their heritage and the role of a few of their ancestors, based on the fact that Black people and others have been oppressed in America. So we're supposed to look *critically* at the role of white people in America and blame them for everything.

First of all, CRT is a sorry-ass excuse for a theory. A scientific theory should include more than ten minutes of critical thinking and review of basic facts. Secondly, this propaganda is called Marxist and rightly so, because it's the same old class conflict song, but instead of rich versus poor, this chorus is all about Black versus white. Any theory you come up with about race is wrong. It usually ends up with some version of "this group is superior and that group is inferior, someone's to blame or someone is not to blame," and always ends with a generalization about race—which is the core of racism.

Ideas like this take away the responsibility of individual achievement and put that responsibility on a group. *If Black people aren't doing well in the United States today, it's the fault of the group of white people that's keeping the group of Black people down.* To me, nothing could be further from the truth. CRT is another ploy to enrich leaders and keep the masses down. Yet some people continue to sing the same old negro spiritual.

> "There are certain right-wing media venues . . . that monetize and capitalize on stoking the fear and resentment of a white population . . . You would think . . . that the Republican Party would be engaged in a significant debate about how are we gonna deal with the economy and what are we gonna do about climate change [but] lo and behold, the single most important issue to them apparently right now is critical race theory. Who knew that was the threat to our Republic?"
>
> —BARACK OBAMA, JUNE 8, 2021

Groupthink is a killer because it squashes individual ambition and accomplishment. President Obama tweeted congratulations to the winner of the 2021 National Spelling Bee, fourteen-year-old Zaila Avant-garde.

> "Three Guinness World Records (related to her prowess at basketball dribbling) and now the National Spelling Bee champ! Congrats, Zaila—your hard work is paying off. We're all proud of you."
>
> —BARACK OBAMA

Let's put aside, for the moment, the skewed Barack Obama and Elizabeth Warren philosophy of "you didn't build that yourself. Somebody else built that road; somebody else made it possible." How did this young, Black lady achieve such success—especially against "systemic racism" in our educational system and so many white people? Obama said it himself in the tweet: *hard work*. Zaila said she studied 13,000 words per day, for several years. By the way, she is home-schooled. That explains why she may have missed the message of CRT from the largest teachers' union in the country.

In July 2021, the National Education Association (NEA) approved a measure saying critical race theory is "reasonable and appropriate" for children, and approved increasing its implementation in K–12 classrooms. The three-million-member union also embraced the 1619 Project.

While it was on a roll, the NEA also voted to go after anyone who disagrees. Here's a quote from its resolution: "NEA will research the organizations attacking educators doing anti-racist work and/or use the research already done and put together a list of resources and recommendations for state affiliates, locals, and individual educators to utilize when they are attacked."

In a July 2021 rally in support of teaching critical race theory in public schools, a Fairfax County PTA leader said this about parents who opposed CRT: "Let them die." The crowd, which was organized by Democrats, was horrified and denounced that statement, right? Wrong. They cheered.

It's on.

But remember, instead of fighting fire with fire, we need to fight fire with water. Let's seize the moment to encourage legislation that supports school choice, so *parents* can decide which schools are best suited for their children.

Systemic Racism

I do believe in systemic racism. It's in every blue city in America.

Look at the failing schools in Democrat-controlled cities. Their liberal leaders and teachers' unions don't care and continue to push Black kids through the school system without educating them.

> *"If enough Americans can be persuaded of all that—that America is inherently racist, that America is and has been a lie—then it's over. That is the objective, and we are in the midst of it. Sometimes you're so close to the forest you don't see the trees. That's what we are in the midst of here: an ongoing effort to erase America by discrediting the entire premise, our culture, our history, our founding. The objective is to create in as many American minds as possible that America as founded is not worth defending." —RL*

The Black politicians who represent these areas remain in power every year because they spout the same old grievances. "Oh, you're victims—and I'm here to help." They receive the votes and the money, but they never help. Where's the money being spent? It stays in the same hands. That's the

Black bloodsucker crowd. Take Maxine Waters, who's living high off the hog in a house that none of her constituents could dream of affording. She's represented them for years, and she's gotten richer. Most of them are still poor.

In Queens, New York—my old neighborhood—over the past few decades, the median income of Blacks often ranked higher than the median income of whites. That's largely because of a high number of two-parent families who came in from Caribbean nations, set up as entrepreneurs, worked hard, saved their money, educated their children, and embraced the traditional values middle-class people hold as part of the American dream.

For the most part, the people who are wealthy in this country earned their wealth, and Black Americans are fully capable of doing the same thing. We are not an inferior people, despite what the left would have you believe. Some African nations are even reconsidering reliance on foreign aid because they see it can stifle self-reliance and economic growth.

But let's remember the inspirational words of candidate Joe Biden—and current disseminator of CRT literature—whose Freudian slips need no interpretation. "Poor kids are just as bright and just as talented as white kids."

The left loves to tell us that institutions are systemically racist. No, institutions are institutions. There may be instances of racist behavior, but we also have legal remedies for discrimination. If there is a discriminatory behavior but no corresponding legal action to counter it, either go to court or stop the slogans and stop lying to gain personal power.

"The bottom line is, liberalism doesn't work; social-ism doesn't work. It's an on-display-in-front-of-our-face failure, and the only excuse, 'Well, at least we're trying. We love people. We're compassionate. We're trying to do something. Our intentions with the Great Society were to wipe out poverty. Our intentions with the war on poverty [were] to wipe out poverty.'

"Well, you failed. 'Well, yeah, but we're not supposed to look at that because my intentions are what count.' But I think it's very plain as day. It's one of the sources of my frustration, because none of this is theoretical anymore. We don't have to rely on theory to tell people this doesn't work. We've been living it since 1964." —RL

Voter Suppression

"I see dead people." That's what the Georgia secretary of state probably said when he reviewed the voter rolls in 2021 and found that over eighteen thousand deceased persons were still in the voter registration database. His office also removed over one hundred thousand "obsolete and outdated" voter files.

I'll skip all the bullshit about "voter intimidation" and go straight to the core of the suppression lie. We're told by folks like Stacey Abrams and Kamala Harris that Black people are too stupid to get valid identification. They aren't as articulate and honest as I am, but that's what their argument concludes. And of course, racist Republicans now want to suppress Black votes by asking people who vote to show some identification.

American companies run by liberal CEOs, like Delta Airlines, go along with this stupidity. Last time I flew on an airline, I needed to prove who I was about three times before I could even get near a jet. No ID, no fly. Yet, the CEO and a swarm of penitent liberals bitch and moan about how unjust it is to ask for proper identification before you vote.

News flash! Black people across America have Medicare and Medicaid cards—and they had to show ID to get them. To have a job, or to receive government benefits, you have to show ID. Want some cigarettes? Bring your identification. How about a COVID-19 vaccination? Most sites required some form of ID.

On one hand, American citizens whose families have been here for generations are told that it is racist that they should have to present an ID to vote. I really enjoy asking my liberal friends about this. "Who runs your city? If it's true that Black people don't have identification, why in the past twenty years haven't Democrats made sure that the Black folks who live in their communities get a piece of ID?"

The second question I ask is, how are Republicans suppressing your vote? Democrats in these districts *own* the districts. Republicans are nowhere near there. How is it possible that Republicans, sneaky little bastards, can go where Black Democrats run the community and suppress Black people's vote? They're not.

Stay with me. I'm just getting started.

At the same time, Democrats broadcast their message to illegal immigrants: "Come to the United States, amigo! We'll

take you to the DMV and *give* you a special driver's license."
In the same breath, Democrats tell Black constituents, "Yeah,
we've been in charge of your neighborhood for a hundred
years, and you still can't get an ID, poor thing," while they
literally create and fund programs to give government-issued
identification to illegal immigrants. Does this make any sense
to anybody except for Democrats?

"Anti-Racism"

I hate the idea that you can't talk about things concerning race
without being called a racist. I don't think people should feel,
or be indoctrinated to believe, that something's wrong with
them because they have a certain shade of skin. I don't like the
whining about "white privilege." Can you imagine where this
insanity will lead? The next outrage will be skinny privilege.
*You've been skinny all your life so you have certain privileges
that fat people don't have.* Well, duh! Human beings discriminate. But we have to learn how to discriminate wisely, and
that's the challenge for all of us.

The best way to show the utter stupidity of anti-racist
rhetoric is to simply quote one of the founders of this garbage
and author of *How to Be an Antiracist*, Ibram X. Kendi.
"The only remedy to past discrimination is present discrimination. The only remedy to present discrimination is future
discrimination."

Really? How can conservatives *not* win an honest and
compassionate debate against this utter crap? Well, we've
managed to screw up the conversation in the past. Let's do
better.

Rush and Race

We had an incredibly diverse staff at EIB. Issues such as race and gender were non-issues in the office. But currently, in our country, the problem with race is that we fixate on it too much.

The EIB family did not have a government mandate to be diverse. We were diverse because Rush believed in merit. We were a meritocracy. People were chosen to work based on their skill set. Their personal lives and ethnicities did not matter. We didn't need sensitivity training and we sure as hell didn't have a chief diversity officer. Rush picked the best people, simple as that.

Nobody wants racism, yet the left's "solutions" seem to increase racial tension. When Obamacare was put into place, everything changed at the doctors' offices. My long patient questionnaires now had new lines asking about my race. I've had to fill out a lot of those forms in the last fifteen years, and when asked about my racial identity, I always choose the final option—a blank line where I write: *human.*

We can keep dividing ourselves up into a million inter- sectional groups. Or we can face the fact that we are all part of one race—the human race. If we started looking at each other through what we have in common, our lives and our world would be a whole lot better. For fifteen hours per week, that's what happened with Rush on the radio. He was equally straightforward about challenges as he was about opportuni- ties we all share as citizens of this republic.

Very few of us go through life without some major chal- lenges. We can let those struggles define us, or we can make a choice to do the best we can. I certainly don't want to stay pissed off at everybody while I'm here. Life is too short.

This might sound flippant to people who are going through recurring disappointment or the worst days of their lives. I understand what it is to go through the worst days and feel alone. I know what it's like to be heartbroken and doubt you'll ever recover. I understand what it feels like to lose somebody, to lose your job, and not have any money. I've been through all this and more. Sometimes I have a bad day, but I try, even on the bad days, to remember that there are good days ahead and the pain doesn't have to define the rest of my life.

SHOW NOTES

Racism is still a problem in this country, and around the world. But I have an answer to racism. The solution is two words: *achieve anyway.*

You may run into racism. Achieve anyway. Don't let someone else limit your success.

If you think someone hates you because you're Black or whatever, and you let that affect your life, shame on you. Achieve anyway. Why do you give others so much power over your future? To allow someone else's discrimination over racial matters to affect your life is your problem.

To my mind, racism is a disease. Some people catch the disease of racism, diagnose it, work to remove it, and heal. Others are infected with racism like it's leprosy—it oozes from them in ugliness. But why would I let a racist affect how I live my life? If you're Black in America, be free. You're free. *Be* free. It's really simple. Achieve anyway.

If you live in the United States, you live in the greatest nation in the world. You can achieve even if somebody throws obstacles in your way.

No matter who or what is trying to hold you back, achieve anyway.

A Recent Message from a Listener

"Sorry for your loss, Snerdley! However, it's our loss, too! I mourn the loss of Rush but I celebrate his legacy. I listened to Rush since New York, late 90, after I came to the US! My English wasn't that great but I can sense I was at the right place. This man keeps telling me the American dream is alive and well. He keeps telling me America is an exception. If there was a conservative party, I would have been a member, because of Rush. His unconditional love for America was untouchable! I love his sense of optimism in the midst of chaos.

"I was able to get through to his radio show, once, while I was living in Miami. It was a great day for me. I exchanged with the man I so long admired and listened to via radio waves. I told him, after you put me through, 'Rush, this your African brother.' I made my point and we laughed. At the end, he offered me an iPhone 7, which I still have! No, I have not met Rush in person, but I met him every single day through the waves! May the heavens celebrate this gain, our loss! Be strong, Snerdley, you are NOT alone!"

I'm just a guy on the radio.

—RUSH LIMBAUGH

12

HIGHEST CIVILIAN HONOR

On the morning of February 3, 2020, Rush gathered the highly overrated staff in the EIB Southern Command to tell us about his diagnosis of advanced lung cancer. He broke the news to his audience that afternoon.

The next morning, while I was still in shock, I got a call from my good friend Sean Hannity. He told me to make sure I tuned in to watch President Trump's State of the Union address that night. "It's going to be special," he said. "Don't miss it!"

Obviously, Rush knew he would be attending the State of the Union address, but I really do believe he was surprised that the award would be presented to him that night. As Rush told the story, several days before the event, he was at the hospital, preparing to start his cancer treatment when he got the call from the president asking if he could come to Washington, DC. "Well, no, Mr. President, I can't." But Donald Trump was insistent. "You have to come," he told Rush. "You have to be here."

"It was a once in a lifetime thing. It's so special and the president was not going to let me miss it. He was not going to let me talk him or myself out of appearing in the House chamber that night." —RL

That evening I watched my friend Rush Limbaugh seated in the halls of Congress between his wife, Kathryn, and the First Lady, Melania Trump. The president went on to praise Rush and announced he would be awarded the Medal of Freedom, the highest civilian honor in the country. I could see the surprised look on Rush's face because the award is usually presented in a White House ceremony. But, no, the president had something else in mind. When Melania turned to present the medal, my heart sang as I saw the astonished expression on Rush's face.

Freedom and Courage
Here are President Trump's words on that special night.

"Here tonight is a special man, beloved by millions of Americans, who just received a stage 4 advanced cancer diagnosis. This is not good news, but what is good news is that he is the greatest fighter and winner that you will ever meet. Rush Limbaugh, thank you for your decades of tireless devotion to our country.

"And, Rush, in recognition of all that you have done for our nation, the millions of people a day that you speak to and that you inspire, and all of the incredible work that you have done for charity, I am proud to announce tonight that you will be receiving our country's highest civilian honor, the Presidential Medal of Freedom. [Applause]

"I will now ask the First Lady of the United States to present you with the honor. Please. [The Medal of Freedom is presented]

"Rush and Kathryn, congratulations."

In the days that followed, accolades poured in, as did the hysteria from the left. I have to tell you, I enjoyed reading and watching it all. The left were beside themselves. *How dare this president give Rush Limbaugh the Medal of Freedom, and how dare he present it on this special night?!* But Rush's fans, millions and millions of Americans, applauded the president. We'd been waiting for decades to see Rush recognized for his tireless work shaping American politics and culture— his defense of freedom, liberty, individualism, and American exceptionalism. We were beside ourselves with joy that evening, even while we carried immense pain from hearing about his diagnosis.

I later thought to myself, *only President Trump could do this. Only he could give Rush the highest civilian honor in America, and make sure almost every elected Democrat attended the ceremony.* It was a joyous celebration for Rush fans, one that we will never forget.

I've probably watched every State of the Union address since Lyndon Johnson was in office. I have never had the kind of reaction I had that night watching my guy, my hero, my boss, Rush Limbaugh, receiving his just due, which was worldwide recognition for the good he had created with his incredible career. I spoke with a fellow broadcaster afterward who is not a political guy. "I don't follow politics," he told me, "but I do know this: there are two names that define conservatism. One is Ronald Reagan, who was often called 'the Great Communicator,' and the other is Rush Limbaugh."

I agree, but not necessarily in that order.

MAGA Dittos

In June 2021, I had the honor of interviewing former president Donald Trump on my WABC radio show. I began our conversation by asking him what he thought Rush's legacy would be.

"More than anything else, freedom and courage. You know, he had guts. [. . .] Rush would talk about anything that was appropriate to talk about. These other people, even the good ones, they're good people but they want to be politically correct. They don't want to say anything that's too controversial. And that's what made him successful, Bo. You know that better than anybody. You may be one guy that knows it better than I do. Rush was a man who had tremendous courage and he had tremendous principle, and if he believed in something, he'd talk about it, and who had an audience like him? [. . .] Nobody will ever replace him. He's a courageous person and he loved our country."

I then asked President Trump about awarding Rush the Medal of Freedom.

"That was a great evening and I've never seen anything like it. One side was going crazy, in a positive way, and the other side was dead silent. But you know what, you looked at the eyes of the other side—they knew he deserved it."

Indeed, he did deserve that honor, and so much more.

Just a Guy on the Radio?

Rush used to acknowledge his influence in a self-effacing way. "I'm just a guy on the radio," he'd say. But he was so much more. He defined what it meant to be a conservative. He could talk policy and make policy understandable to millions of Americans, who said, "Yeah, that's what I believe! You're describing my values." And that's why the Medal of Freedom ultimately found its place near Rush's heart—because he was the heart of American conservatism. And Rush's heart was always focused on his audience.

"I want to get a little personal here, this is the time of year when I often become the most reflective and thankful for all of the blessings that I have had my entire life. And the blessings I have had obviously extend to my family, the people who work, have worked here at the EIB network. Every year about this time, we get the top 50 list, the top 10 list of this or that. The best cars, the best movies, whatever.

"But there is always a group left out and it's you, the most influential audience of all of media is right here on this program. Hands down, no contest.

Because without you, none of anything that happens here would have happened, it would be all academic if it weren't for you. I cannot thank you enough. I am so humbled by it, and blown away by it. So as far as I'm concerned, you're it, you're tops, and I would have to include in this all the great radio stations that make it possible for all you to listen and be a part of this audience. I cannot express my gratitude, and for all of me and all of my family as well, thank you again. You are the most influential audience in all of media." —RL

If Rush had quit radio after he had signed the first of his multimillion-dollar deals, he could have left the brutal spotlight and spent the rest of his time playing golf. Within a few years, his critics would have moved on to other targets and Rush would have become a member of the celebrity class— famous and wealthy and in the media as little or as often as he wanted. I'm so glad he didn't take that path. Truth is, he never considered it—for very long anyway. The proof of Rush's commitment to his listeners is how he invested what would be his final year on this planet.

I watched him get behind the golden EIB microphone every day he possibly could—with courage that humbled the EIB family.

"I want to thank all of you so much for everything that you have meant to me and my family in my life.

"I understand it's mutual. And I hear people— you have made my heart grow so much that it barely

fits in my chest cavity here tonight. But the things that by virtue of your listening to my radio show and being active in this movement that we all cherish and love, you have meant more to me, my family, and my life than whatever it is I might mean to you, even though I know that's considerable.

"You still can't outdo the absolute joy and awe and thanks I feel for all of you. [...] And I can't tell you how appreciative I am and proud to be in a movement with the same passions, desires, and core beliefs that all of you have, because we know that it's right for the country, and we know it's right for people. It's not something that has to be forced on them. It's not something that has to be authoritatively pressed on them. We are what is, and that's why we are an enemy because we're effective. The people that do want control look at us as the enemy. We're always going to be—don't ever measure your success by how many drive-by media reports you see that are fair to us. Never going to happen.

"Don't measure your success by how many people like you. Just worry about how they vote. And then at the end of the day how they live, but that's really none of your business once they close the doors. Thank you all very much. It's been great." —RL

The United States was better because of Rush's voice, not only in his final year, but in every one of his thirty-three years doing the show. So many important issues would not have reached the elevated level of discourse they achieved, if not for his commitment to his audience. Rush took a deeper dive into issues than any other broadcaster. He spent hours and hours every single day researching the topics he talked about, whether it be global warming or societal issues. The way Rush diligently sourced his research is not appreciated enough, and not emulated enough today. He would talk with people in the scientific community and present their points of view into the public discourse. He delivered alternate perspectives that would otherwise not be heard—three hours a day, five days a week, for over thirty years. Few can even comprehend what a monumental task this was. But Rush had an amazing gift.

Rush had a tremendous impact on Republican Party politics, from the point of view of the grassroots voter. Those were his people. That's why he was the symbolic head of the GOP, because he spoke directly to millions across the fruited plain. He also strongly opposed establishment Republicans. For example, party leaders promised to fix immigration—for decades. They did nothing. Rush broadcast the fact they did nothing and fearlessly exposed the special interests driving their policies and their inaction. Decade after decade, so-called conservatives squandered opportunities because, to be frank, some of them are afraid to govern. They walk around in a constant state of fear over losing the next election. Rush would articulate and fight for what he believed was right, the outcomes be damned. This takes a particular type of fortitude that many Republicans apparently don't have.

I've never wanted to portray Rush Limbaugh as some kind of demigod. He was a man, in many respects like any other man. But here is where he was different from most: he was willing to stand and take the arrows the left launched—for over three decades—because he dared to speak political truth. I don't know whether I have the kind of courage to suffer what Rush went through. Maybe I'll find out, as I've now stepped back to the other side of the glass to host my own radio show.

"I always wanted to be older. When I was eight, I wanted to be ten; when I was ten, I wanted to be fifteen; when I was fifteen, I wanted to be eighteen; eighteen, twenty-one; twenty-one wanted to be thirty; when I was thirty, I wanted to be forty; when I was forty, I wanted to be fifty. And the reason is that from the moment I was able to realize certain things, it was very clear to me that older people were freer, they were independent, and they all seemed to be really enjoying things." —RL

My Next Chapter

The broadcast studio is the one place where I feel ageless. During the time I wrote these chapters, ABC shot some video of me in the studio hosting my show. When I looked at the footage, I had a bittersweet realization. The image on the screen displayed an older, bigger James Golden. *Who is that guy behind the mic?* I thought. Because when I'm behind the mic, I feel like a kid. I'm still the teenager who fell in love with radio. It's an ageless passion. I believe I could continue to do it in one form or another until the day I die—and I'd consider it a life well spent.

I've always felt my destiny was not completely in my hands, but in God's hands. *My* struggle is to be aware enough to clearly see what I'm supposed to do. Cosmic design aside, my career wasn't all serendipity. I worked for this. Every summer during my high school years, I shined shoes and cleaned apartments in the housing projects—so I could work in radio without pay.

When I did finally have a job in radio, my pay was twelve thousand dollars . . . a year. But I kept working because I loved it. In my thirties, I barely made thirty thousand dollars. That's no money when you live in New York City. I was in the radio business because I loved it. When Rush and I met, everything clicked in terms of my professional life. But if I hadn't earned a place at the table, we would have never been introduced.

> *"Nostalgia for me is never negative. It's always positive, when I think about the past and remember things of people that I've met and meant a lot to me, it's always positive, always uplifting. Never is any of it negative, never is there any anguish about it.*
> *"Do not lose the faith. Keep the faith." —RL*

When I meet the younger generation in radio today, I look at these kids and see myself—the same energy and the same excitement from simply being in a radio station. They exude the same wide-eyed silliness I used to have. I know how hard they work and how little they are paid. But they're working because they love it.

Rush's Legacy

I won't attempt to define Rush's legacy. But I will offer some thoughts for consideration.

First and foremost, Rush was an extraordinarily gifted broadcaster. His skills were such that he could make the most mundane topics seem interesting. And as I have stated in other parts of this book, he connected with people in a way that no other broadcaster has. Not just hitting listeners' funny bone, and not only appealing to their intellect, Rush connected with the *hearts* of millions of people. He loved them. And they, in return, loved him—not superficially but deeply. They still do.

Rush was also a leader who explained, defined, and evangelized conservatism as a winning political ideology. In so doing, he attracted millions who agreed that the conservative ideology was a reflection of their values and beliefs. He was as much a political leader as he was a broadcaster. He was as much a humanitarian and a philanthropist as he was a political leader or a broadcaster. He was a complex personality. And in everything he did, he strove for excellence.

He loved the United States. He appreciated the people of this country and he felt the love the audience had for him. I was a fan of Rush Limbaugh's before he was my boss and friend. When I speak with listeners about their love and respect for the man, I confess that I feel the same way and say, "I just had a better seat." They were in their cars and I was in the studio. But we grew to know the same man. And I'm no different from the millions of ditto heads who are still grieving because he is gone. I'm just like you.

Rush Limbaugh was a generous, caring, loyal friend.

"I've learned a lot in life, and I hope everybody does as they grow older, it's the whole point of things. And I remember back to the first days and weeks and years when this show started. And there was no grand strategy to it. It had a big, overarching goal: be great, be the best show, be the number one show documented by ratings and audience research, the number one.

"That was the objective. There was no plan on how to do it, and there wasn't any five-year plan, three-year plan, or any of this. It was just me being myself each and every day here on the radio. And then, as that happened, everybody began analyzing it. People that I worked with, people in the media. They could not avoid it. People were analyzing what I was doing. And I had to make sure to never read any of that and to never listen to any of it.

"The last thing I wanted to know was what I was doing so that I could consciously continue to try. Because once you have to consciously continue to try what you already are, you're gonna stop being what you already are and you're gonna start trying to copy what you think you are. The danger when you try to keep being who you are, you stop being who you are. Being who you are shouldn't require any effort at all. Who you are au natural is who you are.

"The minute you start trying to be who you are—I had to resist it. I mean, there were a lot of

well-intentioned people that said, 'Well, if you want to keep this up, you're gonna have to change. If you want to keep this up, if you wanna really be doing this a long time, you'll have to moderate this and change a little bit.' Some of them well-intentioned, some of them weren't, but it didn't matter because none of it was right.

"And it's another reason why I've never listened to anybody else who does this. I don't want to even inadvertently start copying other people and not be who I am. And being who I am in the sense of what interests me, what doesn't. If I start trying to imagine, for example, every day what all of you want to hear, I'm finished. And I don't mean this humorously or ... It's a decent thing. Loving yourself is very important, folks.

"Not bragging about yourself or being sick about it, but if you don't like yourself, if you're not comfortable with who you are, then you're gonna always try to be something you're not, and you're finished 'cause everybody's gonna recognize you as a phony eventually." —RL

Our Legacy

Looking ahead, the question is, *what is our role in honoring Rush's legacy?*

If you'll permit me, I suggest we take what we've learned regarding what is great about our country and put it into action in our local communities and spheres of influence. Go to local school board and city council meetings. Run for office.

Our action does not have to be "big." I'm simply suggesting we take our engagement up *one* notch. If you consider your efforts too small to make a difference, consider the positive influence of twenty-seven million listeners. And consider the impact of Rush's voice. If you've never sent an email to an elected leader, compose one—keeping in mind that new conservatives offer solutions that help people and solve problems. Then send your email this week.

If you've never been to a school board meeting, attend one. The same goes with local, state, and federal government meetings. Ask questions. Meet your neighbors. Support those who hold your values. Show love and respect for those who hold different views. Speak up respectfully in defense of your ideas. Love is our motivation.

Another way to honor Rush is to follow his example in our own lives.

I invested over thirty years of my life in a supporting role. So did many amazing people in the EIB family. Was it worth it? Yes. Do I wonder where I'd be if I had pursued my career behind the microphone? Yeah, sometimes. But there's honor and satisfaction in helping people pursue their goals. If you're in that position today, give it all you have. But don't give up on your own dreams. As for me, I've decided to dust off those dreams and practice what I preach. It's not too late for you to do the same. And it's a good thing *James on the radio* is ageless when he's behind the microphone.

One of the hallmarks of *The Rush Limbaugh Show* was the fact that a significant portion of every episode was about the listener. I know from countless conversations with Rush that one of the most rewarding aspects of the show was hearing from people who were inspired by his example and made decisions to go after their interests.

What would have happened to Rush's talent if he didn't pay attention to—and follow—his love for a certain enterprise? His, and mine, were radio. What's your passion? Will you follow it?

What would have happened to Rush's dream if he had quit radio after being fired for the first time? How about after being fired the *seventh* time? What can *you* accomplish if you won't give up?

What would have happened in Rush's career if he did not relentlessly pursue excellence? Perfection is not possible, but excellence is—and it makes all the difference.

What would have happened to our nation if Rush didn't speak up—and keep speaking up? Will you speak up?

Make your mark, in your unique way.

Talent, on Loan

I'd like to leave you with this. During the last year of his life, more than he permitted himself to in the thirty-two years before, Rush talked about his faith in God and his spiritual relationship with God, as a Christian. I think it helped many of his listeners, including me, realize the "talent on loan from God" phrase wasn't whimsical to him—it was deeply rooted in his core beliefs.

Rush often said that America was a land of "good" people—a place where ordinary people could achieve extraordinary things. His life, his repeated failures, and his ultimate successes proved the point more than words could ever convey. We all have "talents" that are loaned to us from our creator. We are all, as one mystic put it, "drops from the infinite ocean of love." Our talents are on loan, for a brief whisper of time.

"What I have is simply on loan, created by God, and it will be recalled at some point—because we're all going home someday." —RL

We can do extraordinary things with our lives. Maybe not on a massive stage with thousands or millions of people watching, reading, and listening. Maybe those extraordinary things are a thousand "little" kindnesses that nobody but you—and those you are kind to—will ever know about.

One day, like Rush, we will return our own talents back to the God who loaned them to us. I hope, whatever failures or successes might lie ahead of me, that I will be as devoted as my friend to use those talents to the best of my abilities. And when it's time to return them, that God can smile and say, "Well done," as I am sure he said to Rush.

ACKNOWLEDGMENTS

In the preceding pages, I did my best to acknowledge the many wonderful people who have been great friends, priceless mentors, and valued colleagues. There have been so many, I could not possibly have acknowledged all of you, but you know who you are and how important you have been in my life. And again, I say thank you. I wouldn't have much to write about without you.

In addition, when it comes to the book you're holding, I'd like to thank a few people who helped me bring it from concept to completion.

To my literary agent, Tom Winters, thank you for your wisdom. To the publishing team, thank you for believing in me, my voice, and the important message of this book. I'd like to thank Mike Loomis for his guidance and encouragement in the development of the manuscript. And to my longtime friend Debi Pelletier, you brought out the best in me—and occasionally the worst—to make sure the book captured my complete vocal range.

I owe an enormous debt of gratitude to my friends and colleagues at WWRL, WABC, Worldstream Communications, TalkSpot, and Premiere Radio Networks.

To my bandmates with the Fabulous Flames, Cripple Crab, and New York City Part II, we are brothers eternally, and there will always be much love.

A special thanks to Linda Agyapong, Debra Barnes, Grover Belton, Donna Brossmer, Richard and Sheri Chriss, Jon Coleman, DeeDee Compton, Maria Conde, Marina DeValle, Diana DeVeer, Barbara DuHaime, Debbie DuHaime, Somers and Jonathan Farkas, Teresa Felix, Laura Gerking, Dr. Thyonne Gordon, Dale Hill, Deborah Hofler, Veronica Hofler, Melissa Howe, Ana Johnson, Marsha Karopf, Kim, Stephen Limbaugh III, Chris McCarty, Judith Olsen, Star Parker, Kerry Picket, Angel Rogers, Scott Schaefer, Dr. Daniel Weiner, Dr. Brad Weiss, and Marjorie Wolfe.

And thank you, Michele Kirk.

Thank you to my team at Golden Age Consulting Group, New Journey PAC (NewJourneyPac.org), and Lisa Cathie, my friend and business partner, for the excellence you bring every single day.

Finally, I want to thank *you* for reading this book and sharing it with your friends. I hope it has inspired you to use your voice and talents.

Achieve anyway.

NOTES

Chapter 1: On Loan from God

"I became a doctor thanks to you": https://www.rushlimbaugh.com/daily/2020/03/02/caller-to-rush-you-inspired-me-to-become-a-doctor/.

"We lost our best player": https://video.foxnews.com/v/6233560262001#sp=show-clips.

Chapter 2: Meeting of the Minds

"I was brought to New York": https://www.iheart.com/podcast/1119-rush-limbaugh-the-man-beh-81488209/.

"When I moved to New York": https://www.iheart.com/podcast/1119-rush-limbaugh-the-man-beh-81488209/episode/behind-great-broadcasters-82966924/.

"Before Rush's national program": Arbitron "Radio Today," report, 2013, https://www.businesswire.com/news/home/20130801005493/en/The-Rush-Limbaugh-Show-Celebrates-25-Years-in-Syndication.

"Now, 1988 you have to remember": https://www.rushlimbaugh.com/daily/2017/04/24/kate-obeirne-godmother-of-the-modern-conservative-movement/.

"I thought it would be helpful": https://www.rushlimbaugh.com/daily/2019/08/01/31-years-of-donations-to-worthy-causes-by-you-the-people-who-make-the-country-work/.

"I know precisely when I first heard Rush": https://www.steynonline.com/11078/the-indispensable-man.

Chapter 3: The Highly Overrated Staff: Southern Command

"I wanted to issue a special thanks": https://www.rushlimbaugh.com/daily/2018/08/03/thank-you-to-my-brother-and-the-highly-overrated-staff/.

"I'm sorry, folks": https://www.rushlimbaugh.com/daily/2013/09/11/a_speech_about_not_doing_something/.

"I'm just teasing the highly overrated staff": https://www.rushlimbaugh.com/daily/2014/03/28/caller_suggests_new_labor_intensive_project_for_the_highly_overrated_eib_staff/.

"Back in, I guess it was March": https://www.rushlimbaugh.com/daily/2010/06/15/rush_limbaugh_describes_the_happiest_weekend_of_his_life/.

"Dawn Bachinski is a brilliant, hardworking person": https://www.iheart.com/podcast/1119-rush-limbaugh-the-man-beh-81488209/episode/eib-southern-command-family-82708134/.

"You can't have a better prize": https://www.rushlimbaugh.com/daily/2013/12/05/last_chance_visit_eib_southern_command/.

"By the way, Snerdley": https://www.rushlimbaugh.com/daily/2010/08/11/rush_kathryn_s_wedding_photos_posted_on_our_new_facebook_page/.

Chapter 4: The Highly Overrated Staff: New York to Los Angeles

"I knew that I was": https://www.rushlimbaugh.com/daily/2013/04/24/a_college_senior_writing_a_paper_on_why_this_show_is_so_successful/.

"Diana Schneider (Allocco), the editrix": https://www.rushlimbaugh.com/daily/2007/07/19/der_schlick_on_hillary_war2/.

"We don't get a lot of calls": https://www.iheart.com/podcast/1119-rush-limbaugh-the-man-beh-81488209/episode/the-limbaugh-letter-84786282/.

"Snerdley interviewed me": https://www.rushlimbaugh.com/daily/2007/10/03/15th_anniversary_limbaugh_letter/.

"You know, I was telling": https://www.rushlimbaugh.com/daily/2018/08/01/cnns-breaking-news-on-rush-and-trump-sparks-a-monologue/.

"Yes, over 30 years": https://www.rushlimbaugh.com/daily/2018/08/01/rush-24-7-morning-update-58/.

Chapter 5: Background Check

"Unfortunately for a lot": https://www.rushlimbaugh.com/daily/2019/12/23/my-advice-for-young-people-on-how-to-achieve-success/.

"And, by the way": https://www.rushlimbaugh.com/daily/2011/03/30/democrat_party_vs_us_taxpayer/.

"I'm just sitting here listening": https://www.rushlimbaugh.com/daily/2012/04/16/the_grooveyard_of_forgotten_favorites_pre_feminism_edition/.

"He just didn't seem interested in anything except radio": Colford, Paul D., *The Rush Limbaugh Story: Talent on Loan from God—An Unauthorized Biography*, St. Martin's Press, 1994, https://www.latimes. com/obituaries/story/2021-02-17/rush-limbaugh-conservative-radio-host-dies.

"Unfortunately for a lot": https://www.rushlimbaugh.com/ daily/2019/12/23/my-advice-for-young-people-on-how-to-achieve-success/.

"At no time": https://www.rushlimbaugh.com/daily/2014/08/01/eib_ anniversary_el_rushbo_predicts_the_redskins_controversy_on_ firing_line_in_1992/.

"I grew up listening": https://podcasts.apple.com/us/podcast/ rush-limbaugh-the-man-behind-the-golden-eib-microphone/ id1564134812#see-all/reviews.

Chapter 6: Silence Is Not Golden

"The Official Program Observer": https://www.rushlimbaugh.com/ daily/2020/07/17/washington-redskins-ellen-degeneres-show-accused-of-workplace-harassment/.

"If the pattern keeps up": https://www.washingtonpost.com/archive/ lifestyle/2001/10/09/radios-rush-limbaugh-suffers-rapid-hearing-loss/ b9d23aeb-2e34-4982-b819-814629baa8e9/.

"Some in Congress called for": https://www.politico.com/story/2011/01/ fairness-doctrine-fight-goes-on-047669.

"Publications started taking aim": http://content.time.com/time/ covers/0,16641,19950123,00.html.

"When Rush actually took": https://www.heritage.org/conservatism/ commentary/why-liberals-fear-me.

"You remember the orange juice fiasco": October 2007 issue of the *Limbaugh Letter*, James Golden's interview of Rush Limbaugh.

"In May 2021": https://www.foxnews.com/us/virginia-teacher-leave-gender-speech, https://www.foxnews.com/us/virginia-tanner-cross-legal-battle, https://www.foxnews.com/politics/ virginia-loudoun-school-board-tanner-cross-backlash.

"Well, my comment is straight": https://www.rushlimbaugh.com/ daily/2019/07/10/ladies-and-gentleman-transgenders-are-invading-womens-sports/.

"As of 2020, Amazon": https://www.forbes.com/sites/ danrunkevicius/2020/09/03/how-amazon-quietly-powers-the-internet/?sh=51d484b13092.

"The drive-by media hype": https://www.rushlimbaugh.com/daily/2020/02/24/overhyped-coronavirus-weaponized-against-trump/.

"Thank you James": https://podcasts.apple.com/us/podcast/rush-limbaugh-the-man-behind-the-golden-eib-microphone/id1564134812#see-all/reviews.

"Though some people think": https://www.creators.com/read/david-limbaugh/08/18/congratulations-to-rush-for-30-remarkable-years.

Chapter 7: Rise of a Black Conservative

"Let me tell you who": https://www.c-span.org/video/?284357-3/rush-limbaugh-1951-2021.

"During his almost fifty-year": https://www.fbi.gov/history/directors/j-edgar-hoover, https://en.wikipedia.org/wiki/J._Edgar_Hoover.

"Most people want problems solved": https://www.rushlimbaugh.com/daily/2018/11/29/theyve-destroyed-the-conservative-brand-were-problem-solvers-geno/.

"Suppose a brother or a sister": James 2: 15-17. The Holy Bible, New International Version, Copyright © 1973, 1978, 1984, 2011 by Biblica, Inc. Used by permission of Zondervan.

"We want the country to succeed": https://www.c-span.org/video/?284357-3/rush-limbaugh-1951-2021.

"I know that it is a myth": https://www.rushlimbaugh.com/daily/2020/08/19/goodyear-makes-hasty-retreat-after-trump-tweet/.

"I did my good deed": https://www.rushlimbaugh.com/daily/2007/05/14/rush_rescues_turtle_on_golf_course2/amp/.

"No doubt you can": https://genius.com/Pretenders-my-city-was-gone-lyrics.

"She was on PLJ": https://www.rushlimbaugh.com/daily/2020/02/18/a-big-thank-you-to-chrissie-hynde/, https://www.dailymail.co.uk/news/article-8015581/Chrissie-Hynde-praises-Trump-honoring-Rush-Limbaugh-dad-loved-pundit.html.

"Because I don't want": https://www.rushlimbaugh.com/daily/2020/06/02/the-riots-are-an-offshoot-of-the-democrat-party/.

"If you're a sixteen-year-old": https://dos.ny.gov/cosmetology.

"Social Security, as you know": https://www.rushlimbaugh.com/daily/2017/04/17/a-revolutionary-idea-for-tax-reform-is-percolating/.

"In New York City": https://online.wsj.com/public/resources/documents/theforgottenfourth.pdf.

"In July 2021": https://www.foxnews.com/us/oregon-governor-signs-bill-suspending-math-reading-proficiency-requirements-for-hs-graduates, https://www.ksby.com/news/national/oregon-governor-passes-law-that-suspends-math-reading-proficiency-requirements-for-hs-graduates.

"It's a way to further segregation": https://www.rushlimbaugh.com/daily/2020/07/08/we-have-failed-to-fight-anti-americanism-in-public-education/.

"Look at the cheating scandal": https://www.cnn.com/2015/04/14/us/georgia-atlanta-public-schools-cheating-scandal-verdicts/index.html, https://www.cnn.com/2015/04/14/us/georgia-atlanta-public-schools-cheating-scandal-verdicts/index.html.

"Take a look at": https://www.c-span.org/video/?284357-3/rush-limbaugh-1951-2021.

"I just wanted to comment": https://www.rushlimbaugh.com/daily/2010/05/13/the_ignorant_can_make_a_difference/.

"Regardless, the message was clear": https://www.cnn.com/2016/08/19/politics/donald-trump-african-american-voters/index.html.

"A couple interesting stories here": https://www.rushlimbaugh.com/daily/2018/11/26/big-african-american-support-for-gop-in-florida-and-georgia-enrages-the-left/.

"What you probably don't know": https://www.wsj.com/articles/school-choice-moms-tipped-the-governors-florida-race-1542757880.

"We want everybody": https://www.rushlimbaugh.com/daily/2018/11/29/theyve-destroyed-the-conservative-brand-were-problem-solvers-geno/.

Chapter 8: Truth Detector

"Everything was going well": https://www.washingtonpost.com/sports/2021/02/17/rush-limbaugh-dead-espn/, https://www.espn.com/nfl/news/story?id=1627887.

"In a couple days": https://www.cnn.com/2003/SHOWBIZ/10/02/limbaugh/.

"Nothing happened that day": https://www.rushlimbaugh.com/daily/2010/10/04/the_mcnabb_comment_revisited/, https://www.rushlimbaugh.com/daily/2007/04/18/media_jealousy_caused_mcnabb_story/.

"You know, I actually": https://www.rushlimbaugh.com/daily/2009/10/13/rush_on_the_today_show_part_two/.

"Somebody wanted to know": https://www.rushlimbaugh.com/daily/2003/11/24/right_and_wrong/.

"Years earlier, in the fall": https://latimesblogs.latimes.com/sports_blog/2009/10/rush-limbaugh-rams-owner-buy-st-louis-nfl.html.

NOTES

"Jay-Z is a billionaire": https://money.cnn.com/2016/07/01/media/jay-z-business-career/.

"And the lyrics": https://www.businessinsider.com/jay-z-hillary-clinton-concert-2016-11.

"Here comes a Hillary Clinton": https://www.rushlimbaugh.com/daily/2016/11/07/trump_rocks_rally_in_sarasota_obama_repeats_despicable_kkk_scare_in_michigan/.

"Here's a quote from Joe Biden": https://www.usatoday.com/story/news/factcheck/2020/10/27/fact-check-post-partly-false-biden-1977-racial-jungle-remark/6045749002/.

"Look at the 1984 college": https://www.washingtonpost.com/local/virginia-politics/va-gov-northams-medical-school-yearbook-page-shows-men-in-blackface-kkk-robe/2019/02/01/517a43ee-265f-11e9-90cd-dedb0c92dc17_story.html.

"In June 2021": https://www.politico.com/states/florida/story/2021/06/10/gop-rep-byron-donalds-calls-cbc-silence-on-membership-delay-off-putting-1385655.

"Needless to say, Operation Chaos": https://www.rushlimbaugh.com/daily/2008/05/05/operation_chaos_goals_restated_for_all_you_nervous_conservatives/, https://en.wikipedia.org/wiki/The_Ides_of_March_(2011_film).

"But here's what most": https://www.rushlimbaugh.com/daily/2007/03/23/barack_the_magic_negro_explained2/, https://www.latimes.com/la-oe-ehrenstein19mar19-story.html.

"People have forgotten": https://latimesblogs.latimes.com/showtracker/2008/07/what-exactly-di.html, https://www.npr.org/templates/story/story.php?storyId=92421221.

"Even Joe Biden": https://www.nbcnews.com/id/wbna16911044.

"David Brock broke the story": https://en.wikipedia.org/wiki/David_Brock.

"In 2010 George Soros": https://www.theatlantic.com/culture/archive/2010/10/george-soros-gives-media-matters-1m-to-thwart-fox-news/343737/.

"Let me tell you": https://www.rushlimbaugh.com/daily/2007/10/04/who_s_lying_media_matters_for_america_or_mrs_clinton/.

"On June 10, 2021, Amazon's the *Washington Post*": https://www.washingtonpost.com/lifestyle/media/the-media-called-the-lab-leak-story-a-conspiracy-theory-now-its-prompted-corrections-and-serious-new-reporting/2021/06/10/c93972e6-c7b2-11eb-a11b-6c6191ccd599_story.html.

"**And all of a sudden**": https://www.rushlimbaugh.com/daily/2007/05/17/rush-meets-former-president-bill-clinton/.

"**Bill Clinton tried to silence**": https://www.cnn.com/2020/10/15/media/obama-fox-news-rush-limbaugh-qanon/index.html.

Chapter 9: Life Is Show Prep

"**Snerdley brought in a little bird**": https://www.rushlimbaugh.com/daily/2007/10/30/stumpy_and_the_miracle_of_nature/.

"**Super Mega Dittos, James**": https://podcasts.apple.com/us/podcast/rush-limbaugh-the-man-behind-the-golden-eib-microphone/id1564134812#see-all/reviews.

"**A word from one of our amazing guest hosts, Mary Matalin**": https://www.iheart.com/podcast/1119-rush-limbaugh-the-man-beh-81488209/episode/political-odd-couple-84524233/.

Chapter 10: The Divided State of America

"**Make no mistake**": https://www.foxnews.com/politics/maxine-waters-july-fourth-voter-suppression-equality.

"**Rush told the incoming members of Congress**": https://www.washingtonpost.com/archive/politics/1994/12/11/rush-limbaugh-saluted-as-a-majority-maker/e4f879c5-a0d2-43b8-ae56-9e24eeb82b62/.

"**President Clinton insinuated**": https://www.latimes.com/archives/la-xpm-1995-04-25-mn-58741-story.html.

"**Certainly the 1987 Supreme Court**": https://en.wikipedia.org/wiki/Robert_Bork_Supreme_Court_nomination.

"**As I said in my address**": https://www.whitehouse.gov/briefing-room/speeches-remarks/2021/06/02/remarks-by-president-biden-commemorating-the-100th-anniversary-of-the-tulsa-race-massacre/.

"**Go back about 900 years**": https://www.history.com/topics/religion/inquisition.

"**With malice toward none**": https://www.nps.gov/linc/learn/historyculture/lincoln-second-inaugural.htm.

"**It was a political compromise**": https://www.britannica.com/topic/three-fifths-compromise.

"**Can the liberties of a nation**": https://www.nps.gov/thje/learn/photosmultimedia/quotations.htm.

"**Rush was unapologetic about**": https://www.rushlimbaugh.com/daily/2013/09/12/an_explanation_of_american_exceptionalism_for_vladimir_putin_and_barack_obama/.

"Rush articulated this honestly": https://www.rushlimbaugh.com/
daily/2007/03/05/rush_and_derek_from_detroit_talk_race/.

"Liberals do not believe": https://www.rushlimbaugh.com/daily/2007/
03/21/the_difference_between_conservatism_and_liberalism2/.

"Snerdley says, 'You better explain'": https://www.rushlimbaugh.com/
daily/2009/03/20/in_defense_of_individualism2/.

"The Republican Party was born in 1854": https://www.history.com/
this-day-in-history/republican-party-founded.

"In case you were born after 1994": https://en.wikipedia.org/wiki/103rd_
United_States_Congress.

"I grew up listening to Rush": https://podcasts.apple.com/us/podcast/
rush-limbaugh-the-man-behind-the-golden-eib-microphone/
id1564134812#see-all/reviews.

Chapter 11: Let's Go There

"The EIB Network now has": https://www.rushlimbaugh.com/
daily/2021/03/12/another-brilliant-limbaugh-invention-the-official-
obama-criticizer/.

"The *New York Times* even made corrections": https://www.nytimes.
com/2019/12/20/magazine/we-respond-to-the-historians-who-
critiqued-the-1619-project.html, https://en.wikipedia.org/wiki/
The_1619_Project.

"Historians are rediscovering": https://www.pbs.org/wnet/secrets/
secrets-spanish-florida-synopsis/3626/.

"And the very fact that": https://www.nytimes.com/
interactive/2019/08/14/magazine/black-history-american-democracy.
html, https://www.nytimes.com/interactive/2019/08/14/magazine/1619-
america-slavery.html, https://www.americanexperiment.org/the-new-
york-times-1619-project-revisited/.

"So, the *New York Times*": https://www.rushlimbaugh.com/
daily/2019/08/23/is-this-journalism-1619-apple-card-mccabe-hiring/.

"I see dead people": https://www.foxnews.com/politics/georgia-remove-
voter-rolls-brad-raffensperger-list-100000.

"She believed the human race": https://www.nytimes.com/2020/07/21/
nyregion/planned-parenthood-margaret-sanger-eugenics.html.

"Republicans buy sneakers, too": https://www.yahoo.com/now/
michael-jordan-finally-addresses-republicans-buy-sneakers-too-
comment-040215846.html.

"We don't want to tell anybody": https://www.c-span.org/
video/?284357-3/rush-limbaugh-1951-2021.

"This Minneapolis situation": https://www.rushlimbaugh.com/ daily/2021/03/30/rushs-words-ring-true-theres-no-excuse-for-george-floyds-death/.

"As of the summer of 2021": https://www.foxnews.com/us/shooting-police-station-officers-injured.

"Juan Williams wrote": https://thehill.com/opinion/criminal-justice/560470-juan-williams-biden-must-grapple-with-racial-dynamics-of-crime.

"Black Lives Matter, by the way": https://www.rushlimbaugh.com/ daily/2021/06/07/rush-knew-what-blm-was-all-about-right-from-the-start/.

"To a large degree, BLM": https://www.foxnews.com/politics/george-soros-dismantle-replace-minneapolis-police.

"Look how quickly": https://www.rushlimbaugh.com/daily/2021/05/25/ one-year-after-george-floyd-we-are-exactly-where-rush-feared-wed-be/.

"The same goes for policies": https://www.foxnews.com/us/california-prop-47-shoplifting-theft-crime-statewide.

"There are certain right-wing media venues": http://edition.cnn.com/ TRANSCRIPTS/2106/08/cnr.10.html.

"President Obama tweeted congratulations": https://www.foxnews. com/opinion/spelling-bee-champion-zaila-avant-garde-cal-thomas.

"In July 2021, the National Education Association": https://www. foxnews.com/us/largest-teachers-union-critical-race-theory-reasonable-and-appropriate, https://nypost.com/2021/07/05/ embracing-critical-theory-teachers-union-says-they-control-what-kids-learn/.

"Here's a quote from their resolution": https://www.yahoo. com/now/critical-race-theory-opponents-targeted-142228939. html?guccounter=1.

"Fairfax County PTA leader said": https://www.foxnews.com/us/ virginia-republicans-radical-left-democrats-let-them-die-pro-crt-rally.

"In Queens, New York": https://www.nytimes.com/2006/10/01/ nyregion/01census.html.

"But let's remember the inspirational words": https://www.foxnews. com/us/it-was-an-error-to-promote-radical-crt-group-biden-admin-says-following-fox-news-report, https://www.nytimes.com/2019/08/09/ us/politics/joe-biden-poor-kids.html.

"The bottom line is": https://www.rushlimbaugh.com/daily/2021/06/03/ critical-race-theory-the-culmination-of-liberal-good-intentions/.

"Most sites required some form of ID": https://laist.com/news/health/photo-id-la-county-covid-vaccine.

"The only remedy to past discrimination": https://www.foxnews.com/politics/hawley-critical-race-theory-speech-senate-floor-biden-admin.

Chapter 12: Highest Civilian Honor

"Here are President Trump's words": https://www.nytimes.com/2020/02/05/us/politics/state-of-union-transcript.html.

"That was a great evening": https://wabcradio.com/episode/president-donald-trump-interview-6-19-21/.

"I want to get a little personal": https://www.iheart.com/podcast/1119-rush-limbaugh-the-man-beh-81488209/episode/highest-civilian-honor-83475577/.

"I want to thank all of you so much": https://www.c-span.org/video/?284357-3/rush-limbaugh-1951-2021.

"Nostalgia for me is never negative": https://www.rushlimbaugh.com/daily/2021/03/17/one-month-later-rush-still-inspires-we-will-never-give-up/.

"I've learned a lot in life": https://www.rushlimbaugh.com/daily/2021/03/17/advice-from-the-maha-rushie-always-be-who-you-are/.

"What I have is simply on loan": https://www.thelimbaughletter.com/thelimbaughletter/april_2020/MobilePagedArticle.action?articleId=1572178#articleId1572178.

ABOUT THE AUTHOR

JAMES GOLDEN was with *The Rush Limbaugh Show* for thirty years, serving as call screener, "official program observer," and producer with the show's guest hosts. From 2001 until 2021, he was also a producer with Premiere Networks, the largest radio syndication company in the United States. James is currently the host of an afternoon drive-time and weekend radio show with WABC-AM in New York City.

Prior to working with Rush, James was a radio industry pioneer, first as music research director for R&B giant WWRL, then as music director and music research director for WABC Music Radio, and as senior producer and on-air talent for WABC TalkRadio in New York. He was also the VP of programming for the groundbreaking TalkSpot internet multimedia platform.

New Journey PAC

James is also the founder of New Journey PAC, a nationwide action organization that operates both in and outside of election cycles to realign the Black American vote with candidates and conservative values.

You can find us at NewJourneyPac.org.

James on the Radio

For compelling talk and remarkable guests on local and national topics, listen to James on the radio every weekday afternoon during drive-time and Saturday mornings from 8:00 to 10:00 on New York's WABC-AM 770 and online.

For stations and to listen online from anywhere, please visit JamesGolden.com.

Golden Tipp Poll

James continues his thirty-year engagement in the public policy arena in his latest endeavor, a joint effort with TechnoMetrica Institute of Policy and Politics (TIPP). He will be keeping his fingers on the pulse of American values and attitudes by conducting weekly surveys about current events and trends. The TIPP Poll has the much-coveted distinction as the most accurate poll of this century, being the only poll to accurately predict the winner of the last five U.S. presidential elections.

Learn more about James Golden and subscribe
for email updates at JamesGolden.com.